Making Games for Impact

Making Games for Impact

Kurt Squire

The MIT Press
Cambridge, Massachusetts
London, England

© 2021 Massachusetts Institute of Technology

All rights reserved. No part of this book may be reproduced in any form by any electronic or mechanical means (including photocopying, recording, or information storage and retrieval) without permission in writing from the publisher.

The MIT Press would like to thank the anonymous peer reviewers who provided comments on drafts of this book. The generous work of academic experts is essential for establishing the authority and quality of our publications. We acknowledge with gratitude the contributions of these otherwise uncredited readers.

This book was set in Stone Serif and Stone Sans by Westchester Publishing Services. Printed and bound in the United States of America.

Library of Congress Cataloging-in-Publication Data

Names: Squire, Kurt, author.
Title: Making games for impact / Kurt Squire.
Description: Cambridge, Massachusetts : The MIT Press, [2021] | Includes bibliographical references and index.
Identifiers: LCCN 2021001822 | ISBN 9780262542173 (Paperback)
Subjects: LCSH: Video games—Study and teaching. | Video games—Psychological aspects. | Learning, Psychology of. | Video games—Design. | Video games—Social aspects. | Computer-assisted instruction—United States. | Education—Effect of technological innovations on.
Classification: LCC GV1469.3 .S759 2021 | DDC 794.807—dc23
LC record available at https://lccn.loc.gov/2021001822

10 9 8 7 6 5 4 3 2 1

Contents

1 Introduction 1

2 Designing Games for Impact in Context 13

3 Crowdsourcing Knowledge Games in Science 31

4 *Fair Play*: Scaling Teams for Impact 53

5 *Progenitor X*: Zombies, Stem Cells, and Assessment 75

6 Games for Healthy Minds 91

7 Games, Design, Schools, and Markets 109

8 Private-Public Partnerships for Scale 139

9 Conclusions 167

Coda: Making Impact in Universities 185
Acknowledgments and Dedication 199
Notes 207
References 211
Index 231

1 Introduction

In the fall of 2019, tens of thousands of college students in university astronomy courses started their course not by listening to a lecture or reading a textbook but by playing a video game. They learned the "rules" of astronomy by leading a research team through space. Using authentic tools, such as a spectrum analyzer, and concepts such as the small angle approximation, students identified and gathered resources to fight an evil mining corporation. Players were free to complete these goals, roam about the universe, or even travel in time to see how the universe has changed.

This game, *At Play in the Cosmos* (described in chapter 8), is an example of a modern game for impact in which (1) all learning is situated within an authentic role (which communicates why the domain, such as science, is useful), and (2) learning is driven by complex, authentic goals (such as locating iron-rich asteroids). By conducting design research with users, the *Cosmos* team identified a sweet spot where games could make an impact on learning in astronomy, introducing learners to complex terminology, tools, and equations that normally cause students' eyes to glaze over. Stanley Fertig, who reviewed the game for the Amateur Astronomers Association (2019) described it as follows:

> The game's target is that of the level of a college "poet's" introduction to astronomy class, which can also suit a bright high school student, or more advanced users who just want to have fun. Some of the subjects *embedded* in the action include populating a Hertzsprung-Russell diagram, the Schwarzschild Radius of a black hole, relativistic time dilation, radial velocity versus transit methods for finding exoplanets, WIMPS, and a host of other advanced astronomical concepts.
>
> The game even teaches you to use various equations, for example, using parallax to calculate stellar distances, but it does so in a graphical context without requiring you to memorize them. So although most people probably won't

remember these equations, by using them as tools to accomplish missions in the game, you inevitably do remember which variables apply—so you learn what factors are important even if you don't remember the exact calculation. That's useful knowledge.

Oh, and did I mention, it's *fun!* The structure of the game, like any arcade game, is a series of levels which build upon skills and knowledge gained in prior levels. Your role is that of a space search/survey/rescue contractor, your various missions taking you all over the universe. In addition to the scripted missions, the game also has an exploration mode, where you can freely visit and analyze many real astrophysical objects.

Pilot tests suggested that students valued it as a tool, and with some modifications, one can easily imagine using it for younger or disadvantaged students.

How does a game like *At Play in the Cosmos* get made? How do we take social impact goals (such as learning) and express them through a game? How do we build a team, and how do those teams work with experts and outside entities?

This book tackles these questions, using games developed at the Games+Learning+Society (GLS) Center at the University of Wisconsin–Madison as examples. We start small, describing the common scenario of a few programmers and an artist working together to make a small, playable game in a start-up environment, all the way to multimillion-dollar efforts with funders, outside experts, and external constraints. The book touches on key issues developers and researchers must tackle, including choosing platforms, using data analytics to guide development, and designing for new markets. Although it is not a how-to guide, lessons from cases should be valuable. And, for academics, it seeks to synthesize the lessons from these domains more broadly.

Before jumping in, we briefly take stock of where games for impact currently are as a discipline and domain.

Games for Impact Come of Age

Digital games for learning have grown from a theoretical possibility to a hyped (possibly overhyped) technology and now have become commonplace. Games are used from K–12 education to advanced medical training and everything in between. Games for impact almost seem quaint compared with personal robots or biochips. Games for impact are now, in the language of Gartner's Hype Cycle, in the "plateau of productivity" (see figure 1.1, adapted from Fenn & Raskin, 2008). The hype around games for learning

Introduction

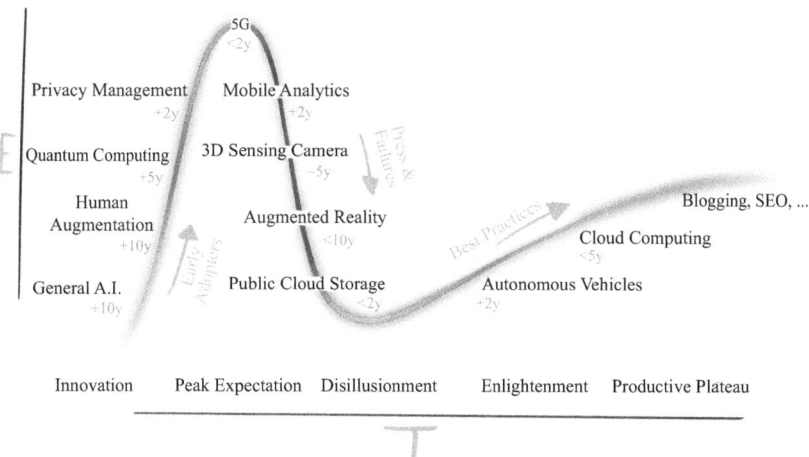

Figure 1.1
Gartner's Hype Cycle, adapted by Nika Persa.

probably crested about 2013, with many associated technologies (virtual reality, augmented reality, knowledge games) peaking shortly thereafter.

Games will continue to absorb new trends, such as intelligent agents, as they move along this hype curve. One of the most compelling features of games as the entertainment medium of the computer, as the predominant model for popularizing popular media, is their capacity to envelop emerging technologies, from the internet to 3D graphics to virtual reality. We can expect games to test the potential of machine learning in artificial intelligence or context-sensitive information in augmented reality (think of *Pokémon GO!* 2.0) in the years to come.

The non-entertainment uses of games should continue to grow. Games are the popular entertainment medium for the computer.

Interactive entertainment technology, or video games, are now accepted as tools for learning (Squire, 2011), modes of persuasion (Bogost, 2007), and simply the expression of complex ideas and emotions. Games encompass a wide variety of media and experiences, and this book explores how to make them to maximize impact. Although it touches on games expansively—from games that increase cognitive function to games for medical training—the book orients to the problem first through the lens of learning. Most lessons apply across domains.

Making impact has become an important function of higher education institutions. Through making impact games, we generate knowledge—in domains from protein folding to forest management—while also making an impact on the world. Other motivations for impact games (e.g., making money) may seem like a good idea, but enacting them is more complicated. Higher education institutions in particular are interested in diversifying income, but, I will argue, they should leverage games to do what they do best: amplify the production of social and cultural capital for participants, rather than make money.

There is no one design process, criterion, or method for making games for impact. Game development is situated in social and material contexts, and specific processes arise in response to local needs and conditions. This book presents multiple cases in an effort to illuminate the considerations in each context.

Before we get to game making, I want to lay to rest two concerns that have driven the field: (1) games for impact are not effective and (2) there is no market demand for social impact games. Both of these questions should be relatively settled; games for impact can be and often are effective, and there is a market for them. However, aligning all of these needs so that game play meets project goals, and the project can be developed with available resources and delivered to the target audience at a reasonable price point and in a reasonable way, is not always obvious. The final key point is sustainability, which is explored in the chapter "Making Impact in Universities."

The Effectiveness of Games for Impact

Multiple reviews and meta-analyses over the past decade have demonstrated the effectiveness of games for learning and behavioral change (Baranowski et al., 2016; Clark et al., 2016; Steinkuehler & Squire, 2013; Wouters et al., 2013; Young et al., 2012). There are nuances to these findings, but the pattern is clear: well-designed games, when appropriately matched to learning objectives, can outperform traditional modes of instruction. Games are effective in promoting sexual health (DeSmet et al., 2014), overall health and well-being (Johnson et al., 2016), and science education (Clark et al., 2016). Earlier research found positive results for games in social studies education (Wentworth & Lewis, 1973). Given the popularity of historical simulation games, one might expect more evidence for history games. However, most history scholars treat games as an interpretation rather than a definitive model, so historians are less motivated to compare learning via a game with learning via another medium. The goal for most history educators is to have students compare and contrast across interpretations to construct meaning, rather than to test students for recall from one source (McCall, 2011). The idea of integrating multiple representations to bolster understanding is a good lesson for the field more broadly.

In fact, comparing learning outcomes and processes across media is famously fraught, as in the Clark-Kozma debate (1983), but games offer promise because they are an embedded instructional strategy as well as media for learning. Restated, games are a way of teaching with embedded practice or reflection opportunities rather than a static presentation of information.

We know that simply changing the medium in which information is delivered does not affect learning outcomes among traditional learning measures. What matters are (1) the instructional strategies employed and (2) the new affordances that media might enable, such as model-based reasoning and procedural thinking (Kozma, 2000). Games can both employ learning strategies within the game (such as embedded challenges) and enable new learning goals. In short, as James Paul Gee, a noted linguist, literacy expert, philosopher, and inveterate gamer at Arizona State University, has argued (2003), they may enable a way out of the progressive educators' conundrum of how to build mastery over specific skills in the context of open-ended learning environments (see Gee, 2004; Kirschner et al., 2006).

A recent review by Doug Clark and colleagues (2016) provides a detailed analysis of how, why, and when games work for learning (in this case, for science). Performing a meta-analysis of 69 studies (out of more than 6,000 studies uncovered), Clark and colleagues (2016, p. 108) concluded the following:

> Overall, results indicated that digital games were associated with a 0.33 standard deviation improvement relative to nongame comparison conditions. Thus, digital games conditions were on average more effective than the non-game instructional conditions included in those comparisons. These results generally confirm the overall findings from prior meta-analyses on the effects of games on learning (Sitzmann, 2011; Vogel et al., 2006; Wouters et al., 2013).

Restated, a meta-analysis revealed that not only have games produced learning gains, but they have averaged one-third of a standard deviation *better* than nongame comparison conditions.

Curiously, perhaps, Clark and colleagues (2016) also found that game conditions were *not* more motivating than nongame instructional conditions (whereas earlier reviews, such as Wouters et al. [2013], found them to be more motivating). For my money, I'd bet on a game being more engaging over other approaches, but we should be aware of the following:

1. The specific factors that make games engaging, such as challenge, fantasy, control, curiosity, competition, collaboration, and recognition (Malone, 1981; Malone & Lepper, 1987), can be integrated into any curriculum, game or otherwise.
2. Making *any* game engaging is difficult, let alone social impact games; simply scan the metacritic scores for entertainment games to see how uncommon good games are.
3. The best curricula may be *more* engaging, particularly when they enable authentic production and participation. The best science curricula that use inquiry-based or constructivist learning principles may be more motivating than games because they recruit personal expression and authentic participation.
4. Games, like any nondidactic pedagogy, may get in the way of memorizing information for the test. In a transactional situation, whereby learning is an exchange of work for grades (a proxy for future rewards, such as college entrance), games based on conceptual understanding will struggle.

Games, particularly multiplayer ones, are a good context for social-emotional development. Clark and colleagues (2016) found that digital games had a significant benefit on intrapersonal learning outcomes as compared with other approaches (mean effect size 0.35). Our own lab, collaborating with neuroscientist and University of Wisconsin–Madison professor Richard Davidson (famous for studying emotion in the brain and documenting the positive long-term neurological effects of meditation, among other things) reached similar findings for games designed to teach such skills; see chapter 6 and Kral et al. (2018). Games that include increasingly difficult challenges grow players' capacity to persevere, also called grit or tenacity. Clark also found evidence for intellectual openness, positive work ethic, conscientiousness, and positive core self-evaluation. Success at games, we now believe, cultivates a sense of resilience, which when applied to academic domains is powerful.

In short, *game design matters*. It matters how the underlying concept is conceived and developed, how it relates to the target domain, and how it relates to learning goals. It matters how the team receives and adjusts to feedback, and it matters how we connect all of this to designing and conducting research on the game itself, even in cases in which students play because it is required.

Clark breaks down games into several subcategories, such as single versus multiplayer, single-session versus replayable sessions, and story versus nonstory, which suggests the broad range of ways one can make a game. But none of them covers whether a game is executed well. We can do research on bad games to tell us that they don't work very well, but that doesn't really teach us anything.

Design also matters when deciding how and when to deploy specific features. In comparing standard versions of games with enhanced versions that test a particular idea (such as embedded coaching), Clark found "a significant positive effect size for the enhanced designs ($\bar{g}=0.34$)" (2016, p. 98). A million design decisions go into a game, and designers manage them artfully (informed by science as well as intuition). In Clark's study, single-player games typically outperformed multiplayer games, but games with collaborative team competition did even better than both of those. Similarly, replayable games typically beat single-session game designs, and, perhaps surprisingly, games with embedded instruction did no better than games without it. This is not to say that designers should make only collaborative-competitive games or forgo embedded instruction but rather *to remind us that design matters*. As Clark and colleagues wrote, "Although this conclusion may appear to be common sense, the role of design is often de-emphasized in debates over whether digital games are better or worse than traditional instruction. The value-added findings empirically demonstrate the importance of the role of design beyond medium" (2016, p. 110). In other words, we need to think beyond "Do games work?" (especially now that we know that they can work) and think about how to employ them for specific ends.

These same patterns are found in domains such as health and health care, in which games are used to help recovering stroke victims (see Krakauer & Cortés, 2018), repel the onset of aging (Wang et al., 2017), and manage diseases such as Friedrich's ataxia (Bonnechere et al., 2016). A meta-analysis of patients found increased knowledge and improvements in self-management behaviors (Charlier et al., 2016). It would be impossible to highlight every medical use of games; the subfield now has its own journal, *Games for Health Journal*, in its eighth year of publication as of this writing (see Johnson et al., 2016, for a review). But for the purposes of this introduction, we see evidence for games creating knowledge gains, long-term behavioral changes, and changes measured by physiological measures (e.g., changes in weight; functional magnetic resonance imaging, or fMRI; blood pressure). A meta-analysis of games for health and medical care finds small but positive effects of games on healthy lifestyles and knowledge (DeSmet et al., 2014).

Broadening Games for Impact

Despite these successes, one can sense disappointment about games for impact. Fifteen years after the first serious games summit, there is no real "killer app" (to use a dated term) that represents best in class. My own elementary and middle school age children, for example, have few learning games in their classes, and the ones they play are interactive worksheets. Their educational games include nonverbal animations and customized practice problems, which make them a compelling alternative to their paper-based cousins, *if* they are well designed. Most, however, lack polish. And creative open-ended problem-solving games haven't yet entered classrooms on a national scale in a meaningful way.

But from another perspective, games for impact are a roaring success. Core ideas from the games for impact community now permeate popular culture. Want a game to increase exercise or fitness? Choose from dozens. Not many are very good, but Nintendo's *Wii Fit* (a $1 billon product), *Dance Dance Revolution*, *Pokémon GO!*, an augmented reality game from Google spin-off Niantic, and iOS indie game hit *Zombies, Run!*, from UK-based Six to Start, are.

In 2008, James Paul Gee and colleagues dreamt up a game to teach game design, and ten years later, Super *Mario Maker* and *Roblox* allow kids to make and play one another's games. Ten years ago, had you said that my son would look to *Roblox* for user-generated content as his favorite game, I would not have believed it. *Pokémon GO!* and *Roblox* were top-grossing titles in 2017 (Conditt, 2017).

The best example of a successful learning game is probably *Plague Inc.*, the 2012 disease simulation game that was runner-up for IGN's Strategy Game of the Year. *Plague Inc.* has *over one hundred million downloads* as of this writing, has stayed in the top ten since its release, and is among the most commercially successful mobile games ever made regardless of genre (see Eadicicco, 2016). The game play is a classic case of "learning through transgressive play," meaning that players learn about a system (in this case epidemiology) by trying to break it (wiping out humanity through disease). *Plague Inc.* wasn't intended to be educational, any more than *SimCity* was, but it is hard to imagine a better introduction to the subject. In 2013, the Centers for Disease Control and Prevention even invited James Vaughan, the founder of Ndemic Creations, to discuss how to use such games to educate the public.[1]

The other crucial data point for discussing games for impact is *Minecraft*. It is safe to assume that anyone reading this book is familiar with *Minecraft*, the second-best-selling game (174 million copies) of all time. Readers can make up their own minds about educational applications of *Minecraft*, including Minecraft: Education Edition, ubiquitous *Minecraft* coding camps, and homegrown applications teaching architecture, design, physics, or electricity. *Minecraft* is, in many respects, a return to the "glory days" of MUDs (multi-user dungeons), in which players create not just characters but entire worlds, including the social policies that govern them (Koster, 2018). When educators such as myself, Henry Jenkins, and James Paul Gee talked about games as productive play and imagined systems that might ramp kids from consumers to producers, *Minecraft* was just the kind of game, platform, and phenomenon we were imagining.

Finally, let's return to *Roblox*. Released in 2006, *Roblox* is a massive multiplayer online game *creation* platform with over 70 million active players.[2] Players (largely kids between the ages of six and nine) play games designed by other players through Roblox Studio. The games feel like interactive LEGO constructions and support an endless array of themes—from the latest manga title to classic superhero themes to the just weird. *Roblox* has made a successful business out of "a game platform about making and sharing games," which, just a few years ago, James Paul Gee and Katie Salen were developing in academic contexts with *Gamestar Mechanic* (Salen Tekinbas et al., 2014). *Roblox* is in essence a creative suite and publishing platform for spreading games that kids purchase, or purchase items for using Robux, its in-game currency. A recent *Forbes* article reported that *Roblox* generates over $100 million per year and is valued at about $2.5 billion. What is particularly cool about *Roblox* is that as kids grow out of *playing* its games, they can start *making* games, and kids are making real money by designing games for other kids. In 2018, Roblox Studio paid out over $80 million to developers; college sophomore Alex Balfanz has made several million dollars through his popular game *Jailbreak*, my son Warner's favorite game

(Weinberger, 2017). At the time of this writing, *Roblox* is a Wild West of game design; there are clones of popular games, brutal roguelike multiplayers, fashion games, and games with guns that Ben Sawyer (founder of the Serious Games Initiative) has theorized are popular in part because parents do not know what kids are doing (personal communication).

Organization of This Book

I hope we have now established that games for impact *can* work, there is a market for impact games (much as with documentary films), and the research community knows something about them. The remainder of this book is dedicated to how we make games for impact. It uses the development of specific games at the GLS Center laboratory as a framework. These include how to form teams, generate ideas, and evaluate which ideas to pursue.

We start with the case of *Virulent* (chapter 2) because it is a relatively simple, straightforward simulation game that reflects the kind of game a new team could build in a class or after graduation. Chapter 2 also introduces the story of the GLS Center itself, which should be of interest to managers in academics or industry who are building a team to last across projects. *Virulent* also enables us to query the multiple factors to consider when deciding whether to green-light a project.

Chapter 3 turns to the problem of how to design knowledge games, games also intended to further understanding of an underlying phenomenon. Following the success of *Foldit*, knowledge games captured public imagination (or at least many academics' imagination), although they have also evolved toward the plateau of productivity. Chapter 3 highlights some of the opportunities and challenges in knowledge games, which also come back in chapter 8.

Chapter 4 describes the process of ramping up to scaling up design teams. It uses the case of *Fair Play* to introduce development of a full 3D art pipeline, multiple teams with competing demands, subcontractors, clients, and staff. Faculty interested in building dedicated game development teams or students building their own companies should find this chapter particularly helpful. The chapter also addresses building games for nongamers and taking games to market.

Chapter 5 addresses one of the hottest areas in games research: assessment and games. Learning analytics, the study of data to improve learning, is increasingly driving all game design—but especially learning games. Chapter 5 uses *Progenitor X*, a zombie stem cell game, to introduce game-based assessment and the use of machine learning to improve assessment.

Chapter 6 returns to the question of improving affective skills such as self-regulation through games. It describes a research collaboration with Richard Davidson, a neuroscientist at the University of Wisconsin–Madison, that resulted in two games that produced long-term neurological changes in players. Chapter 6 also meditates on a perennial question in games for impact: how do we create compelling media that our users *want* to use?

Chapter 7 digs more deeply into the question of how to create games for impact that endure beyond the life of a grant or school project and actually enter the market. It uses the case of *Econauts*, a game that spun out of our lab and into the co.lab accelerator to explore how games need to change to survive in the marketplace.

Chapter 8 describes a private-public partnership between GLS and W. W. Norton & Company to create *At Play in the Cosmos*, an astronomy game that ships with an introductory college textbook. It describes the development of an impact game in detail so as to help readers understand what commercial production looks like. This development process is much more linear than the processes explored in earlier chapters. The chapter ends with a meditation on how our design processes, particularly the constraints required to make games in large organizations, determine the artifacts that are created.

In chapter 9, I close the book with two conclusions. The first conclusion provides a general tying up of game development across these projects, toward creating a more generalized template for developing games for impact. I try to emphasize the real day-to-day work that our teams engaged in to give readers a sense of how we spent our time in each phase. I do not pretend that we discovered the optimal approach. My hope is that this chapter will spark a conversation across different labs and teams.

The second conclusion reflects on the future of innovation and technology in higher education. The story of these projects is also the story of how we innovate in universities and how universities need (or don't need) to innovate in the face of new technologies.

2 Designing Games for Impact in Context

Game design at a small indie startup is different from game design in a university capstone class, which is different from game design by a textbook publisher or an AAA team.[1] An important step in making games for impact is to understand the context—what can be done well within one's organizational and financial constraints, and where one can innovate. This chapter discusses game development by a small, agile team.

Getting Started: Creating Strategic Alignment

The first step in making games for impact is to align the effort with the institutional mission and strategy. Small companies making games about a passion topic, such as iNK Stories making *1979 Revolution: Black Friday* (a game about the Iranian Revolution), face challenges of securing funding and publicizing their work, but they are free to spend money (though they usually don't have much of it) however they want. They can hire staff and contractors or throw lavish parties. They can allow employees to dress in period garb in the office or at events or choose to spark controversy to gather attention. A key issue for these organizations is building and maintaining morale, since early phases are funded by sweat equity.

Publicly traded companies, government organizations (such as the military), and universities constrain development. Almost by definition, their mission is not to make games for impact. They exist in order to do other things.

Large institutions, from universities to corporations, are serious places with internal competition for resources. Game-related projects are vulnerable to questions such as "Is that really serious?" and "Do we know it will work?" in ways that textbooks and online courses are not. Unlike employees in start-ups, those in large institutions can't work for free, so money for staff has to come from somewhere. Project directors spend nontrivial amounts of time merely justifying their existence to skeptical stakeholders. In government and business, game projects are especially vulnerable during annual budget reviews (see Nadella, Nichols, & Shaw, 2017).

Even games developed with financing by grants are constrained by institutions. Grant dollars belong to the organization and are subject to its rules. Employees must be hired according to institutional practices and fit into preapproved job categories, and then academic timelines must be observed. Universities can't give employees bonuses for a job well done or for having survived a crunch period, or even offer promotions or equity. Legacy hires—staff who are brought into a project because they are already there (not trained for the job)—are common. Projects can be held up because requests to buy game equipment are rejected. Purchasing in-game content or currencies such as Robux is basically impossible.

In higher education contexts, project managers wrestle with the fact that learning is basically secondary to efficient credit hour production. Even if a game is the greatest learning tool ever conceived, a good lecturer might generate better ratings, be cheaper, and be just as effective as measured by tests (Matheson, 2008; Wieman, 2007). As a result, a games for impact group is often better off appealing to a different need, such as the game development experience being good job training for undergraduate students. A key to long-term success is to find niches in which there is no other competition, such as online learning. This concept is explicated in subsequent chapters, but games are often most effective when coming from another budget line and addressing other organizational needs.

Start Developing

If you are asking, "How do social impact games even get made?," you are asking a good question. The answer is often that they pull from ancillary budgets with different metrics, such as advertising, or require passion and organizational jiujitsu. The game *America's Army: Proving Grounds* is a good example, having originated in military advertising. The protein-folding science game *Foldit* started in DARPA (the Defense Advanced Research Projects Agency), funded by the US Department of Defense. In fact, most games for impact have strange origin stories. They have champions who steward it through an organization, identifying who will support the game getting made and, ultimately, who will pay for it. The key is to keep an open eye for opportunities and a willingness to experiment.

Many games projects start in university classes. Someone has an idea and recruits friends to build a prototype. In most start-ups, teams are driven by available talent. Most universities have computer science students but few 3D artists or teams with software engineering backgrounds.

Many games for impact projects grow out of entertainment game programs. Game development programs have exploded over the past decade. The same legitimacy concerns that dampen the production of games for impact in large institutions nurture their development on campuses with game development programs. Making games for impact inevitably arises as the answer to the question of "Why have a game development major on campus?" or "What does it contribute to the intellectual life of campus?" Agencies like to fund game development students because their games generally look and play better than those coming from educators.

As a result, most game development programs have launched games for impact initiatives, often with an entrepreneurial spin.[2] A fascinating example is the Rochester Institute of Technology's MAGIC Spell Studios, founded by Andy Phelps. Supported by $28 million in private and public funding, MAGIC created a physical and institutional context for spinning projects out of the university. Putting a game studio on campus gave students real experience in developing games. Rochester was hit hard by the decline of the Eastman Kodak Company, which shed nearly sixty thousand jobs in twenty years (Taddeo, 2017). Could MAGIC help transform the region by encouraging students to stay in Rochester after graduation? Before Andy stepped down, MAGIC students developed and shipped two Xbox games, paving the way for an understanding of games programs as accelerators. There are many ways to think about making impact, and job training will be an important one for the near future.

Design Your Institutional Context

Our approach at the University of Wisconsin–Madison was to build a commercial-quality game studio on campus. UW–Madison is a leading recipient of grant funds in the United States, so we set up our team to partner with scientists. We formed a team of professional game developers who could partner with faculty on grants while also bringing on students to launch projects, products, teams, and companies. We were funded at first by seed money from the Wisconsin Institute for Discovery and eventually stood alone through grants and contracts as we developed the capacity to build games not only for research but also for the market. My codirectors included Richard Halverson, Susan Millar, and Constance Steinkuehler.

As an integrated research and development group designed to support transdisciplinary research, Games+Learning+Society (GLS) included the following features:

- *Cross-industry expertise*. Researchers, developers, and educators worked together "cheek by jowl" in a common space, organization, and culture.
- *Transdisciplinary academic culture*. Faculty, postdocs, graduates, and undergraduates across fields (science education, game studies, computer science, art, design, policy, psychology) worked in the same space.
- *Mixing of game development cultures*. AAA designers, accustomed to industry practices and deadlines, worked with indie developers used to smaller budgets and teams.
- *Integrated staffing*. Teachers who served as outreach staff, communication specialists who helped refine messages, web developers with an eye toward emerging trends (crucial for delivering products at scale), and solution-oriented administrators all shared space.
- *Entrepreneurial funding models*. We sought to leverage the best of public and private funding to advance impact. Partnerships included traditional grant-funded research (e.g., through government agencies) and private entities (e.g., Microsoft Games).
- *Defaulting to open*. We made projects and tools free and open-source when possible. We published materials to established channels (e.g., Apple's App Store, BrainPOP) for market feedback when possible.

Driving our lab was an orientation toward both research (creating materials that extend and test theory) and the market (meeting the needs of users and competing within the marketplace).

Establishing Credibility

This story started in 2009, when the University of Wisconsin–Madison, the State of Wisconsin, and the John and Tashia Morgridge family announced the creation of the Wisconsin Institute for Discovery (WID), a private-public biomedical research facility to support research "from discovery to delivery." WID was funded through $50 million from the state; $50 million from the private Wisconsin Alumni Research Foundation (WARF), a nonprofit funded by faculty inventions that supports the university; and $50 million from the Morgridge family.

The WID steering committee did not direct all of the funds to the university but instead established twin research facilities—a private, nonprofit research entity (the Morgridge Institute for Research) and a public university center, which reported directly to the graduate school, similarly to most university centers—colocated under one roof with shared facilities to amplify the output of each. The university could do what it does best: conduct research supported by federal and private grants. The private institute could invest in high-impact areas to facilitate the translation of research into products, patents, and companies. In short, it was a mix of bottom-up (university) and top-down (private) research.

At launch, WID consisted of six public and six private research groups. Each transdisciplinary group included six to eight faculty members (constructed like an NSF Center). The building itself was designed to support the formation of centers; each wing contained six to eight offices and space for twenty to thirty staff members and students. Each group was expected to generate $2–$5 million annually in funding, largely through competitive research grants. Morgridge targeted some of the biggest stars on campus, including Dr. James Thomson, who derived the first human embryonic stem cell line in 1998 and graced the cover of *Time* magazine in 2001. In fact, a chief reason for founding the Institute was to give Thomson an institutional home for his research should the state decide to shut down stem cell research.

In the spring of 2009, Richard Halverson and I were recruited by Sangtae (Sang) Kim, director of the Morgridge Institute for Research (the private side), and Susan Millar, director of the Institute's Educational Research Integration Area, to explore whether games to improve public science understanding could be a part of WID. Sang imagined we could catalyze innovation by doing the following:

1. *Encouraging communication across research groups.* Designing games requires cutting across multiple domains. For example, designing a

virology game recruits virologists, epidemiologists, immunologists, and medical school faculty. Designing such games might spawn future research collaborations.

2. *Pushing the Institute's technical infrastructure toward emerging trends* (e.g., preparing medical research groups for mobile data collection devices such as Fitbits). Game teams tend to push technology infrastructure.
3. *Improving scientists' educational outreach.* Education researchers can partner on the outreach portions of scientists' grants, and scientists can partner as experts on scientists' learning grants.
4. *Creating copyrightable products and spin-off companies.* Successful projects could become products or even companies that generate revenue through intellectual property licenses (see Shapiro & Squire, 2011).

At the very least, we could conduct transdisciplinary research at the intersection of education, informatics, health, and computer science.

Most game groups, from research firms to textbook publishers, share similar institutional roles. They are tasked with encouraging innovation, collaboration, and discovery and, most important, with identifying and opening blue ocean markets (a new, low cost market that is new and therefore uncontested). In short, game teams live in the place that institutions reserve for exploring innovation.

Grizzled academics familiar with campus politics will spot the land mines. What was a video games group doing in the middle of the shiniest new buildings on campus? Why were educational researchers given space with the university's best and brightest scientists? How would video game people be received by the upper echelons of campus leaders, administrators, and donors? At this time, the games for impact movement was about five years old. Filament Games was only just taking off as a company, hiring its first employees and moving into its first formal studio space. Pursuing games for impact was risky for such a high-profile endeavor.

We needed to establish credibility, and we needed to do it fast. We had to demonstrate that we belonged alongside fellow scientists while also establishing an identity. We wanted to squelch questions like "Could you make a good game that's also good science?" while also laying the foundation for our own grant-raising goals, which were expected to be over $1 million annually. After a year of planning proposals and mission statements, we arrived at two complementary projects:

1. *Virulent*, a real-time strategy game between viruses and their hosts (see Corredor et al., 2014), and
2. *Anatomy Pro-Am*, a crowdsourced game for medical imaging and radiation oncology in which players role-played and ultimately could play as scientists treating cancer.

We hoped that producing two games would achieve multiple objectives. It would prevent our team from being overly identified with one game ("Oh, that's the *Virulent* team"). It would demonstrate a range of genre possibilities (shrinking down to a virus in one game, role-playing as a scientist in another). It would allow us to tackle a straightforward project (*Virulent*) while also chasing a moon shot (*Anatomy Pro-Am*). *Virulent*—a real-time strategy game in which viruses combat the human immune system—was intuitive, was built on existing art, and was easy for newcomers to imagine. In other words, it had a reasonable chance to succeed. *Anatomy Pro-Am*, on the other hand, was unlikely to "succeed" in, say, curing cancer or revolutionizing cancer management, but it was also more reflective of the radically transformative spirit of the institution.

Virulent: A Learning Game Where You Can Fail

Virulent, which was released for the iPad in 2011, situates the player inside human cells, playing as virions (complete, infective forms of a virus outside of the cell) invading and infecting their host cell (see figure 2.1). *Virulent* began through a conversation with Dr. John Yin, a virologist who runs the systems biology group at WID. Dr. Yin described evolutionary battles between cells (including virions, bacteria, and hosts) and thought that these battles could become a game. Dr. Richard Halverson noted that this idea could be explored through a real-time strategy game, and he hashed out the basics, similar to a one-page design document (see Librande, 2010). The biological processes themselves *sound* like a game: virions (players) fight off immune responses with armies of viral proteins while stealing cellular production facilities to create more virions. The core game play in *Virulent* involves the player controlling the "Raven" virus to (1) infect a host cell, (2) replicate inside the cell, and (3) escape from the cell. The team, directed by Halverson, included project lead and postdoc Nathan Patterson (programming), developers Michael Beall (art) and Terra Lauterbach (game

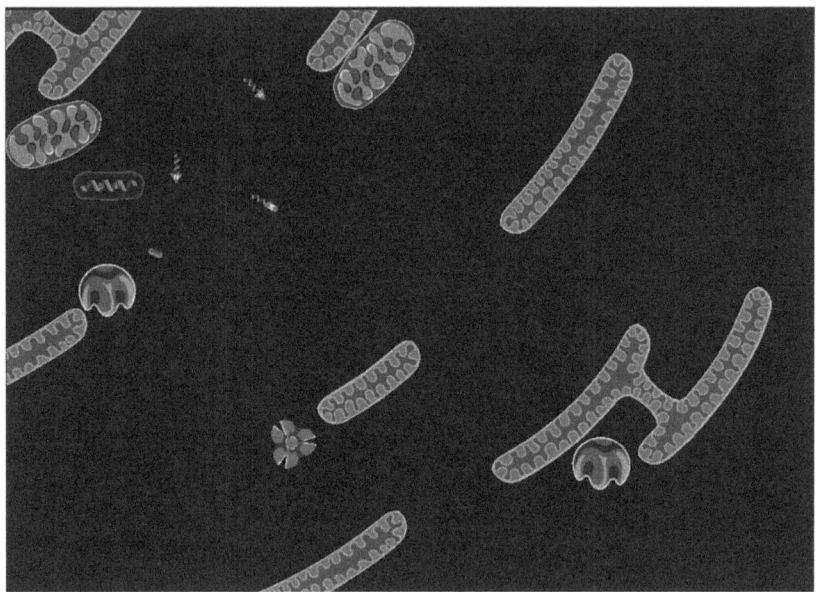

Figure 2.1
Virulent: a game in which the player is a virion inside a cell, infecting the host.

design and programming), and graduate students Kevin Harris, Matthew Gaydos, and Moses Wolfenstein, as well as visiting scholars Javier Corredor and Heinrich Soebke. We had little previous professional game development experience but covered basic game development disciplines.

Green-lighting a Game

Virulent fit our emerging criteria for developing an educational game (see table 2.1). The core idea, "The cell is the battlefield between virions and hosts," was good. A competitive learning game could establish credibility with scientists and gamers alike. Building a team from scratch with the Unity platform would attune us toward mobile games and their associated issues, such as memory constraints, touch interfaces, and the context of mobile use. As an early developer for the iPad, we would build a generative production pipeline. The style of game was reasonable for our team because *Virulent* would consist largely of geometric shapes. Building *Virulent* was, thus, relatively low-risk: the core idea was naturally a game, the production targets were achievable, and in a worst-case scenario we would have an

Table 2.1
Criteria for green-lighting a project

Criterion	Description	*Virulent* as an example
Organizational fit	Does the project align with organizational goals? Is it mission critical to the organization?	*Virulent* had face validity as a science simulation game and represented biological systems that underlie WID.
Strategic positioning	How does the game position the team in terms of competition, academics, and market?	The team made "real, playable games for the market" on a cutting-edge platform.
Professional development	Do team members learn new skills? Does the project nurture team leaders or enable the hiring of new people?	The project enabled us to build a Unity team and expand art capacity.
Technology stack	Is the game on the right software and hardware platforms?	The game positioned us on emerging platforms likely to be stable for 3–5 years.
Partner fit	How do the partner's skills complement those of team members? Is the partner a good collaborator?	Partners understood games and learning, interdisciplinary research, and art.
Feasibility	Is the project likely to succeed? Does its risk profile match the team's needs?	The project was likely to persuade administrative leaders, board members, and scientists.
Team composition	Does the project enable the team to grow? Will it bring in new talent or skills?	We had programmers and educators but no artists. The project enabled us to expand our art, music, and interface skills.
Social value	Does the team see the project as worth doing? Does it achieve social goals?	*Virulent* met few social goals, but we wanted to make a competitive game.
Market potential	What is the game's market potential? Will parents, schools, or the public pay for it?	The project allowed us to test market potential for homes or schools.
Funding potential	Will the project appeal to funders? Will funding agencies or investors value it?	*Virulent* was potentially fundable by the National Science Foundation.
Parsimony or overall fitness of idea	Do these factors hang together in a sensible way?	*Virulent* was a relatively low-risk project for establishing credibility and research.

interactive simulation. I had previously argued for games like *Virulent* as an evolution from text → images → animations → interactive simulated systems, and this project enabled us to explore that intellectual problem space as well (see Games-to-Teach Team, 2003).

The most common question I get is "How do you decide which projects to pursue?" There is no one factor. A good design decision satisfies a confluence of factors. What may be a good project at the beginning of a group's life cycle (such as a conservative one) may not be a good project later, when a forward-leaning project can drive innovation.

The quality of partners is most important. Game design is deeply collaborative. Academics, game designers, and learning scientists have unique skills and values, all of which need to be mobilized to make a great game. Subject matter experts must be comfortable with simplifying complex phenomena, embracing learning through failure, and dealing with the imprecise nature of game design (see table 2.1). Game designers must be curious about the domain. Learning scientists emphasize what's important from the domain for learning, conduct background research into game design ideas, and steer conversations toward generative areas.

This idea of imprecision—the idea that a game designer makes hundreds, if not thousands, of decisions guided mostly by intuition—is often disconcerting for scientists (including educators) trained in a reductionist paradigm in which solutions are broken down into constituent parts. Design decisions can be broken down (indeed, A/B testing is a testimony to this), but the orientation of many scientists—to lean on an empirically supported justification for every design decision—is counter to game design. Scientists with an applied or engineering background usually make the leap to game design more easily. The most important qualities, however, are probably open-mindedness about popular culture, curiosity about the work of game designers, and a desire to share one's love of the work with others.

Making *Virulent*

The first task for new teams is to foster a creative and healthy culture. To beat a dead horse, making games is famously difficult, and digital games perhaps even more so: developers have to come to a unified vision and purpose, get artists and programmers working in concert, and create easy-to-learn, hard-to-master interfaces and conventions, interesting mechanics, and compelling themes in working software. Hundreds, if not thousands, of games are released every day across multiple platforms, most of which never reach an audience. Most games aren't reviewed particularly well, and most entertainment games do not recoup their investment costs.

Making games for social impact increases the difficulty level. Developers must align game mechanics and themes with goals (see Soren Johnson's excellent 2012 essay "Theme Is Not Meaning"). They must account for how and why users will play their game, including the multiple contexts in which they are situated (e.g., homes, museums, or schools). They have to manage a mix of realism and fantasy, balance open-ended, playful exploration with concrete goals, balance multiple stakeholder goals, and manage diverse working contexts and value systems. It is critically important that teams develop shared game values, design pillars, (foundational game ideas fixed at the outset of design) and objectives if a game is to get off the ground.

The first production steps for most small, self-funded teams are to commit to a vision, a technology platform, design pillars, experts who will be creative partners, and a prototyping path. In the case of *Virulent*, we committed to (1) creating a "real" game with winning and losing conditions, (2) deploying to the iPad, (3) having players indirectly manipulate virus particles, (4) working with Dr. John Yin's group, and (5) paper prototyping levels. A series of initial meetings between project directors and virologists led to a general idea, captured on a whiteboard through diagrams with the key game play phases. We had little game design experience and no experience on the Unity platform. We (Patterson, Halverson, and team) embraced agile development, paper prototyping, and a one-page design approach.

Shared aesthetic vision Great games for social impact *can* be made by lone individuals; in fact, unambiguous successes, such as *Plague Inc.*, *Minecraft*, and, for all practical purposes, *SimCity*, were made that way. However, the vast majority of games for impact teams span artists, programmers, subject matter experts, and evaluators or assessment experts. All team members need to work toward the same goal and vision so that they can make good decisions when trade-offs need to be made.

Great teams rarely coalesce overnight. They take time. They have leaders, but they cannot be dictated from the top down. The aesthetic vision arises as teams make progress toward a goal. This often includes playing games together, which provides a shared experience, bonding, and eventually (for better and for worse) inspiration for the design. But, most important, it occurs through actually getting work done. Seth Spaulding (currently senior art manager at Blizzard Entertainment) builds on Tuckman's (1965) "forming, storming, norming, performing" model to argue that alignment, then trust, and ultimately meaning develop as teams make progress.[3]

This last point is worth restating: if a team's goal is to do meaningful work, we need to first achieve alignment, then trust, and then meaning. Alignment requires us to ask: What kinds of games do we like? What are our relative strengths? What can we pull off within our time, scope, and budget constraints? What do we want to learn, and how can this project set us up for future projects? Second, trust forms through work done together. Trust arises through repeated positive social interactions, basically getting stuff done together (Cammarata & Koster, 2018).[4] Finally, in some but not all cases, the work becomes meaningful as each team member feels that he or she is contributing and that the group wouldn't be the same without any of the others involved or with the addition of a new person. There is almost always a formal or informal leader who settles disputes and decides among possibilities (which is explored in chapters that follow).

In the case of *Virulent*, a competitive game-playing culture emerged, with the team identity forged around playing *StarCraft II*, a real-time strategy game developed by Blizzard Entertainment that is a progenitor to the modern esports movement, especially popular in Korea. Not surprisingly, *Virulent* was influenced by *StarCraft*. The first prototype involved manipulating multiple units on-screen by indirectly controlling where they went. This was scientifically more accurate and aesthetically pleasing than a direct 1:1 mapping with a virion. Thus, early on, several design pillars were solidified: (1) competitive, difficult gaming with learning through failure; (2) a feeling of indirect control over viruses to infect the host; and (3) immersion in the battleground of host cells and viruses. The "big idea" was to play as a virus particle, then switch to the side of the human host, and finally to design a virus to fight cancer; the research team we collaborated with was exploring ways to design viruses to act as vectors for drug therapies.

Playing a virus to destroy tissue—which was actually cancerous—was cool. This seemed like great "hard science fiction," a technically plausible scenario that is not yet realized but is possible. What better way to brand the Institute at the cutting edge than the chemical engineering of viruses to cure cancer?

Playing the prototype The goal should be to play a working prototype—paper or digital, and toys that lack goals are okay—as quickly as possible. Team members from different disciplines and backgrounds need to see how the prototype compares with the game idea that is in the other team members' heads. How does the game feel? Do the primary modes of interaction feel right for the target audience? What production or design elements are needed that you didn't consider? Will there be unforeseen technical hurdles?

For any game project—but particularly for those in new genres—prototyping is a critical step for identifying, refining, and validating new forms of game play. Making a quick prototype helps teams isolate and focus on the core game play mechanic. Often, such prototypes are "toys" that lack goals or constraints. Modern game developers now invest up to 50 percent of their time in this preproduction phase in which they focus on prototyping. This method, often called the Cerny Method after Mark Cerny, involves a series of prototypes rather than design documents to develop, test, and verify ideas.

We verified that indirectly controlling virus particles to infect a host was interesting. We showed the games to friends and family and quickly learned that controlling more than seven particles was, for this game and audience, overwhelming.[5] Controlling too many particles diverted players' focus from specific causal interactions and sidelined key science concepts. Game play with larger numbers of particles was really just hurling quantities of virions at cells. We wanted players to encounter specific processes. Dividing attention across particles also created stress for players, and controlling multiple units, which suggests a scrolling camera, created tricky interface obstacles. Still, we liked the idea of players controlling virus particles indirectly, through tapping where the virus would go, and being decoupled from a specific virus particle; instead, we positioned the player as a less embodied third-person "godlike" character that dealt with virus particles dying all the time. Keeping a fixed screen (no scrolling) and fewer than seven particles on-screen at a time kept the game play within working memory and allowed for a single-tap interface, which we felt was critical for nongamers and easier to control. Further (and this is more subtle), having only a few particles might steer us away from action-oriented game play in which players consider where particles were sent and why.

In most projects, teams scrap the prototype and completely rework the game play, and *Virulent* was no different. On the basis of informal internal play tests (internal to the team, other developers in the lab, friends, and family), the team rewrote the game to focus on a single-screen action-strategy game that could be completed in about an hour. This version of *Virulent* (available in Apple's App Store) left behind a computer-based real-time strategy game featuring large maps and micro-heavy game play toward an RTS light (not unlike the way *Clash Royale* did). Despite rewriting and restructuring thousands of lines of code, redesigning game mechanics and player interactions, drafting and creating new artwork, recording new sounds and music, and redesigning with content experts, we still preferred this approach over continuing on the current path. It also meant, unfortunately, abandoning the hope that the game could be used as a computational model by virologists to simulate interactions between humans and virus populations. As discussed in more detail in later chapters, games and computational models often serve different ends.

Production Once the vision has been developed and tested in some way through a prototype, and answers to key questions have been gathered, production becomes more linear. We did not have a deep design document, but we had a relatively coherent feature set, list of levels, art assets, and production goals (see W.W. Norton Astronomy: At Play at the Cosmos, chapter 8, for a full-blown example). The team set out weekly and biweekly sprints, made daily builds, and invited team members to weekly play sessions. From that point on, agile software development methods captured the design process relatively well, with two minor notes.

First, representing complex phenomena bumped into the boundaries of disciplinary understandings. As we interviewed experts, we found places where the virologists' or chemical engineers' understandings differed from those of medical faculty or immunologists. A virologist would know how a virus responds to a cell's defenses but might know less about how bacteria communicate or different parts of the immune system communicate. The team also bumped into the limits of knowledge as they depicted particular components, such as slicer enzymes. Lead artist Mike Beall was taken by the idea of depicting a slicer enzyme with actual blades (to communicate to players what it does) and was tickled when the partner scientists signed off, saying that it probably was close enough and they didn't understand all of the slicing mechanisms anyway.

As developers of learning games interpret one domain into another, they simplify. This design decision—how to make the slicer enzyme communicate what it does—was a classic art-focused game decision that gets at the hard work of design. How much can we change a representation to make a game playable? In the ensuing years, we invested even more in the art team; I came to see that a key missing ingredient in most games for learning is art (see also Squire, 2008, for a discussion of art in *Viewtiful Joe*). Artists turn a flat game experience into something that inspires emotion and, in the case of slicer enzymes, is intuitive to grasp and play.

Second, as the team entered production, we found that there were few, if any, university spaces conducive to game design. Game design teams like open spaces that fit six to eight desks comfortably. They want to gather and review documents without reserving a conference room. They want to huddle multiple people around a screen to weigh in on artwork. They want walls suitable for writing and pinning notes, a central table to gather around for design reviews, and noise barriers to let the team get rowdy. They want to control lighting, sound, and interruptions.

In short, teams want to commandeer a small meeting room, which is exactly what we did. Although we dutifully removed our desktop machines when other groups needed the space, it bothered some that we staked out a conference room. Small meeting rooms are already in short supply on college campuses because they don't count as "instructional space" and thus aren't necessary in the instructionist paradigm. As more teachers embrace group work, pressure for these spaces increases. The lack of appropriate space is a constant struggle for academic and research institutions making games, which inevitably leads to conflict and culture clashes. Game developers talk a lot. Because we were spread out across a cubicle farm (and because many worked with headphones), we took to Nerf guns as a way to gain the attention of coworkers. Medical researchers did not always love this.

Eventually, our team closed the blinds and pretended that we weren't there, which worked surprisingly well. It didn't make us any better friends with the neighbors.

Game-Based Learning Results

Virulent was, in most respects, a success. Internally, *Virulent* legitimized the group. The game represented the underlying science faithfully enough to impress colleagues that we were serious. Few scientists actually played it, but many of their family members reported doing so, and the reviews were positive. As of this writing, *Virulent* has over 25,000 downloads and has a 4 out of 5 star rating on the iTunes Store, across fifty-four reviews. Visiting scholar and team member Javier Corredor translated *Virulent* into Spanish and used the game in schools in Colombia. Reviews revealed that, if anything, *Virulent* was a little *too* difficult, which the team regarded as an indicator of success. There were no major complaints about lack of realism or scientific inaccuracies.

Many students learned from playing *Virulent*. Students who played *Virulent* and read texts outperformed students who read the same texts and viewed diagrams (Söbke et al., 2013). Playing *Virulent* repositioned learners as parts of the cellular system and gave them a situated understanding of cellular functions, which better prepared them for learning, as James Paul Gee's (2004) theory of situated learning would predict. This difference appeared to be a result of two factors: (1) increased motivation in the game condition and (2) better understanding of the functions of cell parts by being "inside a working cell." Analyzing students' drawings, and in particular their talk concerning these drawings, Corredor (2011) found that game play created more social interaction, critically, interaction focused on the content itself. Not surprisingly, the game groups developed better understanding of temporal relationships and the biological mechanisms involved in viral replication. Although *Virulent* is no *Angry Birds* (or even *Flappy Bird*), as an educational research product by a first-time team, its more than 25,000 downloads, good reviews, and positive learning gains meant that it was successful.

Interest in Learning

Virulent's primary value appeared to be the way it raised students' interest in virology. Watching students play *Virulent*, we couldn't help but notice that they seemed to care more about virology than did students in a control group. To follow up on this observation, Stefan Slater, and Shannon Harris (2013) analyzed differences in task engagement between reading and game play and found that students (not surprisingly, perhaps) engaged more with *Virulent* than with readings or videos. Students who played *Virulent* before reading reported that the game was more interesting and fun. Also, outside of class, game players read more information than did those who did not play the game. Subsequent studies (Anderson, et al., 2016) have revealed similar findings, with students frequently choosing to play learning games outside of class on their own time.

The idea that games not only foster learning but also spark curiosity and raise interest in the underlying phenomena is at least as important as gains on pre- and post-test evaluations. We want students to be motivated, curious lifelong learners in an age of rapidly changing information. Longitudinal studies of children reveal that students who are deeply curious outperform those with high IQs (von Stumm et al., 2011). Educators might even rethink the concept of education as an interest-raising enterprise and look to games as a key tool for raising interest in academic domains. Perhaps games make the most sense in domains that suffer from a lack of student interest.

Sustainability of Educational Interventions

So how do we create and sustain educational interventions so that university-derived projects can continue? The traditional model is to constantly raise money through research grants (which are not intended for marketing, maintenance, or polish). Contemporary models of scaling include (1) selling copyrighted materials directly, (2) licensing copyrighted materials to other entities, and (3) encouraging students to spin off companies. Our team explored each of these avenues, which are covered throughout the book.

With *Virulent*, we had a functional prototype with an hour or two of game play. We focused on getting *Virulent* in the hands of more kids. With support from the National Science Foundation, we fleshed out and refined levels, created curricula for teachers, embedded learning analytics tools, and researched the impact of these actions. We were left with the following questions:

1. What mechanisms could pay for the maintenance and updating of *Virulent*? With no support, *Virulent* would become obsolete and unplayable within a few years as hardware and software systems evolve.

2. How might we create *Virulent* 2.0, which would include more chapters, levels, and functions (such as student-authored levels)?

3. Could we publish *Virulent*? Although *Virulent* has face validity as an educational game and is matched to standards, it was designed as a *game*, not as a product to work seamlessly within a school-based curriculum. How would *Virulent* (or any such product) get publicized, distributed, installed on machines, and supported at scale?

Conversations with publishers revealed that for *Virulent* to really work in classrooms, we would need to tightly integrate the game with the textbook.

This integration would mean reworking the art, game play, and levels to correspond to chapters and homework assignments. The content domain fell somewhere between high school, college, and graduate-level biology, and the lack of expository features (outside of a glossary) left its learning goals too opaque for schools. In short, *Virulent* was optimized to be a game, not a textbook. Finally, Chromebooks, not iPads, won the last round of school adoption, so there was no solid distribution platform.

While all of this was going on with *Virulent*, we tackled a second project that employed a social learning model: Pro-Am, or crowdsourcing, communities for learning, which we will explore next.

3 Crowdsourcing Knowledge Games in Science

Educators dream of games in which students not only learn science but also generate knowledge. Can we create games around authentic problems (folding proteins, classifying galaxies), so that game play contributes to science? These "knowledge games" apply the difficult intellectual work that gamers engage in toward solving real problems (Schrier, 2016). To take a very simple idea from the Massachusetts Institute of Technology's Games-to-Teach Project, imagine an engineering construction game (such as the 3 Gorges Dam) in which players terraform watersheds to develop productive and environmentally friendly ecosystems, to invent better solutions while informing the public. As journalist, internet theorist, and attorney Julian Dibbell (2006) proclaimed, that play will be for the 21st century what steam was to the 19th century.

The cleanest model for knowledge games is *Galaxy Zoo*, one of the oldest and most successful Pro-Am (crowdsourcing) science communities (Schrier, 2016). In *Galaxy Zoo*, laypeople help astronomers by identifying and categorizing telescopic images of galaxies (Crowston et al., 2018). According to its BBC News, by its 10 ear anniversary, *Galaxy Zoo* had classified 125 million (of 100 billion) galaxies, resulting in sixty peer-reviewed academic papers across fifteen projects (Gray, 2017). *Galaxy Zoo* has spun out its own platform, Zooniverse, which houses projects ranging from cataloging whale sounds to transcribing British war diaries from World War II. The new steam power indeed.

Foldit, a protein-folding simulation game, has inspired a generation of game designers who make games that produce knowledge (see Cooper et al., 2010; Khatib et al., 2011; Shapiro & Squire, 2012). Initially funded through the Defense Advanced Research Projects Agency (DARPA) to leverage game technologies to crowdfund science, *Foldit* grew out of University of Washington biochemist and computational scientist David Baker's work with the Rosetta@home project, a distributed computation project in which participants donate unused computer cycles at home to further scientific tasks. Baker approached colleagues David Salesin and Zoran Popović to turn Rosetta into a game in which players might do the protein folding so that computers could study which protein-folding approaches are most effective.

In *Foldit*, players solve protein-folding puzzles. As players identify amino acid chains that can bind to protein receptors, engineers can use these data to engineer drugs. In addition to finding specific protein-folding solutions, computer scientists examine *how* players fold proteins and more general protein-folding algorithms. *Foldit* players excelled at problem solving and were especially good (as compared with computers) at searching the problem space for potential solutions. Cooper and colleagues described that players, unlike computers, not only searched the problem space but also searched all of the possible search *strategies*. We are good, collectively, not just at problem solving but also at exploring the different ways one goes about it, especially visually (Cooper et al., 2010). These findings mirror earlier studies of *Tetris* players. Good *Tetris* players don't just solve problems; they manipulate pieces (changing the problem space) to make good solutions easier to see (Kirsh & Maglio, 1994). *Tetris* players rotate blocks until they can "see" good solutions. In other words, good *Tetris* play isn't necessarily about looking at a piece and searching for solutions but rather about manipulating pieces so that optimal solutions can be seen.

In a well-publicized study published in *Nature*, *Foldit* players solved in three weeks an enzyme structure involved in human immunodeficiency virus (HIV) reproduction that had not been solved in fifteen years (Cooper et al., 2010). In talking with the *Foldit* community, Zoran Popovic posted the following:

> Over the 2 years of *Fold.it* life, we have both shown that *Fold.it* players can outperform known computational methods, discovered the structure of an unsolved protein, discovered novel automated methods for protein relaxation, and designed new proteins that are confirmed in the laboratory. Arguably, it would be hard to find any new lab in the world that could boast with these kinds of outcomes in just 2 years of its existence.

The *Foldit* team then gave players tools to see what algorithms they could make. Players' strategies converged on solutions remarkably similar to those created by experts, although the players' algorithm, in fact, offered "faster and more effective energy optimization than previous methods." Publications based on *Foldit* have slowed since 2011–2012, but *Foldit* is active; a recent *Nature* publication described the WeFold collaborative initiative for protein structure prediction (Keaser et al., 2018). The *Foldit* team has created games for other domains, including kids' mathematics games for adaptive learning techniques (*Refraction*).

The field continues to be inspired by these games for scientific discovery. A compelling example is Princeton University's *EyeWire*, in which players compete to map the brain. Funded by an IARPA (Intelligence Advanced Research Projects Activity) grant, the Seugn Lab, working with the Eyewirers, has reconstructed nearly 400 ganglion cells, discovered 6 new cell types, and mapped over 50 cubes during its Countdown to Neuropia in 2014–2015 (Greene et al., 2016). Recent iterations of *Eyewire* leverage social mechanics, such as achievement systems to deepen engagement and sustain participation.

Knowledge games introduce players to scientific tools, open the scientific process, support thinking with models, and deepen affiliation with science. These goals are often overlooked but are crucial to modern life (see National Research Council, 2011). The key threats to human survival on Earth (e.g., global warming, food security, water management) all require fluency with scientific models, projects, and uncertainty within data. In fact, Tom Malone, one of the original theorists of games and motivation, created the Climate CoLab platform for crowdsourcing responses to environmental challenges (see Fisher, 2018).

Nevertheless, these knowledge games are data analysis tools and not learning games. They appeal to enthusiasts but not to typical youths or the general public. They do not claim to "teach" underlying scientific concepts (e.g., molecular biology or neurology), which gives rise to the design challenge in this chapter: Can a knowledge game be both a learning tool and a context for learning biology?[1]

This chapter discusses the development of *Anatomy Pro-Am*, a design effort around a Pro-Am game for detection and treatment of cancers. We wanted to design a game-based learning system to help cure cancer while also teaching kids about the underlying biology and about careers in medical fields (see figures 3.1–3.3). We knew that *Anatomy Pro-Am* was unlikely to exist anytime soon, but we thought it better to try an ambitious project than not to try at all.

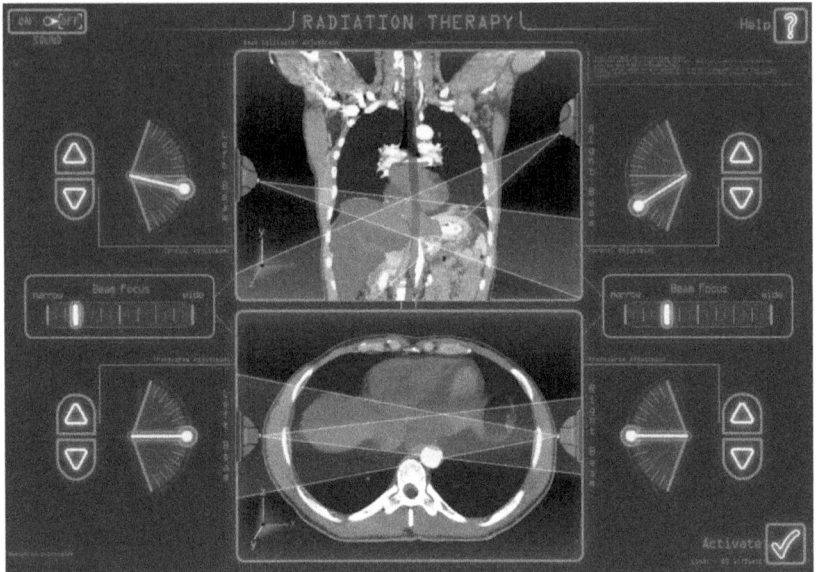

Figure 3.1
Anatomy Pro-Am treatment screens.

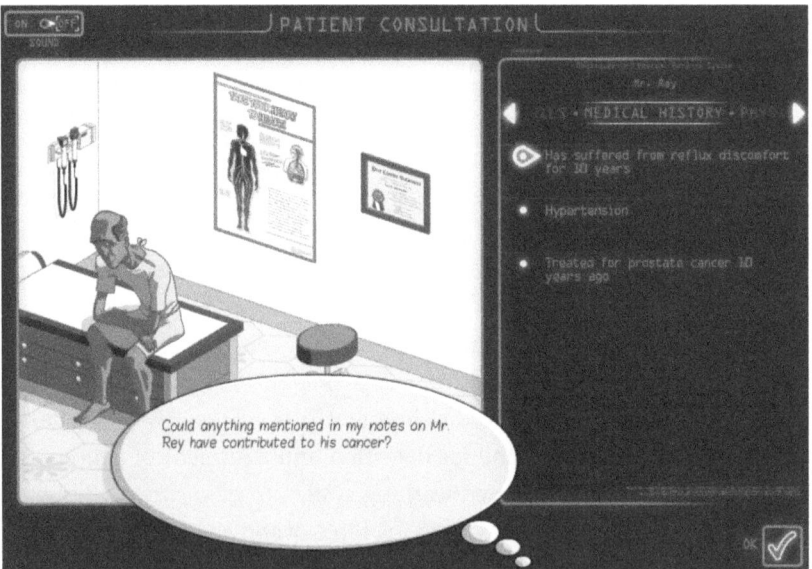

Figure 3.2
Anatomy Pro-Am patient dialogue and patient chart examination.

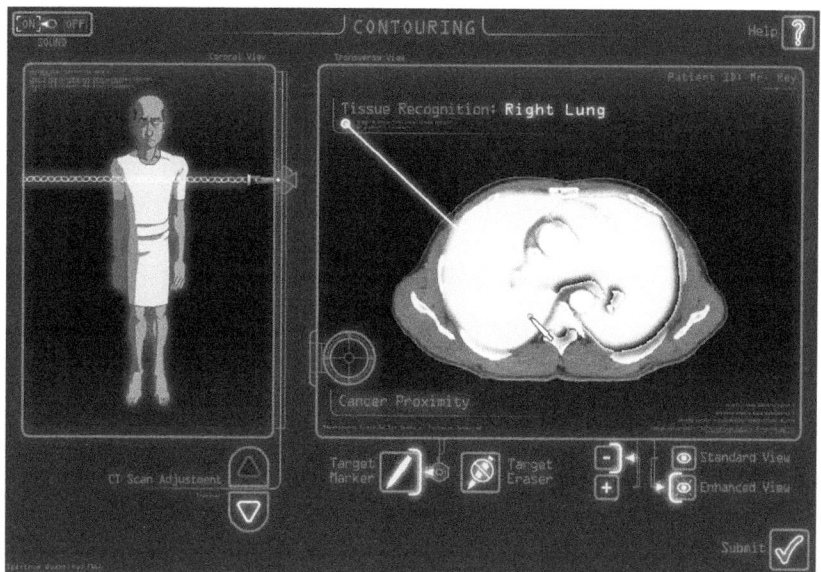

Figure 3.3
Anatomy Pro-Am contouring interface with "hot/cold" tool.

Thomas "Rock" Mackie, founder of the TomoTherapy approach to treating cancer, approached our group with an idea. Rock observed that most physicians struggled to take two-dimensional images of the body and mentally construct models of cancerous growths in three dimensions. When diagnosing and treating cancer, physicians infer the size and shape of anomalous tissue by mentally composing images taken along three planes (axial, coronal, and sagittal) of the body. Rock noticed that doctors who reported playing games seemed to do better than those who did not play games. Could a knowledge game help improve their ability to construct 3D images or, at least, expose the problem by demonstrating how much better gamers were?

Problems in diagnosing cancer are larger than one might imagine. Historically, radiologists have interpreted medical images as they were taught by whoever introduced them to the machine. As a result, there is enormous variation in the way radiologists interpret images and where they see cancer in them (see Shapiro, n.d., for a more extensive write-up). Several studies show massive differences in the ways radiologists analyze images. When asked to color images in which they see cancerous growth, radiologists differ in their treatment of cervical cancer by a factor of four (Weiss et al., 2003). If the area contoured is too small, cancerous growth could be left behind, but if it is too large, healthy tissue would be removed unnecessarily. Each region of the body includes trade-offs. Exposing the head to excessive radiation is more dangerous than exposing the neck (which can be trickier to isolate). Researchers who investigated physicians treating cancer in other areas of the body have reached similar findings.

Rock's theory was that a video game about contouring and treating cancer could help. It could raise awareness of the problem among physicians, could be used in medical education courses, and could possibly form the basis of a Pro-Am community around cancer detection and treatment. Rock imagined that a patient could submit her cancer scans to a Pro-Am community of analysts who would contour the growths, debate approaches, and make a recommendation. Imagine getting not just a first or second opinion but thousands of additional opinions that could be combined into a well-defined consensus.

Rock's enthusiasm for the idea was infectious, so we assembled a team. Led by postdoc Ben Shapiro (now on faculty at the University of Colorado Boulder), we found stellar collaborators in Kevin Eliceiri, director of the University of Wisconsin–Madison's Laboratory for Optical and Computational Instrumentation (LOCI), and Lonie Salkowski, a professor in the Radiology and Medical Physics Departments at UW–Madison. Both had an interest in games and technology, and Lonie had a background in art and medical imaging.

Designing Core Game Play

The idea of a medical diagnosis game is not new. In my previous book *Video Games and Learning*, I described *Biohazard*, a role-playing game in which players are emergency room doctors who diagnose and treat illnesses. In fact, a number of entertainment games (such as the Emergency Room series) tackle similar concepts, and detective games have evolved into a compelling entertainment genre (*L.A. Noire*; *Detroit: Become Human*). Earlier, we had prototyped similar mechanics games for mobile devices in which players investigate illnesses; see *Environmental Detectives* and *Mad City Mystery* (Klopfer, 2008; Squire & Jan, 2007) and *River City* (Code et al., 2013).

Rock and Lonie described the basic process one goes through when suffering from cancer. Patients first note *symptoms*, such as a lump with breast cancer or persistent coughing with blood, bloody stool, or perhaps changes in urination. A patient will then undergo *imaging* as physicians take pictures of the body trying to arrive at a *diagnosis* of what is occurring in the body. On the basis of diagnostic tests, the physician will then prescribe *treatments*. Currently, three main treatments are prescribed (often in combination), which Rock described as essentially "cut, poison, or burn," which correspond to surgery, chemotherapy, or radiation therapy.

At least five additional questions drove the decision to explore *Anatomy Pro-Am*:

1. Could *Anatomy Pro-Am* inspire discussions about acceptable standards for interpreting anomalies on medical images and variances in the way treatments are prescribed?
2. Could we teach science through health and human systems games (an idea of perennial interest, going back to *Fantastic Voyage*)?
3. Could a game increase student awareness of professional opportunities in medical technology?
4. Could a role-playing game (*Anatomy Pro-Am*) complement a simulation-based game (*Virulent*) in an integrated curriculum?
5. Could *Anatomy Pro-Am* create collaborative grants opportunities with medical researchers?

With *Foldit* in the headlines and ourselves located in the Wisconsin Institute for Discovery, we would be insane *not* to try a scientific discovery game.

Minimal Viable Product Prototype

Rather than build one giant cancer detection game for everyone, we created a suite of interrelated prototypes that share a common data infrastructure. We anticipated that students would need scaffolds on how to read medical images (or even an introduction to the domain). The first prototype (*Oncology*) tested the core game cycle: (1) analyze symptoms, (2) analyze images, and (3) treat virtual patients (see figures 3.1–3.3). A working prototype of these game components could direct future development.

In contrast to *Virulent*, which we built in-house, *Oncology* was built in partnership with Filament Games. We wanted to test collaboration with contractors, and Filament's team built consistently high-quality games. We were still questioning whether game production should be a core lab competency (as opposed to design or ideation). *Oncology* enabled us to test embedding of our postdocs and graduate students in the Filament lab.

Partnering with Contractors in a Research Environment
Oncology was relatively straightforward to develop (maybe because we outsourced it!), but we learned lessons. First, the idea of embedding team members at Filament was misguided. Filament had its own management processes, platform, code libraries, and production schedules, which meant that our team had to learn Filament's tools and work around its production schedule. Even though Filament was still a small company, it already had a diverse team with specialized roles. The company would put a team of four to six developers on the game and make fast progress in a concentrated time frame, rather than have people hanging around half-time on a project. Within a few years, that was how we operated as well.

Experienced developers will also spot the managerial problems. Did researcher-developers report to Filament or to me? Who was responsible for the production? Development teams have their own production practices, language, and culture. Enculturating our team into Filament would have slowed them down more than anything. Further, as a for-profit company, Filament had its own proprietary techniques and processes, which they were willing to share, but it didn't feel sustainable. They were fantastic collaborators, but our model mixed roles and responsibilities in unhealthy ways.

Next, and most important, full-time development shops and research groups have distinct work rhythms. Game development (like most software development) has changing project velocity, requires coordination among multiple different disciplines, and involves coordination of overlapping contingencies. Early in development, programmers and artists can exchange information about engine requirements and bugs multiple times throughout the day. Compare this schedule with that of students, who at most have twenty hours per week for production and go for days without appearing in the office. Doing game development on academic calendars is always challenging, and trying to mix academics with typical work calendars complicates it further.

Communication challenges (which we would later have internally) arose between academics and developers. Early in production, a Filament developer (reasonably) questioned whether we could combine stylized characters with CT scans. A researcher sent research articles referring to similar ideas, much as a game developer might mention prior art. Conflicts arose as the Filament developers, who usually own development decisions, designed with researchers, who are used to dictating designs. In traditional structures, these issues are resolved through discrete responsibilities (or clear lines in a contractor-contractee relationship). In the case of a research and development lab, it's messier. Further, trust is a central challenge to all game development teams, and expecting a distributed model to work without significant investments in team building was naive (see Spaulding, 2019).

Dynamics of Outsourcing Development
Outsourcing development to a partner is problematic for game design research. Design is intellectual work. Designing teaches us about the problem space, helps us uncover the affordances of technologies, and helps us learn about the medium. You cannot learn these lessons without getting your hands dirty in design. Playing with ideas is partly how we explore the medium. Even theoreticians (maybe especially theoreticians) benefit from working side by side with designers so as to better understand the material constraints of media (see Dourish, 2017, for great examples of this).

Partnering with developers works when the design is less ambiguous, the expertise of each partner is well articulated, and roles are clear. "Outsourcing" team management, running production cycles, and enduring the headaches in creating working software was nice. Academics rarely, if ever, make software that works reliably and meets market needs. A company such as Filament, in contrast, has methods for developing consistently reliable software on time and within budget. Whereas *academic* groups value experimentation, new ideas, novel solutions to problems, a future-looking orientsation, and learning (with high, regular turnover), *development* groups leverage existing work and patterns, value consistency, and build project management processes over multiple cycles of projects completed with consistent staff (see table 3.1).

In short, game design students are good for exploratory work or research funded by federal grants. An external developer makes sense when games must work *reliably*, in school settings, or for impact beyond research. Academic games are rarely played outside of a prescribed intervention, bribery, or even light coercion. Building an internal team makes sense for multiple

Table 3.1
Academic versus work-for-hire development

Feature	Academic	Work for hire
Expected staff turnover	High	Low to medium
Experience	Little	Lots
Orientation	Future	Present
Development preference	Rolling one's own	Building on established platforms
Design focus	Stretching boundaries	Leveraging patterns to reduce risks

ongoing projects, a game design program for developers to teach in (which can defray costs), a need for faculty and students to learn *from* designers, or a desire to prepare students for careers in industry (where a majority of PhD students end up). An internal development team is particularly important for PhD students to teach in game design programs or enter industry.

Oncology Game

Oncology represents a design pattern that should become common in learning games: case-based game play in which learners role-play as professionals. The game itself is organized around patient cases. The first step is to meet the patient and engage in a conversation to learn symptoms. We had mixed feelings about multiple-choice conversations as a mechanic, but it worked well enough to engage users while conveying information and encouraging players to think about the patient. These same patterns are employed in games from Rockstar Games' *L.A. Noire* to Nintendo's *Phoenix Wright: Ace Attorney* (which are mandatory playing for learning game designers), games that both Filament's cofounder and design director Dan Norton and I find inspiring. Recent games such as Quantic Dream's *Detroit: Become Human* update these mechanics with more compelling models of information gathering and decision making.

Next, players examine a CT image with an afflicted part of the body taken from a repository of cases. Players then contour the image using drawing tools. Notice the sliders on the left side of the screen in figure 3.X_. Clicking the sliders up and down reveals images corresponding to that part of the body. Recall that one of the challenges for physicians was in constructing a mental 3D image from these series of 2D photos. Notice that Filament successfully created an art style that mixes stylized vector graphics with photographic images.

Finally, players aim beams of radiation at the cancer while trying to avoid healthy tissue. The game included minimal instruction on the procedure or how to use the tools. In fact, the entire *Oncology* experience was "simulationy" enough that one might question whether it was a game. The user experience, particularly the aiming of radiation beams, was engaging enough that most students and teachers used it for years on BrainPOP.

Ben Shapiro led a study of this prototype and found that the majority of users had no idea what they were looking at. In some ways, it was okay that players struggled to read images; a strength of games for learning is that they can throw players in over their heads and let them learn (*Phoenix Wright* does this as well). On the other hand, with too much confusion, players lack direction and purpose and may leave the game too early, potentially with misconceptions. We were in the "too confusing to be useful" territory; staring at nonmeaningful images and coloring them was not going to cure cancer.

We faced a new challenge. Was there a way to give players a meaningful experience of reading CT scans, contouring, and treating cancer within the game? How could we create a meaningful context for game play within budget? We wanted to make a series of smaller, more focused games in which people learned to read CT scans through guided game play, but we were just about out of time and money.

The team landed on a compromise to scaffold players. Filament's production lead, Arthur Low, created an on-screen "hot/cold" cancer detector that changed color to indicate when the user had moused close to or over a cancerous area (see figure 3.3). A green circle with a glowing dot in the middle indicated that the user was near cancer and should label that area as a tumor. It changed color to red as the user moved farther away from where the cancer was.

Players still found the cancer indicator confusing. One participant labeled almost everything *except* the tumor as cancer. Even after we enhanced the contrast on images, many players could not discern differences across images. With the project funding running low, we ran out of ways to improve the interface and decided just to explain whatever we needed to verbally. This example is a good reminder that when designing games for learning, it is critically important to test the core mechanics with users early and often.

Pilot Tests with Youth

Despite the game prototype not being done, we wanted to look for *any* evidence that people would learn from playing the game. Would playing *Oncology* raise interest in medical careers? Would players become more familiar with cancer and cancer treatment? We wanted evidence that the project was worth continuing. Working with team members Shannon Harris, Meagan Rothschild, David van Leeuwen, and Katja Halverson, we ran a small pilot study with sixty-nine middle and high school students including pre- and post-test measures.

With very little known about student thinking in oncology, we cobbled together research instruments and asked questions such as "What is difficult about the radiotherapy process?" and "What is the most important way to find cancer using a CT scanner?" Students then played the game in a classic pre- and post-test study, with kids playing *Oncology* for about twenty-five minutes. We found statistically significant ($p < .05$ or better) improvements in students' understanding of (1) what a radiologist does; (2) what tools and technologies a radiologist uses; (3) what contouring is (shading or coloring in areas of unhealthy cancerous tissue); and (4) what is difficult about the radiotherapy process (keeping healthy tissue from being exposed to radiation beams). Finally, researchers noted increased interest in medical careers, and, for female players, increased confidence that they could be good doctors when they grow up.

However, participants also overgeneralized from the "cancer detection" scaffolding tool. When presented with the question "What is the most important way to find cancer using a CT scanner?," almost half (thirty-four) got the answer correct on the pre-test ("Observing minor variations in some tissue as compared to other tissue"). *After* playing the game, almost half (thirty-four) students selected "Watching for the light on the scanner tool to change color." We took this as evidence that our scaffolding was doing more harm than good and needed to be changed.

Role-playing as scientists positively affected students' interest in medical careers and self-efficacy as medical professionals. When presented with statements such as "I am interested in pursuing a career in the medical profession when I'm older (for example, becoming a doctor, nurse, or other healthcare worker)," student responses jumped about 0.5 point on a 5-point scale (and were statistically significant at the p<.0001 level). Likewise, self-efficacy in medical careers increased for females. Male students entered with higher self-assessments than female students, and these actually did not increase significantly, while female students' self-efficacy leapfrogged those of the males. We concluded that a role-playing game about cancer can challenge females' disproportionately negative self-judgments about fitness for careers in medicine.

Overall, the pilot tests were encouraging. We saw knowledge gains (and one loss) in anatomy and physiology, increased knowledge of radiation therapy procedures, and increased awareness of oncology as a career and increases in self-efficacy (Shapiro & Squire, 2011). Role-playing games are a good route for increasing participation in science (see also Barab & Dede, 2007; Squire & Jan, 2007).

Supporting Medical Education with Simulation Games

Now that we had developed a proof of concept for onboarding younger learners, we tackled the question of how to support professional medical students in learning imaging with game-based technologies. We decided to develop this internally because we wanted tighter iterations of research and development. Game design was becoming a core competency.

To build the professional interface, we partnered with Lonie Salkowski, a radiologist at UW–Madison. Ben Shapiro led the development in a Facebook application for medical students to communicate while diagnosing patients. In the Facebook app, medical students were divided into groups and marked up images, which enabled instructors to "see" their thinking (Brown et al., 1989). Most important, putting a game on Facebook created a context for medical students, K–12 students, and teachers at all levels to interact.

Similarly to the *Oncology* pilot, we studied how medical students might use such an application. It was immediately obvious that discussing images in groups was useful in making thinking visible. In particular, medical students struggled with that same dilemma that Rock Mackie presented: medical images are two-dimensional and taken from various angles (axial, coronal, and sagittal views), and physicians must piece together these views to mentally construct a model of the underlying anatomy. As Salkowski

(2017) described in her dissertation, students struggled to connect medical images with physical anatomy on even a basic level. We refocused development on this goal.

A Facebook game supported collaboration and linked social networks, but medical students wanted a reference app for their phones or tablets. To test this idea, we built a prototype of a medical imaging learning app called *Anatomy Browser*. *Anatomy Browser* enabled users to examine anatomical images connected to a 3D virtual human to connect anatomical imaging to human systems. Designed primarily as a reference resource, it included a 3D body, CT scans connected to various views, a 3D fly-through, and rudimentary game and analytics elements (see figure 3.4). Analytic tools enabled developers and researchers to track users as they "flew" through the body to see what users found interesting and see where they were getting stuck. (Learners frequently got stuck flying out of the intestines.) These heat map visualizations became the basis for visualizations of player performance in future games (see Paiz-Rameriz, 2016). We soft launched *Anatomy Browser* on the iTunes Store in 2013.

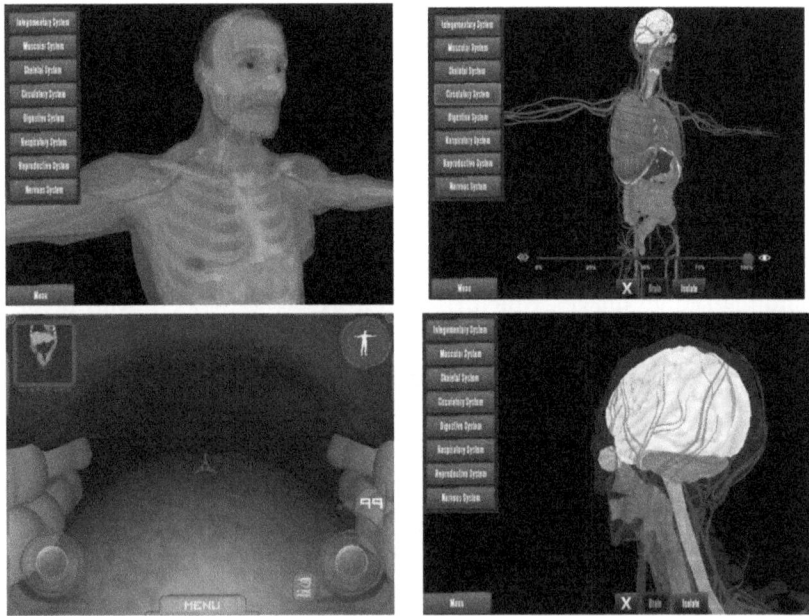

Figure 3.4
Anatomy Browser with fly-throughs.

Medical students valued *Anatomy Browser* as a learning tool and benefited from using it. Dr. Salkowski taught with *Anatomy Browser* in UW–Madison medical imaging courses and found increases in student performance in pre- and post-test evaluations using the materials (from 74 percent correct to 100 percent correct, $n = 50$, $t = 3.61$, $p < .001$, $r = .51$). We are cautious about overestimating the impact of *Anatomy Browser*, given the lack of a control group and the fact that medical students are famously motivated and skilled learners. However, between their learning gains and enthusiasm for the product, we saw sufficiently positive results to continue development.

Integrating Medical Education into K–12 Learning

So far, we had established the capacity to develop and deploy anatomical imaging tools across PCs (Flash-based game for kids), social media platforms to scaffold social interaction (Facebook), and mobile devices for classroom use (iPads). We still wanted to examine the use of *Anatomy Pro-Am* with real kids in a real learning environment. A quick twenty-five-minute lesson with a tool is one thing. Creating a curriculum for use in real schools is another.

We next created *Diagnostic Detective*, a problem-based curriculum that integrates game materials in a live action role-playing game. In *Diagnostic Detective* (created by two partner teachers, Sheri Ebert and Julia Kallio), students role-played as oncology specialists (oncologists, radiologists, and MRI/CT technicians) in a weeklong (five- to seven-hour) unit. We deployed *Diagnostic Detective* over spring break to help with data collection, but it was designed to be a two- to four-week school unit.

The learning objectives for *Diagnostic Detective* were for students to (1) become familiar with basic anatomy and physiology, (2) develop positive associations with medical technology careers, and (3) increase basic medical vocabulary literacy. Learning activities included identifying symptoms by reading charts and interviewing others role-playing as patients, ordering tests, consulting game-based materials, and compiling results to make diagnoses and prognoses. At the end of the week, students created new cases for future camps.

Diagnostic Detectives took place in an after-school setting (spring break). As in other informal learning environments (see Cole, 2006), we struggled to maintain strong engagement in the face of alternatives, such as going home to play. The vocabulary demanded by the unit was a consistent barrier; specialized medical terms from "axial view" to "oncology" put students off. Students' understanding of basic human systems (e.g., the function of specific organs, such as the liver) were weak. Responses to a pre-test reflected this; of the forty-three respondents, only one correctly identified what a radiologist does, with an additional four giving partially correct answers (such as a medical career dealing with radiation). A few students thought that they "listened to radios all day." In response, teachers created whole-group lessons on the fly, which were generally not successful. They next created "fun" activities such as a bingo vocabulary game, which went over better.

Students willingly stepped into the role-play activities, particularly regarding teamwork. They eagerly donned costumes, embraced their roles, and displayed their specialized expertise within groups. This mirrored findings with similar curricular enactments (c.f. Squire & Jan, 2007; Squire, 2008). Seeing this engagement, the teachers created an activity for the final day in which students created videos to demonstrate their understanding.

Students confronted a "final" scenario in which they viewed a new case study, analyzed printed MRI and CT scans, contoured cancerous areas, proposed a treatment plan, developed a prognosis, and shared their results in a video presentation. The teachers reflected as follows:

> The video on the last day was a great activity and kids really got into acting it out. I think it was important that they had to act out and speak the terms because it revealed a lot of misconceptions, some of which we were able to discuss. I would have expanded it to be two days . . . watching the films as a group—it allowed them to see how others interpreted them.

On the final day, teachers declined to administer the post-test because of time limitations and a lack of student motivation. Given students' lack of knowledge in oncology, the lack of a comparison/control group, and the unlikeliness of this curriculum to be enacted in classrooms, researchers supported this decision.[2] We arrived at the following findings:

- Role-playing scenarios are a good model for integrating game-based resources and activities, which can serve as "training exercises" or resources in the role-playing context.
- Face-to-face role-playing promotes scientific literacy because it requires students to speak within roles and develop academic vocabulary; see also Squire & Jan (2007).

- Whole-group lessons failed to hold students' attention, but individualized or personalized learning activities, including tutorials, were embraced.
- Producing a video case created a natural occasion for assessment, similar to Bransford and colleagues' "test your mettle" exercises (see Bransford & Schwartz, 1999).
- Teaching oncology within science classes requires an understanding of anatomy that these students do not have.
- Teachers were reticent to try this curriculum in school because it would invite classroom management risks and require unusually supportive parents and administrators.

Anatomy Pro-Am evolved into two follow-up projects:

1. A line of inquiry in medical imaging directed by Dr. Salkowski with interactive mannequins (see figure 3.5). Dr. Salkowski's (2017) dissertation, "Designing and Using Simulation to Study Expert-Novice Differences in Correlating Medical Imaging with the Physical Exam," used these materials for learning imaging in medical education.
2. A multiyear partnership with DeVry Medical International to adapt materials for medical, nursing, and veterinary schools, directed by Dr. Eric Bauman, a former student and assistant dean at DeVry's Institute for Research and Clinical Strategy.

iPad Apps for Medical and Veterinary Education

After seeing the *Anatomy Browser* and Facebook applications, Bauman developed an idea: Could we create iPad apps to bring these games to medical and veterinary education? How should a game-based medical training curriculum work?

The result of this brainstorm was the PawPad, the first veterinary school iPad rollout. The PawPad contained a suite of iPad apps and tools for medical and veterinary education. Unlike other efforts in which students were given generic tablets, the PawPad included research-driven tools tailored to address needs such as just-in-time tutorials requested by students in needs assessments.

The first issue we tackled was preparing veterinarians for large animal anesthetization. As of this writing, DeVry teaches anesthetization by sending

Figure 3.5
Interactive table and mannequin.

students to a "field of donkeys," located in the Caribbean. Although students see videos of the procedure, they cannot practice it before visiting the donkey field. Common sense would tell you that it's a sketchy proposition to practice anesthetization for the first time on a live donkey. If something goes wrong, it's bad not just for the donkey but also for the school, which answers to boards of supervisors. The penalties for killing animals during training are severe.

Enter *iDonkey* (see figure 3.6). As described in "Building a Better Donkey" (Bauman et al., 2015), players practice suturing a leg laceration on a donkey. They check the patient's health, prepare the patient for surgery, sedate and induce anesthesia, and finally wake the patient and guide it back to its feet. The simulation replicates the hands-on tests students use on real patients: students check the patient's pulse and capillary refill time, or press on the donkey's exposed gums to observe how the blood returns to the surface to gauge healing time. Next, students pick the proper sedative and anesthetic agents and dosages. The game keeps the player on loose rails as they induce the patient and apply their knowledge of drugs to manage the recovery. They calculate proper dosage, anesthetize the donkey, and then deal with complications. Players triage patients and manage the donkey's recovery through simulated monitors and indicators.

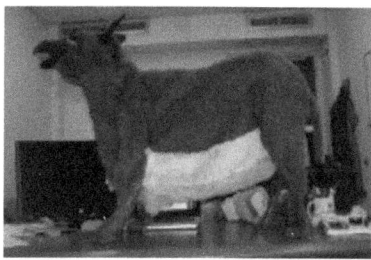 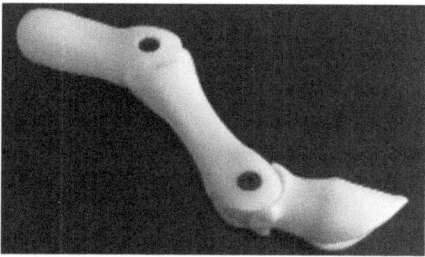

Figure 3.6
iDonkey, a donkey anesthetizing training simulation.

This description highlights one of the more obvious uses of simulation-based games: practicing procedures that are risky or expensive. *iDonkey* made sense for a location-based audience, but it didn't seem like the ideal candidate for scaling; it was difficult to mass-produce, and it was entertaining to us but perhaps not to everyone.

The idea of a shared physical object to organize group problem solving was compelling. While we worked on *iDonkey*, colleague Matthew Berland, the New York Hall of Science, and our team built *MakeScape*, an interactive table for collaborative constructionist learning (see figure 3.7) (Danielak et al., 2014). Seeing the mannequin and *Anatomy Browser* side by side led to the obvious next step: *AnatomyTable*, an interactive large-format 3D touch screen for exploring anatomy. It was designed to support collaborative problem solving around complex spatial relationships (Adams & Wilson, 2011; Bauman et al., 2015). Whereas *iDonkey* remediated the experience of treating a live donkey, *AnatomyTable* remediated the experience of using a dissection table. Thinking of dissection as a game opened new ideas, specifically matching cases, learning objectives, tracking learner movements, and designing for collaboration. Students reported valuing *AnatomyTable* and wanted it available for courses (Bauman, 2016). Although our work uses digital games as the starting point for learning experiences, professional training exercises and practicums are also excellent starting points for building learning games (see Shaffer, 2006).

AnatomyTable led to a veterinary education dissection platform: Anatomical and Physiology Exploration (APEX). In short, APEX allows the exploration of canines (APEXCanine), humans (APEXHuman), and birds (APEXVolucride), but it is expandable to any species. Through APEX, learners treat virtual

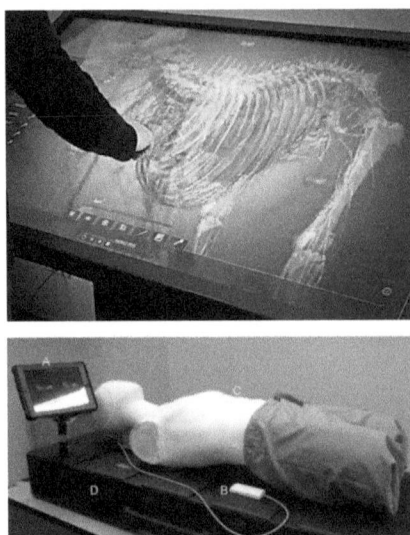

Figure 3.7
MakeScape, an interactive table science game for the New York Hall of Science.

cases in groups and compare and contrast species. In the last phases of the partnership, Games+Learning+Society (GLS) collaborated with DeVry to create and market tables that were distributed to its training sites.

The Role of Research in Transforming Social Institutions

Products generated revenue (and kept staff, especially 3D artists, employed), but more important (and true for academic or industry centers), they validated the value of a product in the marketplace. Most games for impact are built through grants and lead to "zombie companies or products" that no one really wants. Striving to enter the market demonstrates the long-term viability of an approach. *Anatomy Pro-Am*, however, faced the following challenges:

1. Medicine is not a large part of K–12 education. Should we change K–12 science curricula to include medicine?
2. Most teachers do not want to teach anatomy to middle schoolers because of inevitable behavioral concerns.
3. Few government agencies fund health education. The National Science Foundation funds science education; health-related research is funded

by the National Institutes of Health. However, the NIH funds research with a direct impact on health outcome variables (such as obesity or a specific disease), not education (with some recent exceptions, such as Smart Health).

4. *Anatomy Pro-Am* requires sustained institutional support and leverageable social capital (such as Rock Mackie as an advocate). How realistic is it to reform K–12 education and medical practice at the same time?

An ambitious project requires sustained, *exclusive* attention of multiple faculty members, who have the resources, social capital, and motivation to make this a career. Lacking that dedication, we put *Anatomy Pro-Am* on hold.

Anatomy Pro-Am also demonstrated the following.

Transdisciplinary design collaborations. Our best ideas occurred through the mix of game developers, academics, scientists, and industry leaders discussing problems and opportunities. Physical structures of university labs are not set up for such collaborations. Faculty and students are housed in departments, where they know mostly the same things as their colleagues. Labs sometimes share space, but they usually share basic ways of approaching the world and the types of problems they work on. Situating a game lab next to medical scientists, next to science educators, generated new ideas, especially when there was sustained, informal interaction. As an educational technologist, I found it especially valuable to work adjacent to engineers, who also learn through making things and were less jaded by the challenges to education reform.

Social innovation and transformation. Developing technologies, researching their impact, and getting them adopted are all hard. Layering in social innovation—trying to change the work of schools and health-care institutions—is even more difficult. Creating Pro-Am game communities for researchers to passively collect data played for fun is easier than transforming policies and procedures. Supporting games for impact becomes a long-term project of involving multiple stakeholder groups and institutions.

Users in different social institutions with different game requirements. A project such as *Anatomy Pro-Am could* work, but the game experience must be tailored for each audience. A successful product must improve lives for stakeholder groups (students, teachers, doctors, patients) *and* fit within institutional constraints. An incredibly compelling game could help transform an institution, but it is unlikely to do so alone. Projects innovating along multiple dimensions—inventing new technologies and changing established social institutions—require focus and relentless energy. Even *Foldit*, a data generation game created only for researchers, was funded by multiple investigators over years with sustained funding by the US Department of Defense. Future projects would benefit from having multiple committed principal investigators writing grants across their respective areas as well.

Researchers can, however, generate research findings that push a system toward change. As this book went to press, a research study published by the National Academy of Sciences (Mohan et al., 2018) revealed that a serious game can improve the triage of patients. In a study of 320 physicians, those who played either of two training games were less likely to miss patients in danger (undertriage) than those in a control condition, by about 20 percent. Tying training outcomes through a game not just to learning gains but also to medical performance suggests the power of games as training tools and the role of research in catalyzing change. Taking a step back, it's difficult to imagine medical training *not* including tools like *Anatomy Pro-Am* fifty years from now.

Learning experiences as layers of interaction. The multimodal models of medical training that we developed with DeVry may be applicable more broadly. Whereas learning with media research often compares one medium with another, our DeVry model led to a layered model for training in medical education (Bauman, 2016), emphasizing the back-and-forth across didactic explanations, interactive applications, haptic simulations, and real-world practice. Such models are explored more fully in subsequent chapters.

4   *Fair Play*: Scaling Teams for Impact

Most academic games are made by a few students or faculty members working together, perhaps contracting with an artist. This approach works well (enough) for making technology demos or answering (some) research questions. But what about taking projects to market, scaling them in situations in which they don't have "captive" audiences (e.g., in school or paid for in a research study)? Can we make games for impact with the production quality and processes of entertainment games? How can we set up projects from the beginning to be scalable? How does management in such a project look?

This chapter details experiences in building and scaling a team that spans academics and commercial developers from large studios and small independent teams. It articulates a prototype-driven approach to design—suitable to a noncaptive audience with multiple unknowns.

The narrative begins with a grant awarded to Dr. Molly Carnes to explore how digital games might remediate implicit bias. Dr. Carnes, director of the Center for Women's Health Research at the University of Wisconsin–Madison, studies how implicit biases and stereotypes color our actions, especially in relation to women and minorities. For example, scientists rate papers and résumés from applicants with female names lower than identical applications with male names, perhaps because people associate being a quality scientist with being male (Moss-Racusin et al., 2012). These biases are inequitable and detrimental to society; every year qualified women unnecessarily leave the sciences, which leads to shortages of skilled scientists, to speak nothing of the ethical considerations.

Dr. Carnes's grant hypothesized that a game based on her gender bias workshops could mitigate bias at scale. Conducting face-to-face workshops is expensive. Carnes's team hypothesized that an online game could deliver role-playing experiences more cheaply. Creating such a game for faculty and graduate students was exciting, if not harrowing (for a lengthier description, see Paiz-Ramirez et al., 2011). What genre would work for scientists, most of whom are nongamers? Why would scientists, who likely think of themselves as fair and objective, play?

We wanted equity issues in our portfolio, and the chance to work with Dr. Carnes was exciting. Our team had not yet tackled issues with a driving social purpose, which was personally disappointing. We wanted to champion these issues within the Wisconsin Institute for Discovery (WID), which had few senior female, Latinx, or African American scientists. Social justice was not a commitment shared by all team members or, necessarily, by WID as a whole, as it would be in education. This project created an opportunity to define group values (see table 2.1).

Developing a Learning Game for Science Faculty

A game about bias raises production questions as well. Could we represent people with a range of emotions (e.g., surprise, disdain, guilt, anger)? What art style works for this audience? This project began before the Gamergate controversy, but we were aware of potential backlash.[1] We also had concerns common to serious games projects: how to give the player real choices while also ensuring that learning occurs, how to bridge the cultural differences across academics and developers, and how to manage player failure and transgression in sensitive areas. These concerns color almost every games for impact project to some degree, but they were especially salient here.

We committed to a rapid prototyping ethos of "failing early and often," rather than overdesigning on paper and hoping it would work out in the end. We planned to uncover design challenges through cycles of design, testing, and reflection, rather than arguing endlessly. Second, we committed to involve developers from diverse backgrounds. We wanted the game to be built by people with lived experiences of bias events and an active interest in the topic. We wanted to advance the careers of populations underrepresented in games and science.

Prototyping

We built a technical prototype to test early concepts while the full team came on board. The first idea to test was *Research Lab Story*—a takeoff on *Game Dev Story*, an iOS game made by Kairosoft in which the player manages a game development studio. We imagined that players would manage a lab, deal with conflicts between nonplayable characters, and see how *not* attending to bias incidents could hurt the lab's productivity. We liked dealing with bias in utilitarian terms; players could "experience" the impact of bias events on team morale and productivity, rather than arguing on a purely moral basis. We also liked that the game would simulate research labs, which could have secondary positive effects (contemplating how research labs work). Narrative events could be taken directly from research literature that has documented the impact of bias.

User studies of our first prototype (see figure 4.1) revealed the following (see Paiz-Ramirez et al., 2011):

1. *Scientists liked seeing their work environment as a game.* Playing a game set in a research lab interested faculty members (much as game developers like playing *Game Dev Story*). We entertained fanciful scenarios, but a realistic setting ameliorated the concern that scientists would find the game irrelevant (see Keller, 2009).

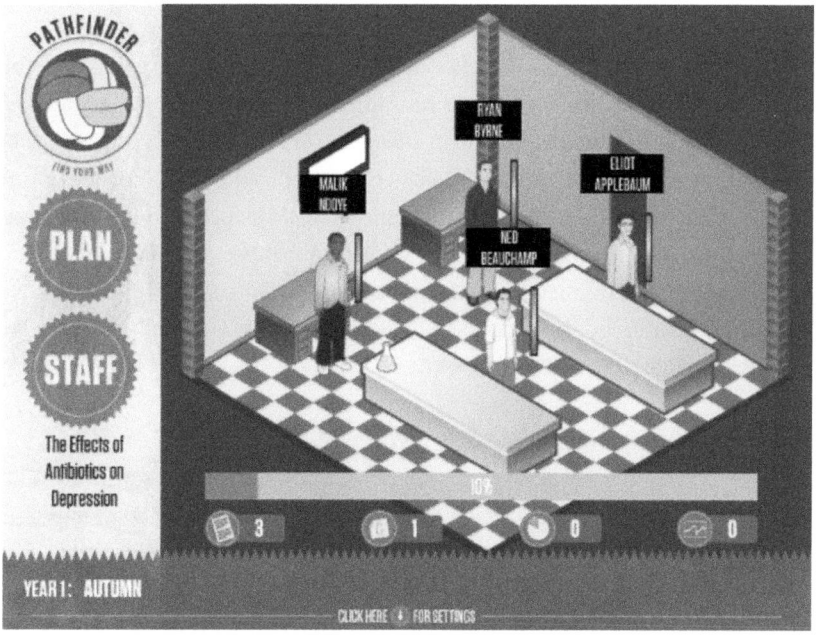

Figure 4.1
Prototype 1: *Research Lab Story*.

2. *Scientists liked the objectives*: writing papers and producing research.
3. *Bias was presented clearly*. Players inferred conflicts on-screen between characters.
4. *Players min-maxed the game to the point of distraction*. Players employed strategies that maximized research production to the point of abusing lab workers. Anything else (including bias) became secondary.
5. *Players ignored bias events*. Bias events were important but not crucial to lab productivity. We would need to either rework the underlying model or amplify the severity of bias events. Otherwise, bias would fall into the background of player experience.
6. *The "God game" presentation detached players from the experience*. We wanted players to feel the emotional sting of bias, for aesthetic reasons (why miss an opportunity for games to provide vicarious experience?) and practical ones (emotionally identifying with bias is important in overcoming it; Todd et al., 2012).

We kept the setting and goals but shifted the player perspective and interface.

This target audience was not literate with games. User tests revealed that most scientists were uncomfortable learning by trial and error. Faculty often sat awaiting explicit instructions and were unable to discern the "deeper meaning" of the game. In response to the user interface challenges, we developed design pillars: always have a clear goal on-screen, simplify navigation and choices whenever possible, and put the game content front and center. To this last point, in "Theme Is Not Meaning," Soren Johnson (2012) described how it is important to distinguish between a game's theme (for example, the fantasy of *World of Warcraft*) and its meaning (evolutionary battle between designers and players in *World of Warcraft*). We needed theme and meaning to be consistent.

Emphasizing the Story in *Research Lab Story*

With *Fair Play*, we needed to consider simultaneous projects and a studio model with dedicated services across projects, including a 3D art pipeline with modelers, animators, texture artists, and postproduction staff. We hired industry-trained programmers and level designers to build robust systems capable of scaling. Seemingly overnight, the team grew from about 12 faculty members, students, and developers to about 30, including 11 developers (5 artists, 6 programmers), 2 postdocs, and 12 graduate students.

Under the advisement of Dr. Rock Mackie, we hired industry veteran Brian Pelletier to lead development. Brian was highly regarded by students and staff, and we wanted someone with experience in managing development teams to help spin out companies.

We recruited Erin Robinson to be the design and production lead for *Fair Play*. Among the many reasons we recruited Erin was that her first game, *Puzzle Bots*, featured players controlling robots to solve puzzles that were reminiscent of rats trapped in a psychology experiment maze. Parts of the game were motivated by psychology experiments that she studied as an undergraduate. *Puzzle Bots* oozes personality and charm, something that we can say of few educational games.

After reviewing the research literature, prototype, and feedback, Erin developed several iterations of game ideas (see figure 4.2), but nothing stuck. We spent weeks discussing ideas. In retrospect, I realize that I hadn't sufficiently empowered Erin to lead the team. I wanted a relatively flat management structure, but instead I was getting design by committee. Frustration built because of the lack of clear roles.

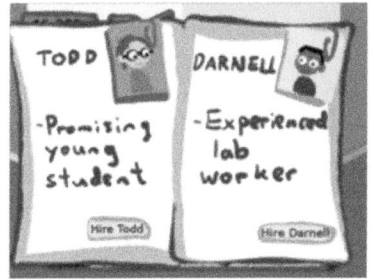
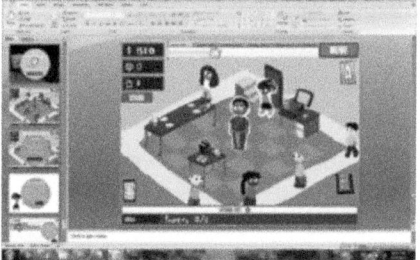

Figure 4.2
Fair Play storyboards by Erin Robinson.

Erin next developed a seventy-slide series of mock-ups of a play experience. Unlike design documents, design mock-ups can provide pacing, timing, and tone so that the reader can get a feel for the game experience. She described this approach in Robinson (2012):

> If you're lucky, a series of mock-ups like this can do more than explain your goal: it can energize and inspire the team to do their best work. These particular mini-presentations were popular enough that sometimes a few of the senior faculty would sit in on our meetings. The goofy placeholder art and the informal nature of the presentation invited questions and discussion. It was a real boost for everyone—and reminded us that we were making something fun.

The mock-ups read like a comic book story of Jamal, a young professor attempting to establish a research lab. Erin discarded related ideas, such as like gender bias, and focused on a narrative of building a career with a secondary theme of facing racial bias. Erin targeted key environments where bias incidents occurred (such as academic receptions), which later became chapters. The mock-ups addressed a majority of concerns, they were feasible, and we wanted to play it.

Erin's redesign immediately struck me as the right approach, but not everyone agreed. Some felt ownership of previous ideas or wanted to tweak the previous game. The team had, until this point, worked by consensus, using an agile process of two-week sprints with weekly reviews. In reality, there was no consensus, but there were strong wills, conflicting views, and then leadership weighing in on what to do. In an effort to facilitate team ownership, I had been passive in leadership style, which was a mistake. Regardless, the strength of Erin's presentation made the next steps easy, as it was better than what we would have come up with.

I started to see flaws in my management approach (see "Building Academic Game Development Teams" later in the chapter). Roles and responsibilities were not sufficiently defined for Erin to truly set direction, direct production, and lead the team. Any project has multiple overlapping forms of power, status, and control, and these are even trickier in academic contexts, in which freelancers, advisors, temporary staff, students, and professionals are working together. The key takeaway, which probably applies to academics more generally, is to ensure that all members of the team have clear lines of responsibility and domains that they control. Even the most egalitarian models (such as Valve's design cabal) typically give ultimate authority to leads in a given area.

Games Come Together: Storyboarding, User Stories, and Vertical Slices
The game that evolved, *Fair Play*, tells the story of Jamal Davis, a graduate student at a large midwestern university. As Jamal negotiates graduate school, he confronts bias incidents. *Fair Play* seeks to induce players' empathy for Jamal through their observing and experiencing these incidents (drawing from social learning theory applied to games; Gee, 2003). Bias incidents begin with his arrival on campus, where he is mistaken for an athlete, and continue to the final chapters, in which he confronts allegations of plagiarism. These bias incidents are recorded in an almanac for review. On the basis of our feedback, we put players on relatively constrained rails so that they were guided throughout and confronted at least two bias incidents within five minutes of playing.

With the core idea created and the team coalescing (and with her own game, *Gravity Ghost*, underway), Erin handed leadership to Dennis Paiz-Ramirez, a graduate student. Dennis further focused on deepening player identification with Jamal, creating triggered events to elicit bias, and polishing to deepen player narrative engagement.

We observed differences in the ways game designers and medical educators approached learning. Game designers' instincts were to immerse players in bias situations to induce emotional reactions. We wanted players to reflect on those reactions. Medical educators were concerned that exposing participants to bias incidents could produce deleterious effects. The concern here is that exposing people to antisocial effects in the game could be a negative stimulus, thus creating further bias. If games are going to include transgressive play, learning through failure, or exploring consequences of actions, designers will need to have freedom to explore such ideas and give a degree of trust to the player, which many are uneasy in doing.

We ultimately introduced bias events to players in a relatively benign way, with clear markers of a "bias radar" (red exclamation marks) to signal that the player experienced bias. By labeling bias detection "bias radar," we hoped to explicitly encourage players to practice identifying bias. Players then practiced reflecting on these biases and naming them. The final chapter, in which Jamal is accused of plagiarism, addresses bias in the direct, emotionally intense way we wanted.

Readers will observe an evolution in art style. We loved the stylized "cute" characters (large heads, larger eyes), but they did not appeal to scientists, who perceived them as childish. The scientists reported, however, being impressed by a 3D game with motion captured animations, which signaled a "real game." The game was set on the UW–Madison campus (although it isn't explicitly named), which provided a Easter egg for locals. They could wander through local landmarks such as the Memorial Union Terrace and WID. Future games might explore using aesthetic approaches, such as setting the game in a highly fictional setting, or including more extreme bias events.

Research results of *Fair Play* Playing *Fair Play* reduces bias for players who show high empathy for Jamal. In an experiment (see Kaatz et al., 2017), participants were chosen either to play *Fair Play* (experimental condition) or to read a text (control) before taking an implicit association test (IAT). High-empathy players who took Jamal's perspective displayed the lowest implicit bias. Many of these high-empathy players were women. We don't know whether this was due to play style or to the experiences of women facing similar biases in the sciences, or to some other factor. In retrospect, we

Figure 4.3
Fair Play scene set on the University of Wisconsin's Memorial Union Terrace.

probably should have designed a female character, given that most women prefer to play female characters in games, but it was encouraging that the game still worked best for female players (Yee, 2017).

A number of follow-up questions could arise. Does *Fair Play* work best for female players because female players in academia are more empathetic? Were they most receptive to this message having perhaps experienced similar bias events in their careers? Is there an underlying phenomena in game-based learning in which people with the most knowledge or direct experience interpret game events more deeply than do those with fewer underlying experiences?

Fair Play has won awards and is used in training. It won the People's Choice Award at the 2012 Meaningful Play Conference, and Dr. Carnes's team's won the Adolphus Toliver Award from the National Institutes of Health in part for this work. *Fair Play* situates experience and enables and provides a safe context for players to discuss experiences and make connections to their lived experiences. *Fair Play* workshops across the country use the game to introduce bias, and then players draw from game play in discussions. Workshops include vignettes and leverage PDFs included in the game.

This success suggests limits for using games to scale ideas without very careful consideration of context. Many grant programs hope that games for impact will scale because the content will be more interesting presented as a game (and, I suspect, many program officers are less interested than the public in entertainment games generally). There is little evidence that people will play *Fair Play* (which is freely available) without incentive or coercion. *Fair Play* could replace required video training sessions. The issue, then, is that most faculty want efficient, quick training, and administrative leaders want to minimize legal exposure (and perhaps address the problem), whereas advocates want effective programs.

Developing expertise in a domain often leads to new opportunities, and our team's expertise in implicit bias led to a collaboration with the University of Oklahoma to build an implicit bias game for the Central Intelligence Agency, funded by IARPA, the Intelligence Advanced Research Projects Activity, which is responsible for forward-leaning research projects. This project adapted *Fair Play* to the CIA's context, reusing the underlying basic research and knowledge gained from prototyping, but retooled for the CIA. Working with CIA agents was a fun change of pace for team members such as Meagan Rothschild, whose expertise is in early childhood education. The game, based on a prototype directed by Dennis Paiz-Ramirez, won Best Business Game and Best Adaptive Force Game at the Serious Games Showcase and Challenge at the major military training conference I/ITSEC 2013.

Building Academic Game Development Teams

A vision for the Games+Learning+Society (GLS) Center emerged to research and develop games with a broad audience, demonstrated impact, and supported scale. Whereas most groups focus on *either* research or development, or *either* education or entertainment, we wanted to explore intersections among them. The center-wide research questions in this phase were as follows: Can games diversify income streams to the university? How should games fit with the teaching mission of a university? How do we leverage games to amplify academic impact? These questions also drove the work at our peer institutions. The following sections detail opportunities and challenges for centers trying to innovate in higher education, with implications for higher education more broadly.

Game development within academic centers. Most research labs and groups organize around tentpole projects central to the group's mission and identity. Our identity was researching and developing science games to increase participation in science, with satellite projects from learning analytics to game design. A key decision for any group is whether or not to develop games internally. Five strategic factors drove our decision to scale up internal development:

1. *A development team is an asset for research.* Studying learning through games (from analytics to identity formation) requires games to study. On-site development teams remove the hassle of finding partners, aligning values, and instrumenting for research. Internal teams remove other faculty needs to manage student-developers.
2. *A development team is a recruitment tool for students.* Students studying game design (or the mindset of developers) can leverage an internal team's connections with industry.
3. *A development team is a teaching tool.* Students entering *both* academics and industry benefit from experiences on professional teams. Professional developers provide enculturation, training, and contacts.

4. *Maintaining multiple projects enabled the development of (a) a full 3D art pipeline, (b) a professional web team, and (c) a community outreach team, which were assets.* These functions are difficult to fund through government grants (which prioritize research) but are valued by researchers. They require roughly $1.5 million annually in projects to support.

5. *Interest in learning games was accelerating, and we had an opportunity to make an impact* through research, products, and companies (see Squire, Gaydos, & DeVane, 2016). Hype for games has waned, but public interest in a technology, paradigm, or approach can be leveraged to diversity funding streams.

These drivers suggest reasons to scale up from a lab, but scaling introduces challenges.

From a Research Lab to a Research Center

Teams of fifty or more are organized differently from teams of ten or twelve, and most academics do not have experience working on large teams that require full-time managers (see table 4.1). Research lab cultures emerge through sustained, directly collaborative work (analyzing data, designing materials, or writing); decisions can be made by consensus and disputes resolved with everyone present. A research *center* culture requires more top-down intervention and layers of management. Most academics are not experienced with layers of hierarchy and disputes involving layers of management. The work of a research *lab* falls largely within one's own skill set, whereas game development (particularly once 3D pipelines are involved) extends beyond one person's skills.[2]

Managing growth   Despite our best efforts to manage growth, we experienced pain.

Table 4.1
Contrasts between research labs and research centers

	Research lab	Research center
Size	2–12 (small group)	20+
Faculty role	Maker-manager	Manager
Primary management technique	Sustained interaction	Vision setting, supporting, and enabling
Layers of management	1–3	3+

Our strategy was to encourage students and staff to form companies so as to stay around twenty people. Rock Mackie, who had successfully launched multiple companies, advised us to (1) encourage interest groups to form around projects, as those groups are proto-companies, and (2) staff teams so that core business roles (CEO, COO) are fulfilled. Just as Filament Games originated through staff (Dan Norton and Alex Stone) collaborating with students (Dan White), we hoped that more teams might form. Two more teams spun out of the lab this way.

Game management literature distinguishes between teams under and over 15 people (see Spaulding, 2009). With groups around 10 people (which is also how academic labs look), leaders split time between "making" and "managing." Smaller companies have a 15:1 ratio of makers to managers. In contrast, a midsize game company that runs multiple projects will have 70 or more people. Here, the group leader should be managing, not making. Large teams typically have a 10:1 ratio of developers to managers, so a group such as GLS can have 4 or 5 full-time leads without specific production tasks. Enter middle management dynamics. To quote Spaulding, someone needs "to devote their full time and attention to department-management issues like career management, scheduling, hiring, and training and mentoring new leads" (2009, p. 32).This is not something that academic managers are experienced in doing.

Academic Game Development Production

Creating and maintaining a culture cutting across any large group is difficult. Our challenges were in spanning research (both education and science) and development (both independent and AAA), including fault lines within these sectors.

Scientists and Gamers versus Educators

Within academics, *game studies* (the study of how and why games are engaging), *learning sciences* (how people learn), *educational areas* (e.g., science education), and *scientific domains* (e.g., disciplinary fields in WID) have different cultural norms. In fact, there are subfields within those, but we will hold off on that for now. A weird fault line emerged between those identifying with science and games (heavily male-dominated fields) as compared with education (which can be gendered female). Participants were of different genders, but patterns formed that aligned roughly with gendered ways of constituting acceptable talk, ways to disagree, and ways to behave. Postdocs trained in other fields exacerbated issues of clashing value systems and cultural norms.

AAA versus Indie Game Development
Seasoned AAA developers tend toward waterfall development (a linear process of progressing from step to step), well-defined roles, and hierarchy. In general, indie developers lean toward prototype-driven development with minimal documentation, flatter hierarchies, and riskier ideas. The "artists versus programmers" issues that define many teams were replaced by different values about games altogether. Academic development falls between indie and AAA development. As with indie development, academics ask, "What should be built and why?" Academic games change direction during development, and marketing departments don't dictate features. Like indie games, academic games are largely driven by passion. However, unlike indie games, academic games exist in larger institutions with HR policies and norms. The norms of academics are unlike those of AAA games. AAA jobs are *highly* competitive, eighty-hour weeks are routinely demanded, and employees are terminated easily. Try applying the management techniques of AAA in academia and see what happens. Thinking in terms of an integrated technology that understands academic *and* contract development works better; game development requires highly functional teams with a shared understanding of work processes, flows, and personalities and trust. If a good game dev team who knows how to work with academics forms, the last thing you want to do is lose it.

Individualistic versus Team Cultures
The extent to which academia is individualistic and built on a "star system" becomes evident when compared with game development. Academics are judged as individuals and, in even the most collaborative team environments, become associated as authors of ideas. Game developers, in contrast, work in teams. Work goes into enculturating identities as team members. Individuals taking credit for a team effort can poison game development. PhDs and postdocs look for ideas to own.

Many professors feel that their groups have a team culture because the culture is built around them. Some groups surely have a collaborative culture, but most academics work on a star system and have labs named after the professor to reflect that.

Commitment to Growth

Managing employee growth is a full-time job in game development, which turns over technology about every five years. Companies invest in individuals as leaders and create career ladders that exceed the pace of academic labs. A game employee might grow from entry programmer to advanced programmer within five or six years and earn multiple promotions and increases in job responsibilities. When our studio director developed advancement ladders and growth curves for the university's HR department, they thought we were crazy. Academics do (hopefully) commit to students' lifelong growth. Academic advisors look out for students (again, hopefully) in ways that are atypical in game development, although informal networks of developers are powerful (and difficult for outsiders to crack).

Different Workflow Rhythms

A key challenge to game development in an academic context is the rhythm of workflow. Academic calendars (conferences, meetings, classes) require teams to meet once or twice per week and work independently, which is not good for game development. In contrast, most game developers have daily stand-up meetings, work concurrently, schedule daily play sessions, and work at a faster velocity. Game development requires making a million small, interrelated decisions that come together to form user experience. If I left the office for two or three days, projects drifted as they responded to new challenges. The idea that a graduate student would "disappear" for a week or two is anathema to game design. Students who are integrated into core development need to be in the office twenty or more hours per week (and hopefully compensated on overload).

Lessons for Teams

To help the team grow, I eventually took leave from UW–Madison to work at WID full-time. My presence on the ground all day, every day provided leadership clarity and feedback for teams, which I believe is required to lead such a center. Academics considering similar efforts might also do the following:

1. *Expect conflict.* Managing interpersonal conflict is not a routine part of most academics' jobs. Passion-driven creative enterprises generate conflicts over vision, priorities, or personalities. Resolving them is a large part of the job.
2. *Empower and rely on strong team leaders.* Game development benefits from strong leadership. There are many viable answers to development decisions, and many of them end up being wrong. Reasonable processes and good leaders manage this (Spaulding, 2009). A collaborative, flat model may emerge (such as Valve's design cabal), but the number of moving parts and sheer number of decisions to make requires delegation.
3. *Promote team leaders on the basis of disposition.* Team leaders can come from academics or industry, but they must be good at integrating perspectives, ensuring that voices are heard, and managing clients. Leaders must have expertise in game development and in the subject domain and a clear sense of research goals, methods, and outcomes. We rotated team leaders for professional development and group cohesion.
4. *Empower self-sufficient subdisciplines.* Teams that spanned projects (web services, art, analytics, Institutional Review Board procedures, statistical analyses) were slammed and constantly balanced competing demands. Designating a strong, self-managing team lead for such disciplines to meet with project teams, plan services, and allocate team time is essential. Such groups are best when they self-manage, which requires exceptionally strong and trustworthy dispositions.
5. *Design for redundancies.* Games for impact teams include specialized skills, and losing any one of several employees can tank a project. Performing work for private funders, from foundations to companies, is demanding because if a funder wants a feature (such as web functionality), the funder expects it to be done regardless of team composition or university HR policies. Developing secondary skill sets, such as training a game programmer to also do analytics programming, helps.
6. *Help teams prioritize efforts.* Games for impact tend toward too many things at once. A good game for impact must simultaneously (a) interest target users, (b) appease funders or partners, (c) satisfy domain experts, and (d) generate research results. Design decisions might suffice one condition (e.g., satisfy domain experts) at the expense of another (appeal

to users). Leadership helps team members understand priorities, particularly with regard to resource allocation.

Managing teams or, more accurately, managing the managers of teams, is time intensive, and academic developers must be careful to have clear management, roles, priorities, and, critically, time, such as twenty or more hours of face time per week.

Game Development in Academic Institutions

Game centers are at the forefront of attempts to remake universities for the digital age. Viewed from the top down, universities need to evolve in a context of decreased government funding, increased competition for students, and competition from nontraditional entities and support games for impact centers in testing ideas. Viewed from the bottom up, academics see game development as opportunities to attract funds, support research goals, educate students, and maximize impact. Efforts to launch innovative centers such as game centers will face three types of problems: (1) accepting money on contracts, (2) spending money to develop games, and (3) investing in proactive business development. Anyone seeking to grow such a center might use this list when negotiating with administrators.

Problems Accepting Money in University Settings

Private contracts are challenging for most universities, which do not process them in a routine way. Most universities have policies in place for patents, copyrights, and indirect rates but fewer processes for royalty negotiation or contract arbitration. Negotiating contracts is laborious and can involve months of negotiations. As an example, one contract negotiation with a UK-based company became stuck over which country's laws would adjudicate breach of contract. The university does not live on contract work, so honestly it was easiest for legal staff to let the project die. If a negotiation stalls or fails, no one in the legal department loses their job. Jobs *are* lost, however, if a project is approved without proper safeguards, so as a whole, the university is incentivized to dismiss them. It is difficult for a university to assure stakeholders that private grants and contracts will be processed in a timely fashion with sensible copyright-sharing and indirect cost policies.

Problems Spending Money for Game Development

Spending money for game development is equally difficult. Hiring game developers challenges an human resources processes for nontech companies. University job titles and descriptions make little sense, especially for artists, who are hired as instructional support specialists. Game developers may not have college degrees, which might require administrative approval. Pay scales are significantly less than even in private nonprofits with hard pay ceilings (such as $62,500 for senior programmers at UW–Madison, which may have changed). Game development frequently requires contractors for short-term (e.g., sound design) or emergent (e.g., technical artist) needs, whereas in public universities, paying contractors is laborious, for good reasons. Funds for other unforeseen expenses, from power tools to subscription services, can be difficult, if not impossible, to procure. Partners in private contracts have little patience for bureaucratic hassles.

Investments in Business Development

Working with private entities requires spending money to (1) identify and procure business leads, (2) develop and maintain relationships (which means unplanned travel), and (3) follow-through on partners' requests. For example, one partner required us to fly to the Caribbean and present work before its executive board on a week's notice, which the university was not wild about. Private funders, from foundations to companies, do not care about an organization's rules about expenses; if they've given money for a job, they expect it to be done if it's legal and paid for. Setting aside money and negotiating expectations with administrators is imperative.

Supporting a Skunkworks through Private-Public Partnerships

Our group developed a private-public partnership with the Learning Games Network (LGN) to support game development. This arrangement is explored in some detail because more research labs are creating nonprofits to accept gift donations and perform work that falls outside the scope of the university. Our model, established through a memorandum of understanding with the university, enabled the university to partner with LGN to support games for impact. The university led research grants, with subawards to LGN, and LGN led development projects, with subawards to the university. LGN agreed to rent space (a renovated nightclub affectionately called "the purple building") and hire administrative staff. We continued the vision of the Morgridge Institute for Research but in a lean, creative, and sustainable way fit for games.[3]

A professional game development studio in the heart of the UW–Madison campus was a boon for creativity. It drew faculty, game developers, graduate students, postdocs, and undergrads from different disciplines to work side by side in integrated teams. Unlike Morgridge or university spaces, which have policies appropriate to large organizations, such as which employees get desks, LGN was flexible and responsive. Undergraduate programmers set up camp and joined teams. We prohibited hoarding of resources (a common university practice) and created an ethos of "use it or lose it." We openly encouraged a culture of "asking for forgiveness instead of permission."

The space, location on campus, mix of talent, and culture fostered creative collaboration. For example, let's return to the example of *AnatomyTable*. It began when Dr. Matthew Berland was awarded a National Science Foundation grant to build interactive table exhibits for the New York Hall of Science. The academic team ran into problems with contractors, and within days we had cleared space and built a makerspace. This table led to the aforementioned interactive table for veterinary care. Dr. Lonie Salkowski saw this table and improved upon it by developing an interactive mannequin (working with LGN) for teaching anatomy, which was given a grant for further development by the university. A game studio on central campus promoted the group internally and externally. Graduate and undergraduate students cited it as a deciding factor in their coming to Wisconsin. Alumni valued it as an example of applied work on campus. We hosted all kinds of such events, from ESPN Game Day to department retreats.

Flexible, unallocated space is important to innovation but nearly impossible to find at universities. For example, we created an audio recording studio with vintage equipment to attract musicians. The makerspace for artists to physically sculpt brought Jordu Schell, creator of the aliens for the film *Avatar*, to hold a daylong workshop for local artists. Artist Mike Beall created a Baby Groot for Nicole Perlman, who cowrote *Guardians of the Galaxy*. We encouraged these as hobbies, understanding that some might have tangible benefits later. Key to this space (and, I argue, to any good lab) is a large open area in the middle for hosting tours, play sessions, and design jams. We wanted end users to have a physical presence in the space so that they were in our minds (as well as available for "Kleenex testing," the quick and dirty kind of play testing that you throw away afterward).

Taking a do-it-yourself approach to running a research and development lab was an investment in ourselves not easily understood across the university. When we started the experiment of renting the purple building, we had funds to cover costs for two years, which, at over $200,000 per year, was nontrivial but enough to cover the lease. Yet we were routinely asked, "What if it doesn't work?," as if a lab should continue indefinitely, which for me, highlighted the difference between an entrepreneurial, innovative spirit and a university. Should something living forever be a precondition to trying anything?

We tried this arrangement for two years to test the idea. We figured one of three things would happen: (1) the group would thrive and perhaps require even more space; (2) we would quit, either failing to generate enough income or just growing tired of it; or (3) the university would value these activities and provide on-campus space or funding.

A mix of all three happened. The arrangement created new business in the form of multiple contracts. Yet the stress of working with a separate nonprofit mounted. Accounting and management issues created liquidity issues. LGN was a small organization with an operating budget of a few hundred thousand dollars that grew overnight to more than twenty-five people and millions in annual expenditures, including federal grants. Federal grants bring with them substantial cash flow issues and require extra oversight. We spent a year reorganizing the business, responding to a mandatory federal audit, and fighting administrators at the university who did not want us to exist. This became my life for about two years.

Innovative work requires supportive leadership. At the end of our lease, WID director David Krakauer and Dean Julie Underwood left their positions, and within weeks, the university decided to audit LGN, which had already completed a mandatory federal audit. For six months, all payments to subcontracts at LGN were paused, which shut down LGN-university business and closed the purple building. Without an administrative champion at the university, there was no incentive to forge such an innovative partnership, and in short, I am now (happily) at the University of California, Irvine, and not Wisconsin. Our lab was subsequently hired by UW–Madison and became GEAR Studios, where it exists as of this writing.

Reflections on Innovative Academic-Industry Partnerships

The most critical factor for academic-industry partnerships is for leaders *with decision-making authority* on all sides of a project to *want* it to happen. This statement may seem self-evidently true, but it is worth restating. If top leadership does not want innovative partnerships, they will not happen. All incentives align for middle managers to avoid new, risky, or innovative partnerships, and they routinely terminate projects by slow walking or stalling them out.

Leadership support is essential for executing contracts. University-private partnerships usually involve firsts for both organizations. New legal situations are confronted and new policies adopted. Observing contract negotiations (inherently an adversarial process), one might reasonably conclude that legal teams would prefer that deals not be completed. Those with decision-making authority must interpret feedback from legal counsel, push to solve roadblocks, and nudge parties to flexible terms. Academic administrators, who are not known to be risk-takers, must be comfortable with risk exposure.

Academic-industry partnerships may be more difficult in older, more established universities, with guarded business processes, than in younger organizations that create new programs, procedures, and policies routinely. In many universities, administrative teams are autonomous and operate as their own fiefdoms; they make their own HR decisions and, critically, select, train, and enculturate the next generation of administrative leaders. Business decisions, such as the appropriateness of contract terms, are made within business offices (the deep state of universities), whose role it is to protect the university from faculty who will break the university or fly-by-night leadership that doesn't understand the university. They aren't *entirely* wrong, but they also prevent innovation.

Lifelong innovators report that the two biggest hurdles to innovating in big organizations are (1) the "culture of no" and (2) the related response "But we've always done it that way." Most readers know what a culture of no is; it is the cultural expectation of arriving at an answer of no, to *not* try something new, to *not* take risks. In the words of Clay Johnson (2015), "not how to make something work but to ensure that it does not fail." As Johnson observed, a culture of no is an authentic desire to protect the institution. Administrative staff (particularly those second and third in command) are what Johnson calls the "Be" team, meaning that they were there *be*fore administrative leadership arrived and they will *be* there after they leave. In universities, these are the program managers and business office directors who feed information to directors and deans and thus shape institutional perceptions. Pursuing projects that challenge existing practices means that you are now in the business of organizational change.

In fact, most games for impact leaders find themselves managing organizational change. Organizational change requires (1) explicit administrative support and (2) a mindful approach to the act of change itself. In *Rebels at Work*, Kelly and Medina (2014) distinguish between "bad rebels," who are characterized as pessimistic rule breakers who alienate others, and "good rebels," optimistic creators who build better systems through forming coalitions. Building on surveys of change managers across government and industry, Kelly and Medina articulated a tactical approach to organizational innovation. Rebels must, for example, be *more* trustworthy than their peers, must learn to pitch and sell ideas to leaders, must never openly criticize the character of leaders (particularly superiors), and must inspire and mobilize colleagues.

Universities are averse to failure. Within technology, the mantra "Fail early and fail often" is used to the point of parody. In this age of innovation and the "faculty entrepreneur," universities may claim to embrace failure but are more often uncomfortable with initiatives closing. Even those institutions (such as WID) that are held as sites of innovation are expected to do amazing and interesting things with 100 percent success rates. In fact, most university innovations are just achieving existing goals more efficiently, such as improving student retention rates. Innovations that suggest new goals (increasing private partnerships, fostering student start-ups) or call into question existing practices are less likely to be valued. Tellingly, five years after the experiment of WID began, none of the leaders involved in its creation were on campus. To the extent there is *any* story told about GLS within the university, it is told by Clay Johnson's "Be" team. I'd bet the story is framed as a cautionary tale.

5   *Progenitor X*: Zombies, Stem Cells, and Assessment

One afternoon, our team struck up a conversation. With our new capacity, what kind of game *should* we make? For the first (and perhaps last) time, we had a financial cushion, an experienced team, and visibility. Games for impact were hot, and investors were looking closely at games. New game design competitions appeared every week. Maybe we could create a hit, or at least capture public imagination.

"Why not make a game with zombies in it?," someone (I think Mike Beall, an artist) asked. "You've always wanted to do that, Kurt," which was true. Ever since playing Ska Studios' *I MAED A GAM3 W1TH Z0MBIES 1N IT!!!1* (a lovable $.99 Xbox Live game), we'd wondered, "Could you make an educational game with zombies? (The classic typing tutor game *Typing of the Dead* did not count, since it was reskinning drill and practice, which means simply taking an existing format like a matching game, and giving it a new theme.)

"You know, if there was a zombie invasion, that would be a good time to grow organs," Mike commented, after learning about the regenerative biology group. Scientists with the Wisconsin Institute for Discovery (WID) were (reportedly) growing a circulatory system in the Discovery Building. In fact, in 2017 they did something like that, publishing a study in *Proceedings of the National Academy of Sciences* about growing arterial cells.[1]

The idea seemed feasible. What if there were a game in which you had to engineer stem cells to fend off a zombie invasion? A zombie invasion would provide the perfect backstory for using regenerative biology. We imagined a zombie invasion starting with a virology engineering experiment gone bad. The bulk of the game would be a science fiction shooter/survival game in the spirit of *Deus Ex*: back at the lab, players would engineer, grow, and trade stem cells. The stem cell growing phase could be like the hacking camera puzzles in *BioShock*. The legal team at Morgridge would hate the idea, which was a bonus. Better to invite controversy than shy away, and better to ask for forgiveness than permission.

The idea stuck. We could not imagine a better thing to do than build a zombie stem cell game. We hoped to reach as wide an audience as possible among the gaming public, aged twelve and up. Although we had designed most of our games to work in a classroom context, we challenged ourselves to make a stand-alone game for the broad public. A "puzzle game inside of an action game" suggested a new model for hard science fiction educational gaming. For the demonstration version, we could tell a story through cutscenes and dialogue. If a billionaire or another agency funded the shooter version, then the game would be set. Otherwise, we would still have a functioning game.

Mike Beall, along with PhD students Liz Owen and Shannon Harris, started studying regenerative biology to find the "game in the domain." This design work was difficult even to imagine outside the context of WID, where we talked with scientists every day. Because WID scientists were explicitly committed to collaborating, it was easy to approach them with half-baked ideas. The best facilitator of this process was the three o'clock daily teatime created by our director, David Krakauer, during which researchers would gather over tea to talk informally. Teatime created both rapport and extended conversations in our usual routine of short, frequent interactions.

Dr. Lonie Salkowski introduced us to Dr. Gary Lyons, who worked in regenerative medicine. Project lead Mike Beall spent two weeks in Lyons's lab observing and studying regenerative medicine. Regenerative medicine is an approach to medicine that leverages the body's natural healing ability. Examples range from relatively ordinary interventions (e.g., using healthy knee cartilage tissue that is harvested, grown in a lab, and then reinserted into the body) to cutting-edge experiments in growing tissue outside the body with scaffolds. We consulted with Dr. Rupa Shevde, our neighbor and one of the world's leading stem cell educators.

The stem cell lab scientists spent most of their time isolating and growing stem cells. What if we turned this into a growing/gardening game?

For the next few weeks, Mike talked to stem cell scientists in James Thomson's labs (Thomson's is one of the two foremost stem cell labs in the world), visited their lab benches, and kicked around ideas. After a few more weeks of talking with scientists, reading about stem cells, and sketching ideas, lead designer Terra Lauterbach developed the core game play loop: players proceed through three phases of cultivating stem cells (see figure 5.1). Players (1) treat cells to transform pluripotent stem cells into specific cell types; (2) group these differentiated cells and collect them; (3) layer these transformed cells into tissue segments; and (4) arrange these tissues into organs. Players jump back and forth across levels assembling cells, tissues, and organs to complete missions.

The resulting game, *Progenitor X*, is a puzzle game set in an apocalyptic world overrun by zombies. Players grab the controls to a cellular growth robot and try to save the world (Owen, 2014). The regenerative biology content model is manifested in the main mission of the player: to cultivate and differentiate stem cells, assemble tissues, and replace organs that have been contaminated with a zombie virus. Despite its supernatural story line, *Progenitor X* is designed to teach cutting-edge knowledge and processes in stem cell science and is rooted in collaboration with regenerative medicine scientists at WID. Collaborators include Dr. James Thomson, director of

Figure 5.1
Progenitor X: treating zombie outbreaks through regenerative medicine using stem cells.

regenerative medicine at the Morgridge Institute for Research (MIR); Dr. Rupa Shevde, director of outreach experiences at MIR; and Dr. Gary Lyons, a professor of regenerative biology at the University of Wisconsin–Madison.

The art style, led by Brian Pelletier, was designed to cultivate player interest. In an email, Brian described *Progenitor X* as follows:

> A modern interpretation of pulp horror comics with thick brush ink lines and heavy shadows and low camera angles for a more dramatic imposing scene. The coloring was muted and grainy with subtle halftone patterning to mimic the look of coloring on newsprint paper. The look was heavily inspired by those great horror comics from the mid 20th century. The color palette used analogous or split complementary colors with a focus around yellowish green, the zombie skin tone, used throughout all the images.

Hearing Brian and the other artists work from conceptual to final art, I was constantly reminded of the sophistication that talented artists employ to evoke an emotional response, and how researchers frequently reduce art to a simple variable, such as 2D or 3D.

The puzzle-based game play builds from matching games, in which players manipulate shapes and match patterns, similar to games such as *Candy Crush Saga* and *Tetris*. These matching games simplified the work stem cell biologists do in the research lab, but they were authentic metaphors for what they do. Scientists apply chemicals similarly to the way *Progenitor X* depicts it. Lab workers isolate and gather cell types and affix them to structures that guide their growth. We hypothesized that students would better understand the cycle of how undifferentiated cells become specific cell types, which become tissues and then organs. Of course, they might also better understand the broad purpose of regenerative medicine (regrowing cells, tissues, and perhaps organs).

In early 2012, we conducted a play-test with stem cell scientists. The goal was to generate enthusiasm for the project, validate the general approach, and identify glaring inaccuracies. The feedback was wildly encouraging. One lab technician asked if she could send a copy to her spouse "to explain what I do all day." To our surprise, we had created a zombie stem cell game that scientists were proud to be associated with.

Progenitor X went through several rounds of user testing with hundreds of people. Interpreting the results of this one was easy: students, parents, and teachers loved it and immediately wanted to play it. Whenever we play-tested another game on our website, many students would deviate and try to play *Progenitor X*. Other than one group of scientists, who were concerned about the cultural sensitivity of depicting the dead, there were no concerns about the zombies.

With *Progenitor X*, we saw an opportunity for its use in homes and informal settings (museums, after-school clubs), so we created context and backstory and embedded tutorials. The cutscene seeks to induct the player into the role of a junior-level stem cell scientist who comes across Robotic Advanced Medical Integrated Systems (R.A.M.I.S.), which cultivates stem cells to repair cells, tissues, and organs. The player meets Dr. Yeong, a stem cell scientist who guides the player through each game phase. Although it was never implemented, there was a lengthy narrative arc for the player as the zombie outbreak traveled across the country.

The working demonstration game consisted of fifteen cell, tissue, and organ puzzle cycles. An average play-through of all game cycles took middle school players twenty to forty minutes (the average time was twenty-five minutes). Table 5.1 provides an overview of missions and goals.

Assessment in Games

Releasing *Progenitor X* as a stand-alone game was an opportunity and a challenge for research. On the one hand, we could (possibly) attain far reach by getting the game in the hands of thousands or millions of players. On the other hand, it is impossible to individually observe players, to understand the contexts in which they are playing. Are they playing out of curiosity or because they are being somehow coerced? Are they playing seriously, to learn something, or just haphazardly, with no intention to finish?

Designing Assessment Systems

How do you design an assessment system? What events should be recorded? What are left out? In this era of big data, when bandwidth and storage are cheap, it is tempting to frame this task as simply creating a giant log file of every mouse or cursor movement or screen touch. And, to an extent, it is, because everything happening on-screen can be recorded, but as illustrated in table 5.3, which shows the data generated by a single click in *Progenitor X*, any single data trace is extensive, complex, and devoid of meaning outside of context. What does any of those data mean? And what do they mean for learning? And what parts of the game state itself need to be recorded in order to contextualize a player's actions?

Imagine, for a moment, that you want to make inferences about the player of a relatively simple game, such as *PAC-MAN*. The designer would want to record the position of *PAC-MAN* at short intervals, as well as the inputs (turn left, right, up, or down). It might also help to know key aspects of the game state, such as whether the game is in "normal" or in the mode immediately following power pellets, where *PAC-MAN* eats ghosts; a player running straight into a ghost would mean a different thing in each circumstance. But regardless, simply noting the player's position as x, y coordinates would not capture whether the player was chasing a ghost, whether the player was going for a bonus fruit, and so on. Minimally, the game would need to record the player's position, the position and status of all four ghosts, the status of all four power pellets and bonus fruits, and also perhaps the lives remaining.

Our team learned that designing a game-based assessment system was more complex than simply recording every movement and reporting findings. Embedded learning analytics within game play is a complex undertaking that involves optimizing game play for analytics, engineering data collection systems, and creating models of user behavior. As figure 5.2

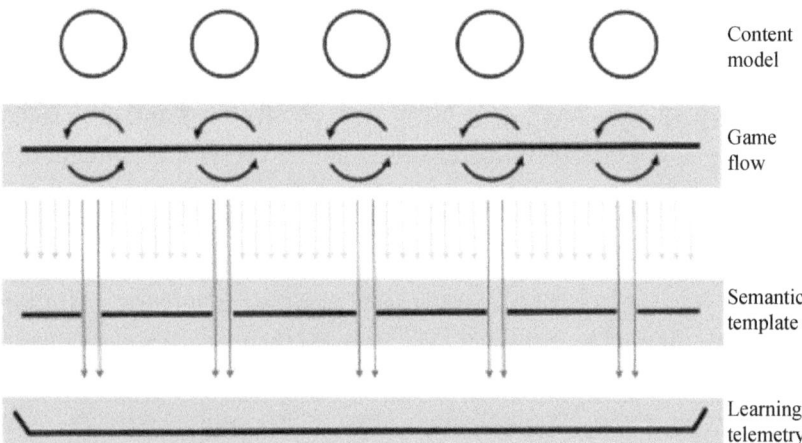

Figure 5.2
Game-based assessment model.

illustrates, there are several steps between designing the game and querying game play data to answer research questions. Researchers must create data collection schemes, organize data to be analyzed, and develop tools that query data. The following section describes the data collection and engineering process behind *Progenitor X*.

Data Design and Collection

Under the direction of Dr. Richard Halverson, the team created the Assessment Data Aggregator for Game Environments (ADAGE), an open Application Programing Interface (API) for data collection, storage, and analysis for academic games (Owen et al., 2014; Stenerson et al., 2014). ADAGE is a low-cost open-source approach to collecting and storing game play data for learning. If we were going to create a data collection and storage mechanism for one game (log-ins; mechanisms for recording player actions, connecting them across sections, and analyzing actions across games), perhaps we could do it for all of our games. And if it were available for our games, why not make it available to anyone making a learning game? We envisioned a system in which researchers could study a learning trajectory from one game to the next, potentially drawing inferences across a longer time span.

ADAGE was unique in its time, but commercial cloud services and associated middleware solutions make such custom services easier. Other contemporary approaches are detailed in Mislevy et al. (2014), Clark et al. (2016), and Shute et al. (2016). Most often, these techniques follow this model: Designers begin with a content model, which is articulated into a game flow model. This game flow is broken down into a semantic template, which is a system for making meaning from data. Underlying this semantic layer is the actual learning telemetry layer, or layer of game play data that are fed into the system. To work in the opposite direction, we might say that assessment experts begin with data generated from game play. They organize the data into meaningful units for analysis. These units are a part of game flow, which feed up to a model of the target learning domain. Building learning analytics is common enough that most larger teams have data scientists on the game design team. As an example, even the small team of undergraduate and graduate students in our lab at the University of California, Irvine, building an Apple iWatch application are basically building these functions ourselves.

Three principles drove this approach:

1. Designers should capture as much data as possible so as to preserve the original data stream. Researchers need to revisit data and query data as new questions emerge.
2. Assessment and game design should go hand in hand. Designers can and should build in choices that generate data that can become moments for generating inferences on learning.
3. Theory should inform and guide data collection. There is a seemingly infinite amount of data to collect from a game. Theory can help guide researchers in deciding which data to collect.

The first step in setting up a data collection framework is to organize and define the data to be collected in the telemetry layer. Our team (see Owen et al., 2014) conceptualized game data in three ways: (1) game units (e.g., completing levels of game play); (2) critical achievements (e.g., completing achievements specified by learning designers as important), and (3) boss levels (e.g., completing levels designed to test for mastery).[2] To apply this framework to *Progenitor X*, we might track (1) how many levels players complete; (2) responses to in-game directives, such as "Hand me the pluripotent stem cells," and (3) failure or completion on boss levels. This conceptual framework is intended to guide thinking; there is no one right answer for what kinds of data will or will not be collected.

Recalling the *PAC-MAN* example, there are two broad categories of data to be collected: player actions (such as moving *PAC-MAN*) and system information (status of the game world; see also Danielak, 2014). This coupling of player actions and feedback is essentially the action-feedback loop that constitutes game play (c.f. Salen & Zimmerman, 2008). Halverson and Owen (2014) further explicate that a useful data layer should include relevant game data such as time stamp, map levels, and x, y coordinates.

When designing methods for collecting, aggregating, and storing data, it is useful to group actions into clusters of meaningful activity, which Owen calls the semantic layer. In the case of *PAC-MAN*, this semantic layer would be players gobbling power pellets and eating ghosts, which are meaningful events (see also Habgood & Ainsworth, 2011). By grouping actions into semantic layers, designers can identify meaningful activities and connect them to other events. In the case of *PAC-MAN*, one might try to correlate perfect scores on levels with saving power pellets until the end of a level, which could then be correlated with other measures (such as learning gains on a test). Of course, no one gives post-tests to *PAC-MAN* players, although one could imagine correlating *PAC-MAN* scores with other measures, such as measures of intelligence or executive function.

Learning Analytics in *Progenitor X*

To illustrate how the assessment design works, let's return to *Progenitor X*. Recall that in *Progenitor X*, the core game play cycle involves (1) setting up, (2) treating, (3) organizing, and (4) collecting cells (then tissues and organs). Players tackle increasingly complex cycles of game play, which we might simplify into start → treat → collect as they move from cells to tissues to organs (and then back and forth). The following data were collected for *Progenitor X* (Owen & Baker, 2018):

- *Player actions* included taps and drags, user interface buttons, almanac usage, manipulation of the cell/tissue/organ lab view tabs, and use of laboratory tools.
- *System events* included tutorials, changes across lab views, and cutscenes.
- *Progress units* included game, objective, and cycle starts and ends.
- *Context* for each event included who, where, and when for events (player ID, session ID, time stamp, location, screen coordinates, device used, operating system, game version, etc.).
- *Result* related to player actions within a cycle (start, treat, collect) and the end of units, such as cycles or objectives, and was populated with data types as required (e.g., a categorical success or failure).

Thus, a robust, relatively intact data stream was recorded. These data-recording tools were implemented within the game client developed in Unity, and the event-stream data were stored in a MongoDB database.

Feature Engineering

As the design, collection, and feature engineering for data systems comes together, researchers start modeling players' decision making. Modeling users is iterative; it is common to invent new forms of analysis during game design. For example, while designing *Progenitor X*, we observed that players weighed whether to create organs with cells they had or to return to earlier phases to create more cells. Observing play practices generates opportunities to check understanding and even embedded assessments. Some game-based learning approaches foreground assessment so that assessment specialists define the domain and learning tasks. This type of "backward design" is just backward in my mind. I can't think of a clearer way of violating interest-driven learning principles than having psychometricians design learning experiences. Assessment specialists should be on teams shaping ideas and generating data to lead to valid inferences on learning.

Game data analysis With data collection systems in place, researchers aggregate and transform data for analysis. With *Progenitor X*, researchers transformed data into usable units, driven by observations, instincts, or theoretical reasons. A sample of the data transformations that were used on *Progenitor X* are included in table 5.1 (adapted from Owen & Baker, 2018). It is worth noting that these transformations are interpretations of data, so that from the earliest phases onward, data are not "a pure, uninterrupted stream" but something interpreted and organized.

As a part of her dissertation work, Liz Owen (2014) administered a pre- and post-test evaluation to students to connect patterns in play to pre- and post-test scores. Overall, a 19.5 percent increase was found in pre- and post-test scores for players. Further, there was a significant positive correlation between learning and overall game play progress and success, meaning that on average, players learned about regenerative medicine, and the better they did in the game, the more they learned. There was a significant *negative* correlation between off-task failure in the tutorial and learning, meaning that those who were off-task in the tutorial were less likely to display

Table 5.1
Examples of data transformations and sample features

Data transformation examples	Sample features
Total counts by event	Total failures in objective 1
	Total tissue cycle failures
	Total objective 3 successes
	Total failures (entire game)
Ratios	Tissue failures: cell failures
	Total game successes: total game failures
	Tutorial objective failures: total failures
Averages	Average failure per objective completed
	Average success per objective

learning gains. Finally, and most critically to this study, success on the boss level was significantly correlated with learning.

This last finding is worth examining further: researchers found a positive correlation between success on the final boss level and learning. Early analyses showed that success on the final boss level predicted the game play pattern of "thoughtful exploration." Subsequently, data scientists drilled down on higher-resolution data on boss levels (e.g., percentage of successes on boss level and number of successful moves in the most difficult portions of the boss level). Using the machine learning software Weka and ADAGE data (Hall et al., 2009), Owen and Baker (2019) analyzed data with a J48 classification tree. They found that players' game completion could be predicted by their success rate in earlier objectives, such as the number of times they attempted the first level or their success on the final level (see table 5.2). These data revealed that improvement *within* the game (doing better at the game on the boss level, compared with early levels) predicted learning. We might infer from this that players who applied themselves within the game (as opposed to guessing or being already familiar with the content) learned from game play.

Educators have long known that failure is a key contributor to learning. Using learning analytics, Owen (2014) demonstrated how *not all failure is the same*. On the one hand, we knew this intuitively; button-mashing, or simply hunting and clicking on solutions, isn't the same as thinking about a problem and getting it right. In some games (e.g., action games such as *Virulent*), players won't get far without understanding. Puzzle games such as *Candy Crush* and *Progenitor X* lend themselves to *some* learning through trial and error. Owen's work with *Progenitor X* shows how games can help

Table 5.2
Patterns across all *Progenitor X* players

	Pre-post gains
Total game play	19.5% average increase
Objectives completed	Significant positive correlation ($r=+.272$, $p=.002$)
Number of successful cycles	Significant positive correlation ($r=+.216$, $p=.012$)
Tutorial level off-task failure	Significant positive correlation ($r=-.617$, $p=.04$)
Boss level success	Significant positive correlation ($r=+.272$, $p=.002$)

Table 5.3
Objective-level aggregate results summary

	Pre-post gains
Objective 1 far failure	Significant negative correlation ($r=-.167$, $p=.04$)
Upper extreme: players with objective 1 far failure	3.9% average increase (15.6% lower than aggregate)
Objective 8 success	Significant positive correlation ($r=+.272$, $p=.002$)
Objective 8 efficiency ratio	Significant positive correlation ($r=+.193$, $p=.022$)

educators detect guesswork early on. As designers, we might engineer features that steer learners on course.

Situating Game Analytics

This coordination of data streams inside and outside of game play is a fruitful area of research, but it is one that we should explore with caution. Making strong claims about learning requires connecting in-game activity with activities occurring outside of the game, including things such as tests. Ideally, we would correlate them to more authentic performance measures and a variety of out-of-game indicators. The temptation to engineer everything into games and extrapolate from them is great.

To explore how in-game data connect to out-of-game contexts, Dr. Constance Steinkuehler and team (Anderson et al., 2018) examined the game play data generated by *Virulent* and connected it to out-of-game conversations and interactions. Recall from chapter 3 the *Diagnostic Detective* curriculum in which students explored oncology in a one-week after-school program. That same week, they also participated in a program based on *Virulent*. In the *Virulent* curriculum, they were given an iPad and role-played as agents at the Centers for Disease Control and Prevention investigating the fictitious Raven virus (the virus depicted in *Virulent*). Students were charged with investigating how to stop the virus from spreading. The game itself was recast as a medical simulation tool. The iPad allowed students to view patients' internal workings. Participants were assigned to groups of three, in which they played the game, studied the reasons for the virus spreading, and built physical paper models of the virus life cycle and the immune system. Solutions were recorded and presented to a mock CDC panel, where they debated solutions. Participants were also encouraged to play the challenge levels on their own or at home.

Similarly to earlier studies, researchers observed learning gains through playing of *Virulent*. Forty-three people completed a pre- and post-test assessment, with a statistically significant increase in biology and virology knowledge over the five-day intervention [t (42) = 5.47, $p < .05$]. Digging more deeply using learning analytics, the team identified several factors that predicted learning:

> Factorial ANOVA showed that number of failed attempts before success across all levels (F(1.75) = 7.330, p= 0.005, η2 = 0.087), total attempts at main levels (F(1.75) = 4.119, P = 0.046, H2 = 0.043), and pre-assessment scores (F (1.75) = 6.235, P = 0.015, η2= 0.065) were significant predictors of post-assessment scores. Other time on task measures including game progression (F(1.75) = 1.194, p= 0.278), and total time playing the game (F (1.75) = 0.631, p= 0.430) were found to be non-significant. Total number of failures at main levels including attempts after initial success were also found to be non-significant (F(1.75) = 0.023, p= 0.880) (p.139).

Thus, with *Virulent*, changes in failure rates were not predictive of learning, but instead overall attempts were. This could be, in part, due to the design of *Virulent*, but it could also be due to the influence of other learning activities.

Because researchers had a full data record of all discussions, they were able to dig into interactions and examine conversations. To examine these patterns, researchers selected ten-minute segments of activity to transcribe. These transcripts were analyzed using MAXQDA (v. 12) software. Researchers mined data for negative value statements around level failures, including "lost," "hard," "difficult," "impossible," "hate," "dislike," and "fail." They then reviewed hand text to gather context and identified 550 utterances to examine. Discussions that included failure often led to collaborative discussions. As groups tried to ameliorate failure, they discussed game mechanics, which required them to use game vocabulary to decipher what was happening, as in the following exchange:

Participant 78: I got sucked into this blue thing . . . The B cell.

Participant 86: Okay. So what I did was like I pressed the little red thing in the corner when you first start and then you press virion or something like that. And then you start guarding it. Then if it doesn't pop up, you get it right there.

Participant 78: So I'm supposed to be sucked in?

Participant 97: Isn't it the brain? A B cell?

On the basis of this interaction and others like it, researchers studied whether talk progressively became more sophisticated. Using the length of words as a rough proxy for talk sophistication (after Flesch, 1948), they examined how discourse evolved. Student groups used longer words (on average) on late days in the intervention, word length increased for all participants by day 5, and students used biology vocabulary more frequently in the final days. It is but a start, but this study suggests how games might spark deeper discussions through play.

The Future of Learning Analytics

The analysis by Steinkuehler's lab suggests the potential, but also the pitfalls, of applying big data techniques to game play analysis. On the one hand, for researchers, having an intact data stream of player activity is exciting. How valuable would it be to identify where players struggle, or where they are off-task, to provide nudges that return them to task? Discerning between productive and nonproductive failure might help students refine their thinking in the context of problem solving. This just-in-time coaching is just the kind of formative feedback that educators have long hoped for, particularly as we attempt to capture some of the magic of tutoring.

The discourse analysis of Steinkuehler and colleagues further suggests the potential of applying learning analytics to large data corpuses, such as classroom talk. As tools such as Apple's Siri, Google Assistant, and Amazon's Alexa proliferate, it is possible that educators will have access to a full, uninterrupted data stream of student activity. My own son's classroom employs voice-activated Google Assistant, which his teacher uses to look up information on the fly. It is easy to envision a not-far-off future when an embedded assistant might coach students in context, providing formative assessment or, perhaps more likely, providing data to teachers and parents so they can study students' work.

I also worry (as do, I think, Steinkuehler and many other researchers) that by creating such technologies, we may be inviting surveillance technologies further into students' lives. Is whatever knowledge we gain worth this intrusion? Part of the fun of games is their escape from consequence and their invitation to explore new ways of being. By designing assessment opportunities into games, are we removing that escapism that is also part of their appeal?

In reflecting on this work on assessment and games, for now, we may be saved by the sheer work involved in getting anything meaningful from it.

In her keynote address to the Assocation of Testing Publishers, "Next Generation Assessment: The Power of Games," Steinkuehler (2015) described how, currently, game-based assessments are provocative, not deterministic. Nothing from this research suggests that games will be particularly well suited to automatically assess learning. Game play itself captures only a fraction of the interactions, and as the case of *Virulent* suggests, how and what are discussed also constitutes learning. Similarly, a great deal of the work goes into cleaning data, which is about 80 percent of the work (Steinkuehler, 2015). Currently, "collecting and analyzing data" is far from "automatic." Tremendous conceptual leaps are made as researchers code, chunk, and organize data. Further, the work itself is quite intensive; consider the work of several full-time PhD students and researchers that went into this chapter, all for findings that are encouraging but also limited. To be sure, tools will evolve that automate that work over the long haul.

As educators, we might consider, however, how the inclusion of tools such as games for assessments is changing who does the work of assessment. How might these technologies displace interpretations further from students, teachers, and parents and further toward programmers and analysts, who are distant from students? I believe that as a principle, the best assessment decisions are made as close to learning as possible, as students, teachers, and parents (and other stakeholders) reflect on student activity. Students should have more, not less, voice in assessments. I worry that despite our best intentions, offloading that critical interpretive work of deciding what does or does not count for assessment, and what patterns we will or will not look for, will exacerbate inequities in assessment.

6 Games for Healthy Minds

The tropes around brains and games are so established that they are tired at this point. Think of "brain" and "video game" and the images that come to mind are something rotting or perhaps fried. Games are the enemy of thinking and school, and we don't usually associate video games with prosocial behavior.

There is another, equally strong current underlying games in the popular imagination, and that is of games as a training tool, sharpening youths' minds and perhaps training a new generation to become warriors or pilots. This observation was perhaps first (and most famously) made by Ronald Reagan (1983), who, speaking at Disney's EPCOT Center, extolled the virtues of games to train cold war pilots. Subsequently, an extensive research literature has developed around game-based training tools in military training (Tobias & Fletcher, 2011). The mechanics of skills such as piloting can be relatively straightforwardly translated into flight simulators, but the military uses games for training in about every way one could imagine (see also Mead, 2013).

Reagan's observation has been borne out in research literature regarding the brain and games more generally. Neuroscientists studying action game players have shown that the regular playing of action video games trains the visual systems of gamers such that they can detect and track objects on-screen more readily than nongamers (Green & Bavelier, 2003). This skill can be detected through functional magnetic resonance imaging (fMRI) scans; gamers trained on action games (typically around thirty hours on a shooter such as *Unreal Tournament*) are better able to locate and track targets while blocking out extraneous information. This includes tracking such information moving in space as well as in time (better ability to track rapidly appearing and disappearing information—attentional blink). Subsequent studies using fMRI technologies reveal that expert gamers require fewer attentional resources than nongamers to complete these tasks, meaning, essentially, that it's much easier for them.

At the same time, three negative trends associated with games complicate the pattern: (1) a rise in attention deficit hyperactivity disorder (ADHD) diagnoses, (2) a rise in autism spectrum disorder (ASD) diagnoses (Baio et al., 2018), and (3) rising concerns about gaming addiction. It's beyond the scope of this chapter and, frankly, beyond my expertise to go into much depth on each of these issues. Briefly, though, ADHD diagnoses are on the rise, and over 6.4 million school-age American children (about 10 percent) have been diagnosed with ADHD. On the one hand, one could imagine arguing that games should be training youths' attentional systems, so we should, if anything, see fewer such diagnoses. We might also argue that games (and perhaps even more so for social media) are training youths to become highly skilled in high-feedback-reinforcement systems such that "reality is boring" in comparison. Or we might point to increased awareness, better patient advocacy groups, changes in the structure of schooling, or marketing from drug companies (see Hinshaw & Scheffler, 2015). Academic studies of the phenomenon point to changing social attitudes toward the phenomena and engaged parents seeking to advocate for their children (Davidovitch et al., 2017).

People (children, youths, and adults) with "autism spectrum disorders (ASD) have strong preferences for screen-based media, particularly video games," wrote Micah Mazurek and Christopher Engelhardt (2013a). We know through self- and parent reports that people with ASD spend much more time with games. In a national sample of participants, Mazurek and Engelhardt (2013b) found that over 40 percent of youths with ASD spent *most* of their free time playing video games (compared with 18 percent in the general population; Marshall et al., 2006).

People with ASD have a clear affinity for video games, although they report the same features as compelling as does the general population (stress relief, immersion, social connection, achievement, story—see Bartle, 2003; Mazurek et al., 2015; Yee, 2014). No correlations were found between hours of game play and attention, hyperactivity, or oppositional defiant behavior. Oddly, perhaps, researchers found that boys with ASD who played primarily role-playing games (such as *Pokémon GO!*) were more likely to exhibit oppositional behaviors than those who didn't, which strikes me as just weird (Mazurek & Engelhardt, 2013a, 2013b). Advocates for individuals with ASD, such as the Els for Autism Foundation, argue that the routines, repetition, puzzle solving, and safe space for socialization provided by games make them responsive to their needs. One could imagine role-playing games being appealing, given that they are opportunities to play with social interactions in a safe way.

Finally, gaming addiction is most certainly an issue worth attending to. My own thinking on gaming addiction has evolved over the past twenty years. Like most, I've encountered cases of people who engage in problematic gaming. The same can be said for food, work, and sex. In 2018, the World Health Organization added gaming disorder to the *International Statistical Classification of Diseases and Related Health Problems*. Although this addition was debated hotly among gamers, the actual language operationalizing the condition seemed reasonable:

> The behaviour pattern is of sufficient severity to result in significant impairment in personal, family, social, educational, occupational or other important areas of functioning. . . . The gaming behaviour and other features are normally evident over a period of at least 12 months in order for a diagnosis to be assigned, although the required duration may be shortened if all diagnostic requirements are met and symptoms are severe (p. 428).

Gamers and game reviewers (and game designers) toss around words like "addicted" colloquially, but it is clear that this description—which requires twelve months of impaired functioning—describes substantial problems.

Designing Games for Good

Are there opportunities to leverage the engaging, attention-focusing qualities of games? Could we design a game that helps students control their attention or develop empathic accuracy (the ability to accurately read the emotions of facial expressions)? Could we apply the brain-imaging techniques that have been used to study action game players to study learning with a game for impact?

Beginning in 2014, with support from the Bill & Melinda Gates Foundation, our research team began studying these phenomena through a collaboration with University of Wisconsin–Madison neuroscientist Richard Davidson. Richie is the founding director of the Center for Healthy Minds and is known for his work studying emotion and brain. He is also a friend and confidante to the Dalai Lama, which leads to such things as Richie bagging out of team meetings at the last minute to fly across the world to be with His Holiness. The dog ate my homework, too.

Our teams met with the simple goal of understanding one another's work. What questions were we working on? What was known and not known from our domains? Two areas emerged: (1) how might neuroscience ideas and methods for studying learning be applied to game-based learning (especially as we study learning as a biological and social phenomenon)? and (2) could we design tools to encourage healthy minds?

If you want to see an awkward gathering, try convening game developers with neuroscientists and mindfulness experts to discuss screens, violence, and mental health. One is about quiet contemplation, the other distraction, or perhaps transgressive play. One the height of productive prosocial work, the other the essence of "wasting time." Add to that competing visions of health, wellness, and healthy society.

Through time, we established shared values. More video game developers practice meditation than you might anticipate, and when you look across the entire "production pipeline" of studying meditation, you find fMRI technicians, practitioners, and people searching for work-life balance, most of whom have played games at some point. Both groups share an irreverence born of operating at the fringe. Using mindfulness or video games to do anything useful might seem normal now, but ten or twenty years ago, both seemed crazy.

As learning researchers know, this kind of long-lasting, deep structural change to the brain is difficult to induce and measure. Transfer—or the ability to show that something has been learned in one situation and used in the next—has proved to be among the most elusive quests in the learning sciences (Barnett & Ceci, 2002; Woodworth & Thorndike, 1901). How we apply learning from one context to the next depends on myriad factors, including contextual factors such as self-efficacy, motivation, and the fit between the learning environment and the lived one (Blume et al., 2009). Finding enduring, widely transferable changes in brain functioning is relatively wild for researchers used to trying to get kids to use algebra to solve math problems. Could we design an app to help teenagers develop these same skills?

A Game for Mindfulness?

The following are reasons to pursue a mindfulness game for youths:

1. We already turn to phones in times of anxiety, restlessness, arousal, relaxation, or boredom. Think of how we pull out *Candy Crush Saga* and the like after a stressful situation. Could we provide an app that actually helps with the underlying issues? (See Ito & Okabe, 2005.)
2. A digital game would be eminently disseminable. Put it on a digital store such as the iTunes Store and it could immediately get to millions of youths.
3. Digital games deployed to phones are portable.
4. Social games and activities can connect people readily in a shared activity.
5. Games already recruit focused attention.

Once one goes deeper, the challenges to a game for mindfulness also present themselves. Games are good at *recruiting* attention. Few teens worry about their mind wandering during a *Fortnite* battle. Design techniques such as challenge, reward, narrative, and amplified feedback grab our attention and deepen our experience, and as such game play is somewhat orthogonal to mindfulness. Can we create game mechanics that *deepen* mindfulness yet are not boring?

Game play does, however, recruit serious attention. In this respect, games share qualities with activities that develop mental strength, such as martial arts and exercise. When played at high levels, games recruit focus, sustained attention, and metacognition. Any parent who has struggled to regain their child's attention while gaming understands this. (Or, in my case, being yelled at by *my* children for getting sucked into *Hearthstone*.) Whether it be action games such as *Fortnite*, which recruit visual attention, or games involving deep strategy (such as *Civilization* and *Hearthstone*), games recruit focus.

Attention, however, is something a little different. Davidson reminds us of how foundational attention is to psychology. As William James (1890) wrote: "The faculty of voluntarily bringing back a wandering *attention* over and over again is the very root of judgment, character, and will [emphasis added]." So, again, how can we develop learners' ability to mindfully capture this mind wandering and develop mastery of their thinking through a game?

Breath Counting: The Game

A way forward presented itself through the work of doctoral student Daniel Levinson. Levinson, with members of Davidson's group, developed and validated a breath-counting task as a way to measure mind wandering (Levinson et al., 2014). The idea behind this task was deceptively simple: Focusing on the breath is a foundational activity in meditation, and to relaxation across a variety of traditions. Breath counting is simply the technique of counting breaths. Levinson and colleagues found that successful breath counting (e.g., being aware that one is on, say, the tenth breath) is a good measure of mindfulness. The more one's mind wanders, the more one miscounts breaths. Because breath counting includes a challenge, it is implicitly a form of a game. Could a breath-counting app be a starting point for a mindfulness tool? (See Beall et al., 2013.)

Davidson's team received a grant to build a proof-of-concept prototype. *Fair Play* designer Erin Robinson, together with David Gagnon and Nathan McKenzie, developed a simple breath-counting prototype. Players would focus on a candle and press a button with every breath. On the nth breath, they would press a different button. With just a few simple checks (such as making sure that they weren't simply quickly tapping), we could induce and measure mindfulness.

The game was great for assessment but not super engaging for middle school students. It is pretty boring to stare at a screen while breathing. The core metaphor of a candle worked well enough, but we thought other visuals might engage this audience. In a research study, we *could* require youths to use the application, but it seemed antithetical to force people to use it.

We moved forward, hoping to resolve the problem by designing the application for smaller, quicker hits and themed to students' interests. The Center for Healthy Minds eschewed competition, transgression, and violence as a part of its values. We were intrigued by the idea that youths would turn to an app such as this to "strengthen" their minds at moments of anxiety, fear, stress, or fatigue.

We rebuilt the game *Tenacity* as a breath-counting application for the iPod Touch (for an in-depth discussion, see Binzak et al., 2015). We scoured the sales charts to identify popular prosocial, nonviolent themes that might be calming. We were quickly drawn to nature, and most themes revolved around deserts, space, and flowers (see figure 6.1). In each case, the game

Figure 6.1
Tenacity prototypes.

world becomes more populated as players do better. If they successfully count breaths, they go farther into space or more flowers bloom. We toyed with presenting distractions to tap on but did not feel comfortable deviating significantly from the core breath-counting task, which had been validated for this purpose.

Results. To investigate the impact of *Tenacity*, researchers Constance Steinkuehler and Richard Davidson recruited 115 middle school students and randomly assigned them to either *Tenacity* or *Fruit Ninja*, a control condition. The games were about as similar as we could find as far as types of interaction, use case, and so on. Both groups were asked to play their game for thirty minutes a day for two weeks. The pre- and post-test measures were extensive, the most thorough I'd seen in a learning study. They included neuroimaging, pre- and post-test behavioral tasks measuring attention (i.e., continuous performance task, mind probe task) and telemetry data (breath count accuracy, level progressions) as well as pre/post affective self-report from each individual's game play.

Researchers found promising findings as a result of playing *Tenacity (Patsenko et al., 2019)*. The longitudinal randomized control study showed that playing *Tenacity* for two weeks induced functional and structural changes in key attentional brain areas, and many of these changes related to improvements on attentional tasks (see figure 6.2).

> Adolescents who played *Tenacity* for 2 weeks showed a significantly higher resting state functional connectivity (rs-FC) between left dorsolateral prefrontal cortex (dlPFC) and left inferior parietal cortex (IPC) compared to adolescents who played *FruitNinja* (Figure 6.2). In addition, the increase in structural integrity of white matter tracts that connect left dlPFC and left IPC related to the increase in accuracy on an attentional task only in the *Tenacity* group (Figure 6.2). We also found group differences in structural changes in another key attentional region—right cingulate gyrus—a significantly lower RD (lower radial), marginally lower MD (mean diffusivity), and marginally higher FICV (neurite density) for *Tenacity* after only 2 weeks of game play. There were no group differences in the DTI indices at Time 1. Importantly, *the changes in DTI indices were associated with improvements in accuracy on an attentional task.* (p. 3, emphasis added)

Restated, researchers found increased links for *Tenacity* players between the left dorsolateral prefrontal cortex, which is central to executive functions including working memory, planning, abstract reasoning, and inhibiting behaviors, and the left inferior parietal cortex, which is involved in the perception of sensory information, perception of facial stimuli, body images,

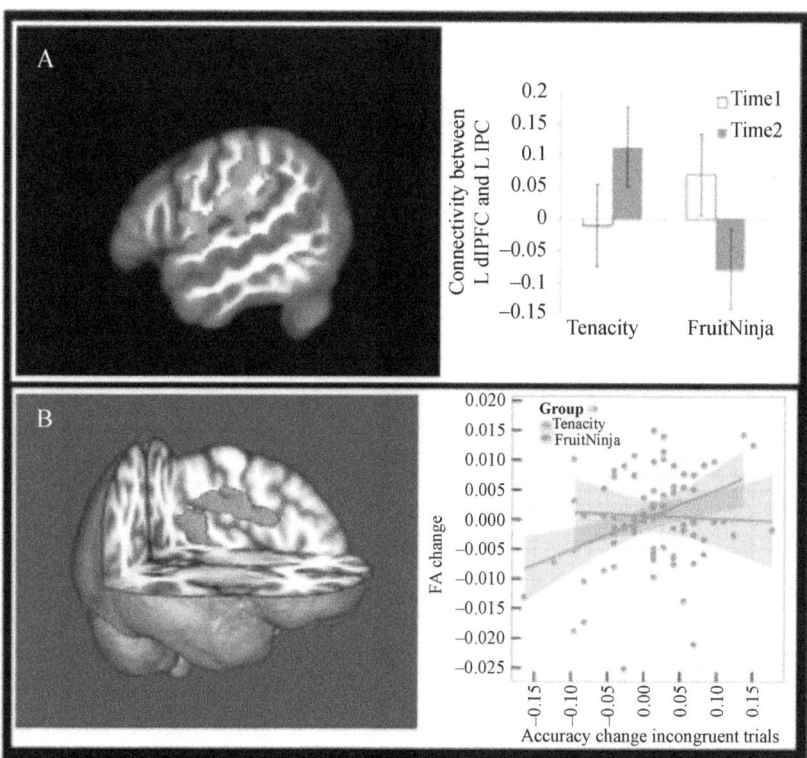

Figure 6.2
Comparative images of brain scans on *Tenacity* and *Fruit Ninja*.

and mathematics, and language processing. In addition, researchers found structural changes for *Tenacity* players in the parts of their brains responsible for forming emotions, memory, and learning.

On the downside, self-reports from players revealed that most really didn't like *Tenacity*. The hope that youths would voluntarily turn to *Tenacity* did not come to fruition. Most reported using it only as part of the experiment. The modest findings that we saw were encouraging; something positive was happening. Meditating can be hard work, and even uncomfortable, but millions of people voluntarily, regularly meditate, and there was little risk of our *Tenacity* app replacing that. We needed to resolve the contradictions around capturing versus focusing attention, managing screens, and framing the activity.

With the support of a gift from an anonymous donor, we recreated *Tenacity* as an iPad app for adults. We added challenges, quests, timers, and new levels more appealing to parents as a proof of concept for what a market-ready meditation app might look like.

Games for Empathy

A research grant from the Gates Foundation supported further collaboration. Whereas *Tenacity* seemed likely to succeed, we also wanted to try something more high risk and high reward. We wanted to explore a game for improving empathy, the ability to understand the emotional experiences of others.

Crystals of Kaydor is a game for increasing empathy in adolescents. The production process behind *Crystals* was short, at nine months. Through design jams, we developed the idea of the player controlling a robot to explore another planet. The player navigates the planet, traverses obstacles, and neutralizes monsters. Along the way, she encounters aliens with whom she does not share a language. She must (a) interpret their facial expressions, (b) gauge the intensity of their emotions, (c) communicate back through an expression, and (d) interpret the aliens' response. In this way, the player can have a conversation of sorts with the aliens. In some cases, the aliens need to be consoled; in others they might just be expressing joy.

This facial recognition was both the core learning mechanic and the core game play mechanic. The game play of trying to recognize the aliens' emotions was fun, and it was quite clearly the exact practice that was the target learning goal. Lead artist Adam Wiens developed a sophisticated facial animation system that responded dynamically to player input and supported dynamic game play. Considerable effort went into designing creatures that were engaging, induced sympathetic responses, and were nonthreatening, while, frankly, looking really good on an iPad. We tested all of the creatures with dozens of youths and gained consistently positive responses.

Research

Similarly to our process with *Tenacity*, we conducted a research study with adolescents to investigate whether playing *Crystals* would increase empathic accuracy (EA) and related brain activity. We recruited 74 youths for the study (27 female; mean age(sd) = 12.8(0.7) years; age range 11–14 years). Thirty-four played *Crystals* while 40 played the commercial game *Bastion*, an active control condition. Researchers chose *Bastion* because it

Figure 6.3
Crystals of Kaydor.

involves similar game mechanics and is legitimately a great game that we felt good about asking kids to play.

Results. Overall, there were no group differences in EA improvement following game play, but engagement with specific training parts of *Crystals* was associated with a higher increase in right temporoparietal function following game play (see figure 6.3). Kral et al. (2018) wrote:

> Moreover, rs-fMRI connectivity in empathy-related brain circuits (posterior cingulate–medial prefrontal cortex; MPFC) was stronger after *Crystals* gameplay compared to *Bastion*. The more individuals' EA increased following *Crystals* versus *Bastion*, the stronger their rs-fMRI connectivity in brain circuits relevant for emotion regulation (amygdala-MPFC). These findings suggest that a video game designed to increase empathic accuracy produces behaviorally-relevant, functional neural changes in fewer than 6 h of gameplay in adolescents. (p. _TK_)

Crystals of Kaydor is, to the best of my knowledge, the first longitudinal study demonstrating neurological changes as a result of a game-based intervention. The game was popular among youths, who liked the characters and game play.

From a design perspective, the "facial recognition conversations," the core learning mechanic, worked for learning and was, for me, a high point for our lab's work. It was interesting for us to play with, and it was a design innovation for games more generally. This way of interacting with characters was a welcomed addition to the clunky conversation tree solutions in narrative-driven games. We imagined many innovations stemming from this "conversation engine." *Crystals* is the kind of research and development work that is well suited for academics.

In regard to design, we never resolved the tension between the world-based game play and the conversation engine. The world-based game play (which looked a little like *Diablo*) was thin in comparison with other games in the genre, and the interplay between these phases was a bit forced. We intended for this phase to draw in more typical gamers, which it may have, but evidence suggests that those same gamers may have focused too much on the world-based game play. If I were to redesign *Crystals*, I would pull out the conversations and focus on them to drive all of the game play. Instead of the players' time being split between phases so that 60–70 percent of the game is spent exploring the world, I would reverse it so that 80 percent of the time is spent in conversations, and then I'd work on making them as interesting as possible.

Scaling Out Products

Upon completion of the grant from the Gates Foundation, we had two strong prototypes and a good working relationship, but we were at a crossroads. It would be years before the data from these trials would be published. This delay between design, production, data collection, and product release created an unanticipated snag that is endemic to this space. The market for games shifts rapidly. Five years is a *generation*. Simply stopping production for two or three years is akin to a death sentence. Standards, conventions, and, critically, business models change so quickly that anyone restarting a project after a few years of downtime is starting back a few steps.

This problem between research and product timeliness is not impossible, but it's also nontrivial. Consider, for example, *Crystals*, which is fairly typical example of a three-year grant project. The first six months are mostly spent hiring staff, setting up production pipelines, and creating a team culture. An established team such as ours at the GLS Center could produce

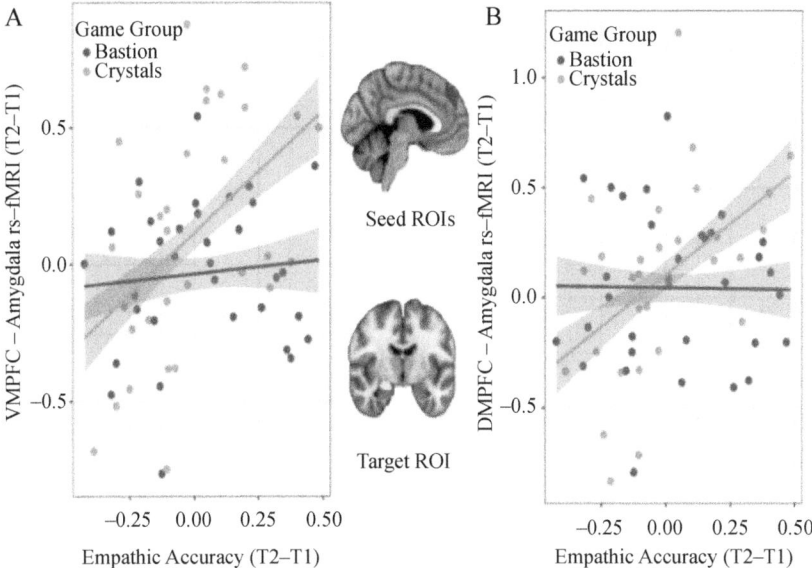

Figure 6.4
Comparing *Bastion* and *Crystals of Kaydor*.

large time savings here, but working on multiple projects also meant that staff were pulled across projects and into other activities. Data collection itself typically takes another three to six months, and then data analysis and reporting take the next year, and this is under the best conditions. More often, as in *Crystals*, the project bleeds over into another year or two as staff changes (such as a postdoc landing a job), delays in IRB documents, or other unforeseen problems push back the project. Researchers navigate these hurdles routinely, using no-cost extensions (saving some money for an extra year) or analyzing and writing data after the grant is done.

Even with a relatively forward-leaning design (we aimed for next-generation iPads), the main development occurred in 2013 on a truncated nine-month production cycle. The marquee research paper was published in 2018, a full five years after the grant. Had we restarted development in 2018, planning for a 2020 release, we'd have faced a multitude of challenges: most development staff would have moved on unless we had significant projects to keep the team going *and*, critically, professional development opportunities, which is how industry-grade talent furthers their careers (and compensation). These problems are solvable, particularly if an institution will commit to hiring and keeping staff employed or to strategically investing in projects.

A Participatory Approach to Healthy Minds

As we reflected on next steps, a logical move was to port *Tenacity* to wearable devices. The use case we imagined (a youth pulling out a device before a test, while in the car, at the store, at a social gathering, before bed) made more sense for something like a watch, which doesn't require full visual attention. Fidget spinners were taking off at the time, and that seemed like another competing use case. Imagine if, instead of playing with fidget spinners, youths were playing a collaborative breath-counting activity in which they tried to collectively count a thousand breaths before a test?

Participatory Design Workshops

Because we were starting new in California, with a few years having passed between studies, we wanted to re-engage with youths in the target demographic. We partnered with Sherry Skipper-Spurgeon, a teacher at MacArthur Fundamental Intermediate School in Santa Ana, California, and recruited twenty-nine middle school students for an eight-session curriculum in which they would design a wearable device for mindfulness. This was a voluntary after-school program with minimal compensation, and all of the youths were free lunch recipients (see figure 6.5). Whether it was the change in time or in geography, we were stunned by how differently youths in 2018 Orange County, California, approached this task than did youths in 2013 Madison, Wisconsin. All of them were eager to discuss mental health, mindfulness, and meditation. Most had engaged in these practices in some form.

The biggest takeaway was a shift in our mindsets. We had, until this point, used something like the medical model, in which we would develop a technological solution, hand it to youths, and observe whether it "worked" (see also Vacca, 2017). The moment we engaged youths in conversations about their emotional lives, they lit up. They readily reported stresses, from tests to schools to grades to family life, to friends who "tilted" while playing video games. They all reported techniques they used for relaxation and attention focusing. Music was central to most of their practices. The "winning" designs (see figure 6.6) were most often watchlike devices that (1) recorded their physiological state, (2) allowed them to engage in a short, focusing

Games for Healthy Minds

Figure 6.5
Participatory design workshops.

activity such as rhythmic action game play, (3) communicated their emotional state with friends, and (4) reflected on and guided their progress. The energy in this group designing applications was stunning, particularly when compared with the way youths used the *Tenacity* tool.

The next-generation design refocused the activity from one of game playing to one of developing mental strength. We had used a model of "use a device for thirty minutes a day as directed by the doctor." We wanted, in contrast, for youths to take responsibility for their health so that they were

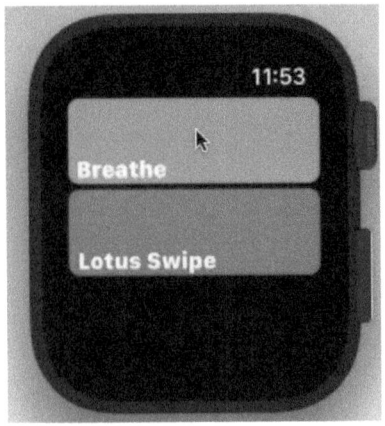 

Figure 6.6
Wearable *Tenacity* for the Apple iWatch.

setting goals, reflecting on their practices, and evaluating their progress. This shift was triggered by multiple factors. Partly, we were increasingly concerned about the ethics of situating ourselves as experts shaping youths' mindsets in this way. We wanted to empower youths to achieve their own goals. Second, examining the data, we recognized that we had put the format of games (specific design patterns, interfaces) ahead of the deeper idea of choice. One reason games are so compelling is that we choose to play them. Force people to play a game—any game—and they will likely hate it. Games researchers who suddenly find their love of game play sapped because it is a job will understand. Finally, we thought the real opportunity was to make a game out of getting mentally stronger, in the same way that we might use fitness trackers. Ironically, embracing gamification strategies felt more genuinely respectful to users than a traditional game-based learning approach.

The core experience was redesigned to employ a schedule → enact → evaluate approach. The experience begins with a short diagnostic assessment, followed by a scheduling exercise in which youths set goals and routines to take command of the experience. In the enact phase, players use interactive versions of many common attention-focusing practices, including breath counting, pattern matching, and rhythmic game play. We honored the fact that music is a key enactor of their identities, an important way that they control their emotional lives. Whereas in the previous study we focused on the art styles that appealed to youths, this design sought to amplify healthy mental health practices already in use and start a conversation around them.

Conclusions

Video games are often maligned as a cause of social ills such as attention deficit hyperactivity disorder and autism spectrum disorder. The evidence for these relationships is not clear, in part because diagnosis of the disorders is so recent and patient advocacy has grown so rapidly that the data are difficult to parse. As a parent of two school-age gaming boys, I feel these tensions myself. If, for example, one of my kids were diagnosed with either condition, he might qualify for extra tutoring or school services, which is a coveted status in the high-achieving Southern California schools. The idea that my son's inability to concentrate on ninety minutes of homework each night after a full day of school with virtually no recess might be due to video games seems disingenuous. At the same time, we likely all know youths who have been diagnosed with ADHD or ASD and whose lives have been improved through treatment.

Games *can* help attention focusing and empathizing, but a practice-based approach may be most helpful for producing these changes. Situating the locus of control within youth, so that they are developing and practicing higher-level executive functioning, is parsimonious because the ultimate goal of any such activity is to help people better manage their mental health. Youths have a natural appetite for the topic, and (again perhaps paradoxically) the rise of competitive gaming has helped fuel this as kids discuss and debate tilting and rage quitting. It's tempting to think that youths are starting at zero here, but actually they already have sophisticated ways of managing their mental health that can be leveraged.

An underdeveloped area, which we are exploring now, is how to use social tools to promote healthy minds. We know, from other areas of research, that healthier minds are developed through complex social phenomena, ranging from Alcoholics Anonymous to martial arts. These practice-based approaches use rituals and routines, social connections, and personal responsibility (among other elements) to improve mindfulness. These same kinds of routines and connections can be built into applications. We imagine, for example, choosing a friend who also seeks to improve mental fitness, setting collaborative goals, and earning achievements after completing these goals together.

The role of games in such an approach is more than using a particular development tool set or design pattern or even thinking in terms of roles and goals. A game-based approach, in my mind, means getting inside the minds of players and understanding their goals, interests, and desires, as well as their use case scenario. It means developing tools and techniques that will help them better achieve these goals and reflect on their successes. In some indie design circles, this principle is called "respect the player," which stands in contrast to medical models or even the attention-driven model behind most media, game, and social algorithms. As of this writing, such media companies, including Google, Facebook, Apple, and game companies, do not allow us to own our data, reflect on the use of the data, or really sculpt our experiences; instead, they seek to sculpt our attention so that it is sold for profit.

Game designers of all sorts—but designers of educational games in particular—are going to be forced to reckon with the ethics of these attentional decisions. Almost ten years ago, designer Jonathan Blow caused a minor storm by declaring that "social games are evil" for precisely this reason: they manipulate our attention so that designers are exploiting users' attention, keeping them on the game longer or getting them to spend money they might not ordinarily spend (Caldwell, 2011). All game designers, but designers of games for social good in particular, will need to develop ethical models for how to help learners establish goals, pursue goals, and reflect on their experiences. It may be that "game design" will fail as a label and we will want a descriptor that emphasizes how players themselves are designers of their own experiences.

7 Games, Design, Schools, and Markets

Imagine a game like *Civilization* in which players competed on realistic maps to build farms, towns, or factories and the game itself was a simulation of human-environmental interactions. Now imagine (1) a predictive simulation so that scientists, conservationists, and land developers were all playing on the same tract of land (in this case Vilas County, Wisconsin) and (2) scenario design tools so that stakeholders (activists, landowners, policy makers) could explore how these ideas play out. My previous work on the *Civilization* series explored similar ideas: could we create game systems in which players explore choices and consequences in land use decisions to inform the public and promote better policy discussions? We were especially excited about using multiplayer games to generate cross-generational, cross-sector discussions about our futures.

My understanding of these issues is indebted to the work of Stephen Carpenter and his colleagues at the Center for Limnology at the University of Wisconsin–Madison. Carpenter's group studies lake ecosystems, particularly eutrophication, the process by which lake ecosystems become so over-enriched by nutrients, usually from land runoff, that they are overrun by "blooms" of plants or algae. These blooms can cut off sunlight and cause hypoxia, depriving the water of oxygen. Some algae blooms produce toxic chemicals (Chislock et al., 2013). Eutrophication can be triggered by specific spills (point source pollution) or can be caused by diffuse runoff across a watershed (see Carpenter et al., 1998). Most commonly, eutrophication is driven by human activity, including nitrate and phosphate discharges from residential or agricultural fertilizers.

Over decades of researching these problems, Carpenter has also worked with local groups to help them better manage their ecosystems. When engaged in direct dialogue, free of political spin or impugning of one another's motives, most communities arrive at good solutions for managing their local resources. We share common interests, such as clean water, meaningful, well-paying jobs for local residents, and protection of natural spaces, whether for the purposes of recreation, conservation, or fishing and hunting.

Scenario planning is a technique in which system stakeholders gather in diverse groups to envision multiple plausible futures. The benefits are "(1) increased understanding of key uncertainties, (2) incorporation of alternative perspectives into conservation planning, and (3) greater resilience of decisions to surprise" (Peterson et al., 2003, p. 358). In their scenario for Wisconsin's Northern Highland Lake District, for example, Carpenter and colleagues described planning around Northern Wisconsin's lakes, an area that covers five thousand square kilometers and was rapidly being developed for tourism and second homes (often from Chicago). Comparing these scenarios, Carpenter and colleagues found that in all likelihood, different lakes would evolve toward different foci (such as recreational motorsports versus fishing), and the interactions among lakes would be the source of friction.

In our earlier work (see Gaydos & Squire, 2012; Squire, 2012), we developed an adventure/role-playing game, *Citizen Science*, around similar ideas. In *Citizen Science* (developed by Filament Games), players are teenagers trying to save Lake Mendota from eutrophication. We wanted the game to play like an interactive scenario so that players could watch the lake evolve in response to their choices. The successes and challenges of developing *Citizen Science* are covered elsewhere. One of my lessons from the game (which was under development when I began writing this book) was that it is hard to do design-based research with a for-profit company (as described in earlier chapters). After further reflection, I see *Citizen Science* as a complete, satisfying game experience completed under an aggressive budget, and the partnership generated multiple design ideas I never would have considered.

If *Citizen Science* was a sandbox for exploring scientific investigation, we envisioned a simulation game that would be more like a fieldwork site, where students, citizens, activists, and developers could all have a sustained discussion about issues related to sustainability (see Bell-Gawn et al., 2013). *Citizen Science* was admirable as a single-player game with a theme of conducting a virtual investigation. However, it didn't use real data, did not engage players in socially authentic (real) investigations, didn't really appeal to the broad public, and had a limited "ceiling" in its long-term impact. It's worth noting, however, that it was used in classrooms years after the grant was completed; when we were forced to take it down because it no longer was compatible with current versions of Flash, we received numerous inquiries from teachers around the country who had been using it.

Trails Forward: **Knowledge Games for Public Policy**

Early in our years at the Wisconsin Institute for Discovery, we were approached by Dr. Michael Ferris in the Optimization Group, who was interested in using games as a tool for studying human decision making regarding conservation issues. Could a simulation-based game be used to enact scenarios such as the Northern Highland Lake District but allow researchers to investigate the ideas humans make and their impact on the underlying simulated environment? This idea built on the concept of contested places from our earlier work on local games by identifying locations and issues in which there are contesting agendas and building game play around them (Squire et al., 2007). Ferris was interested in using a large-scale multiplayer simulation game, which became *Trails Forward*, to test this idea.

Building a model-based toy. The core content around which the game would be built was still undefined; it would need to pull from multiple physical, natural, and social sciences (think ecology, biology, zoology, chemistry, economics, sociology). We began by partnering with the Conservation Conversation Group, an interdisciplinary research effort by Ferris and scientists in disciplines from forest and wildlife ecology (Volker Radeloff) to agriculture (Jennifer Alix-Garcia).[1] Could we build an interactive model that integrated research from across these groups to help synthesize the research? Such an interactive model could function as a toy to play with (Macklin & Sharp, 2016).

As we had done with other projects, we began with a design jam. In this case, however, we explicitly included a range of scientists, practitioners, and designers to develop truly diverse ideas. Many groups quickly coalesced around map-based interfaces (see figure 7.1) and tested ideas around sharing resources, much as in a *Civ* game. Through this exercise, we arrived at the idea of taking a real piece of land (Vilas County, Wisconsin) and making it the game board. Player roles would reflect real-life ones, and players

Figure 7.1
Scientists, officials from the Wisconsin Department of Natural Resources, and game developers creating *Trails Forward*.

would compete as land developers, recreational boaters, and other key constituencies so that they could observe emergent interactions.

Working with PhD student Adam Mechtley, Ben Shapiro built a minimal viable single-player prototype in Unity. This prototype featured a tile-based system that recorded landscape type (land, water), trees (density, species, and size), housing density, population density, zoning, land use, road connectivity, and density of key indicator species (see figure 7.2). Each tile represented a three-by-three-acre plot of land. This tile-based system could simulate a variety of phenomena; through "recipes" applied to each tile (which were equations defining anything from an endangered species to water flow to phosphorus), we could change the underlying game state at each turn and then let players make choices on top of it as they saw results. Shapiro and Ferris taught an advanced undergraduate course in which they developed models for the basic phenomena; these were captured and published to a wiki. This wiki became the "design bible" for both the game and the underlying science.

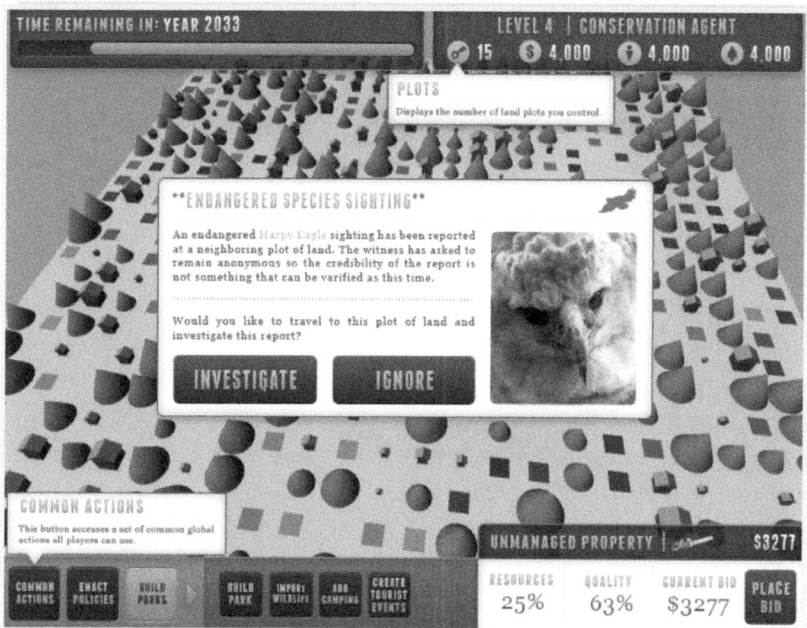

Figure 7.2
Triggered events in *Trails Forward* prototype.

A simulated model map of Vilas County. The next step was to build a map (which also required building a rough model). We chose Vilas County, Wisconsin, a rural county in the upper reaches of Northern Wisconsin, for its capacity to support contested spaces and emotional resonance. Home to 20,000 people and 1,327 lakes (covering 93,200 acres, 15.6 percent of the county), Vilas County has some of the finest fishing in the Midwest, including walleyes, northern pikes, and muskies (the latter of which can get up to fifty inches or forty pounds).[2] Vilas County has over 245,000 acres of public hunting land, and hunters kill 1,500–6,000 deer (with a record of over 14,000 in 2001), grouse, and woodcocks. These same forests host snowmobiling, snowshoeing, cross-country skiing, and ice fishing in the winter.

Vilas County's economy is based on tourism in these lakes and forests. Over half (62 percent) of the homes in Vilas County are vacation properties. In 2013, Tourism accounted for $203 million annually—or, in direct spending, about $9,000 per capita (Sheehan et al., 2014). Top employers are accommodations and food services, retail, and health care, with logging and construction rounding out the economy. The median household income is $42,720, with about 15 percent living under the poverty line (DataUSA, 2020; Faster, 2017). Logging, while an important part of the local economy, is more piecemeal than one might think.

The bifurcation of the American economy is reflected in the economics of Vilas County. Multimillion-dollar lakeside retreats sit near inland $130,000 two-bedroom homes in foreclosure. Seasonal homeowners spend about $75 in the local economy for every day that they are present, totaling about $1 million per occupied day. Locals depend on seasonal homeowners for work (everything from retail to maintenance), but animosities can emerge as visitors from Madison, Milwaukee, Minneapolis, Chicago, or beyond descend upon rural Wisconsin in luxury vehicles to occupy their second homes, a dynamic that was captured in Katherine Cramer's excellent *The Politics of Resentment: Rural Consciousness in Wisconsin and the Rise of Scott Walker*. With the vast majority of work dependent on seasonal homes or tourism, working-class males in particular struggle to construct identities around dignified work.

Modeling Vilas County required spanning environmental and human factors. These include chemical processes (such as phosphorus flows), ecology (forest models), zoology (deer behavior), and human processes. Shapiro realized that modeling property values would be important, and his team wrote scripts to extract property values from online tax records, developing a model of land value based on location, access, and neighboring tiles. To illustrate, 77 percent of Vilas County's property land value is in waterfront property. Whether or not a property has waterfront access is not the only determination of value; whether the lake is big or small, well stocked with game fish, loud or quiet, and part of a bigger lake chain that provides access to other recreation all contribute to its value. Shapiro's model predicted land values with a high degree of accuracy and allowed us to model the economic consequences of conservation.

Land development is more complex than a layperson may think. People buy and sell property, but the real challenge in a game and for long-term impact is zoning for particular uses (such as high-density construction) and the roads that make lands accessible to particular issues. Both of those require indirect lobbying, which became a key verb (or action) for players. We knew that buying and selling land would be a key verb, but we decided that if political influence was a key interaction, we needed to have economies of political influence as well. As a result, players could invest political capital into lobbying the state for roads or zoning changes, which would occur over longer time scales. In fact, how to deal with time scales became a critical issue; one reason *Civilization* is so interesting is that it lets us see patterns across hundreds or thousands of years. How do we create decisions that are meaningful for players, model real choices, and yet allow us to see patterns across time scales, particularly when there are delayed effects?

Keeping with the simulation aesthetic, we shied away from distinct player classes and instead left all verbs open to all players. We wanted to see which verbs players chose, including whether players entered with one goal (such as developing land) and those goals evolved through time. We created three archetypical play styles (or player goals): (1) rangers, who are conservationists interested in caring for the land and enforcing law; (2) developers, who want to build properties to maximize profits (imagine a casino or factory on a pristine North Woods lake); and (3) timber companies, which maximize profits by cutting down trees. Good game to call out (or seduce) the player with interesting goals.

As in a *Civilization* game, we designed around short-term, midterm, and long-term goals. Long-term goals were about transforming Vilas County to align with the player's vision of the future, whether it be a well-developed, wealthy region, an island of conservation and/or sustainable living, or an economic engine fueled by logging companies and the industries using them (such as lumber and paper mills). Unlike the situation in a *Civ* game, no one player could achieve these goals; they require alliances and probably compromises. This aspect of game play was entirely a research and development project with uncertain outcomes. We had no idea if it would be interesting or frustrating, especially the idea of not having an immediate direct impact on the world. Midterm goals were to build functioning subsystems, such as an industrial chain of logging and lumber mills, a green corridor for endangered species, or a bustling housing development alongside a pristine lake stocked with muskies. In the short term, players would buy and sell land, log land, bulldoze land, build homes, build factories, or enhance properties through solar panels. We loved the idea of players studying the map, looking for strategic spots to make an impact, and competing to enact their vision of the county.

The simulation-based game play was augmented by critical events (such as an endangered species sighting) to amplify conflict and create excitement and potentially memorable moments (see figure 7.2; for more on memorable moments, see Squire, 2011). Conflicts were hand-coded in for play sessions but could be triggered at inflection points in the model. In *Civilization III*, for example, barbarian uprisings were triggered by a second civilization entering a golden age. Critical events would be triggered by variables (e.g., human population density, phosphorus concentration in water, land values) crossing thresholds. Game pacing could be managed by configuring these critical events and short-term goals.

Technical Infrastructure

With a (somewhat) working simulated map of Vilas County, Ben Shapiro and team created a server architecture that was at the forefront for its time (we later learned that groups in industry, such as Raph Koster's Metaverse, were doing the same thing). Writing a server architecture for a multiplayer game to host dozens of players was achieved by integrating (1) the Unity client, (2) a game server built with Ruby on Rails, (3) information pulled from the underlying map database, and (4) JSON calls to plug in new components to the game. These JSON calls enable researchers to write scripts for new species, or even bots. Bots—artificial intelligence agents—would be included to fill up empty games as well as provide models of user behavior. Co–Principal Investigator Michael Ferris was especially interested in developing algorithms that described optimal solutions so as to help us (1) understand players' implicit assumptions, motivations, and values, and (2) generate optimal policy.

Forested Dairyland: Creating a Predictive Simulation

Before Wisconsin became "America's Dairyland," it was blanketed by forests of white pine. Before white settlement, 80 percent of Wisconsin was covered in forests, which were almost entirely logged by 1900 (Dhungana, n.d.). Today, Wisconsin is 46 percent forested, and growing, as marginal farmlands are reclaimed for forests. This logging history created allied industries around forest products, including sawmills, paper mills, and a processing plants. In fact, Wisconsin is the leading US state in paper producing. Forestry employs 60,000 people, including 30,000 in paper production, and Wisconsin generates $23 billion in paper products annually (Wisconsin Economic Development Corporation, 2020). Logging employs relatively few people; machines have made logging less labor-intensive, and roughly four thousand Wisconsin residents work in forestry and logging today (in estimated $300 million impact; Wisconsin Economic Development Corporation, 2020). Vilas County remains one of Wisconsin's top lumber-producing counties (21,391 million cubic feet of timber, much of it oak and maple), but this accounts for less than 2 percent of Wisconsin's production (Dhungana, n.d.). Logging remains important economically and culturally, but it is relatively diffuse across Wisconsin's sparsely populated North Woods.

Forestry and landownership. Logging isn't as straightforward as a logger grabbing an ax and chopping down trees or even a large industrial company clear-cutting forests. About 57 percent of Wisconsin's land is owned by private, nonindustrial individuals (Wisconsin Department of Natural Resources, 2020). Thirty-two percent is owned by a mix of federal, state, and county agencies that manage forests, including logging. Only 11 percent of forests are owned by corporations because corporately owned forests are a relatively new (and limited) phenomenon in Wisconsin (Perry, 2014). Corporations have the capacity to clear-cut large swaths of land (which is more profitable), locate lumber mills on-site, and manage forests not as an integrated part of the regional ecosystem but as sites for maximizing the extraction of profits for shareholders who live miles away.

Currently, the majority of logging in Wisconsin is carried out on private or public lands through bids for contracts to local loggers. Forest owners or stewards develop management plans, working with forestry experts, and manage their land, attending to wildlife needs (recall that hunting is important), water management (forests drain water before it enters lakes), timber development (and sales), and aesthetics. The aesthetics portion of the Wisconsin forestry handbook is my favorite; I could get into sculpting and grooming forests as a sort of landscape architecture (see Wisconsin Department of Natural Resources, *Multiple Benefits from Forest Management*). Wisconsin's public lands are considered by most to be very well managed; twenty-seven Wisconsin county forests meet sustainable forestry standards (see Congressional Research Services, 2011; Wisconsin County Forests Association, 2013).

Logging contracts and forest management The central land management process, which became a core game play loop, is bidding on logging contracts. To open land for logging, landowners typically consult with a forester, who helps (1) analyze the forest (marking boundaries, identifying trees, and preparing roads and landings), (2) prepare the contract and prospectus (which includes everything from how the timber is weighed to acceptable stump height), (3) solicit and select a winning bid, (4) monitor the sale, and (5) administer postharvest activities. Foresters help landowners ensure that their goals are met, such as maximizing long-term forest growth or short-term financial gains or minimizing impact on the watershed. To design the logging core loop and ensure fidelity to the underlying practice, we consulted online guides, studied sample contracts, consulted with Wisconsin Department of Natural Resources (DNR) officials, and conducted a focus group with loggers. Our basic logging game play of presenting and bidding on contracts (see figure 7.3) satisfied all groups.

Stakeholder groups Foresters and DNR staff welcomed us and were eager collaborators because they wanted to improve forest management and foster dialogue about forests. Most foresters and conservationists are realistic about the role of trees in modern life. The average person uses about 1,664 pounds of forest products—or an 18-inch-diameter, 25-foot-long tree—annually (including paper, newsprint, paper towels, mail, and building supplies). The question is how to provide these needs most responsibly, and Wisconsin is a leader in sustainable forestry. In developing the idea, we met with the DNR's Kirsten Held and the forestry outreach team's Phil Miller, who wanted to use *Trails Forward* to train fire response teams. Comparatively speaking, loggers and senior officials from the DNR were suspicious

Figure 7.3
Logging choices in a *Trails Forward* demonstration.

of our activities. Both groups started with the assumption that we were Madison liberals hostile to business. The political appointees at the DNR came from building and economic development, not forestry, or even timber, for that matter. Despite reservations, all stakeholder groups signed off on the project and committed to supporting its use. Getting loggers to validate this game as representative of their practice was especially rewarding.

Pilot tests in classrooms We began pilot tests with *Trails Forward* in the fall of 2012 in classrooms in Sun Prairie, Wisconsin. Even with the game less than halfway working, we wanted to explore game play, see what kids would do with it, and explore the kinds of thinking that game play produced. The partner teacher, Ann Brown, was excited by the game's opportunities to address Common Core scientific reasoning standards. These standards align with *Trails Forward* game play very closely:

Knowledge of Environmental Processes and Systems

B.12.2: Describe the value of ecosystems from a natural and human perspective; e.g., food, shelter, flood control, water purification

B.12.10: Identify and evaluate multiple uses of natural resources and how society is influenced by the availability of these resources

B.12.11: Assess how changes in the availability and use of natural resources (especially water and energy sources) will affect society and human activities, such as transportation, agricultural systems, and manufacturing

B.12.12: Evaluate the environmental and societal costs and benefits of allocating resources in various ways and identify management strategies to maintain economic and environmental sustainability

B.12.16: Analyze how natural resource ownership and trade influences relationships in local, national, and global economies

B.12.21: Research the roles of various careers related to natural resource management and other environmental fields

Environmental Issue Investigation Skills

C.12.1: Compare the effects of natural and human-caused activities that either contribute to or challenge an ecologically and economically sustainable environment

C.12.2: Explain the factors that contribute to the development of individual and societal values

C.12.3: Maintain a historical perspective when researching environmental issues; include past, present, and future considerations

Decision and Action Skills

D.12.6: Identify and analyze examples of the impact beliefs and values have on environmental decisions

D.12.7: Analyze political, educational, economic, and governmental influences on environmental issues, and identify the role of citizens in policy formation

These standards are included partly to remind the readers just how many of today's science standards are organized around problem identification, pattern matching, and analysis. Few classes teach these standards in depth, and they are difficult to teach through canned activities. *Trails Forward* hoped to be a springboard for these activities.

Pilot test results For the Sun Prairie pilot test, we did not have a working server architecture, so we created a turn-based multiplayer game augmented through pencil-and-paper trading (which could also be done over chat). The main findings were as follows:

1. Students enjoyed the game experience and found the roles appealing, but the detailed and complex nature of the game interface was opaque. The game would require significant onboarding, and potential redesign would have to be manageable. The high-level game purpose and mechanics were advanced for this age and would require some scaffolding.
2. Technologically, there were hurdles to implementing a working MMO-style game in classrooms. Between blocked ports, lag, and other issues, we knew that requiring large real-time online interactions would be a challenge.
3. The teacher feared the game risked becoming a high-fidelity forestry simulation too far removed from core ecological systems. She said something to the effect of "This would be great as a logging career simulation."

In fact, the game *needed* to simulate logging with enough fidelity to generate meaningful data. *Trails Forward* looked, felt, and played like a simulation because it was one. The art style, pacing, and game flow were optimized for a broad swath of the educated gaming public, which middle schoolers are right on the cusp of.

Evidence for game play producing environmental investigation practices Game play produced generative practices in which students analyzed game play data, consulted outside resources, and compared them toward generating sustainability plans. Ms. Brown, together with researchers, generated a curriculum in which players would record actions and data. One challenge related to sighting an American marten. The American marten is an exceptionally cute little creature that inhabits the North Woods of the United States and Canada but is endangered in Wisconsin. It is a good indicator species of the health of North Woods ecosystems because it requires large tracts of forest to thrive. We included an American marten sighting as a critical event to encourage youths to analyze data and consider wildlife corridors. Students readily studied physical maps in support of their game play, a phenomenon I had previously observed in *Civilization* units.

Trails Forward as an Ecological Simulation

Trails Forward is, at its core, an ecological simulation platform. Its strength is as an agent-based modeling system in which scientists can build and study simulated events on extensive maps in the context of human decision making. In one such study, Stephen Wangen, Ben Shapiro, and Michael Ferris (2012) used *Trails Forward* to investigate under what conditions the American marten might be reintroduced to Northern Wisconsin. Wangen and colleagues modeled how American martens move through the environment at a tile-by-tile level, including their foraging for voles (a small rodent), mating, and territorial behaviors. Using *Trails Forward*, Wangen and colleagues were able to demonstrate under which future scenarios American martens could return.

Reflections on *Trails Forward*

After about a year of *Trails Forward* development, we were at a pivotal turning point. On the one hand, we had a promising demo for a simulation game. We had evidence that the game play could produce forms of scientific thinking, and Wangen and colleagues were successfully using it as a tool for ecological modeling. On the other hand, we were anxious about getting the server-based game play. Simply getting the game to work reliably was nontrivial. The production pipeline for developing new scenarios was intensive. We had evidence for promising game play around logging, but we still ran the risk of creating a logging simulation.

A subset of the team argued for a simpler game (which eventually became *Econauts*) created in Unity appealing directly to the core audience of middle school players. The idea was to use Unity's built-in networking tools so that one player could host the game and two more could connect in a lightweight, faster-paced game, more like a real-time strategy game for environmental management. The team (specifically Mark Stenerson and Terra Lauterbach) imagined players competing on real maps to do all of the same verbs (logging, building, farming, developing) but in shorter, replayable sessions so that they could play, analyze, and reflect on multiple games. For those familiar with my earlier work on *Civilization* (see Squire et al., 2005), it is like going from one twenty-plus-hour, six-thousand-year game played on giant world maps to smaller scenarios focused on particular eras and designed to illustrate key ideas. Scenarios would be easier to develop, and editing them would be as simple as editing a text file.

Conceptually, this contrast between *Trails Forward* and *Econauts* reflects a classic distinction between high- and low-fidelity simulations (Thiagarajan, 1998) or, using a scientific modeling framework, predictive and idea simulations (Feurzeig & Roberts, 2013). In both cases, the idea is that we can build models or simulations to capture, describe, and illuminate ideas or to make predictions about the world. The challenge in trying to do *both* within one model is that predictive models require researchers to account for every relevant variable. Idea models, in contrast, can leave out variables (even ones that have an impact) if they are not useful for a particular situation. Focusing on just a handful of variables (in this case, links among ground cover (or logging), water runoff, algae, agriculture, indicator species, and land value) can make relationships among them more apparent.

We hoped that *Trails Forward* would avoid these issues by simulating select processes (about twelve). In order for *Trails Forward* to be relevant to forestry policy, patterns of landownership, specific logging procedures, and real estate valuation needed to be modeled with precision. The game play was becoming bogged down by logging, and we hadn't even explored fishing, hunting, or real estate in fine detail. On top of that, the basic multiplayer architecture (Ruby on Rails) was exciting but not yet working reliably.

From a Simulation to a Game

We decided to take a different tack on the problem and study how a more simplified model might compare with this larger simulation. Much as *Anatomy Pro-Am* created a trajectory for people at different levels to play the game, we hoped that we could connect environmental science players into a community through a series of interconnected games. We hoped that players might begin by playing *Econauts* and then a subset might continue on to *Trails Forward*.

A Real-Time Strategy Game for Ecological Management

After playing a rough prototype, we settled on a simple, replayable real-time strategy game for ecological management. This idea is not new; it has floated around games and learning conversations as long as I can remember. This version would

- be created in six to twelve months for $300,000;
- be ready for the iTunes marketplace *today*, working on iPads and iOS;
- target youths aged eight through twelve in after-school or home markets and, secondarily, schools;
- unapologetically be a game; and
- include an engine design for modding.

Like *Trails Forward*, *Econauts* would be built on an evolving world with simulated chemical cycles, species, and economies. Like *Trails Forward*, it was an agent-based model, in which each tile was an agent with inputs and outputs that interacted with entities on that tile (such as trees, bulldozers, or farms) as well as on neighboring tiles. In this way, phosphorus flows, for example, could be modeled through giving a tile a starting value, which would then be modified by improvements on that tile or activities on neighboring tiles (see figure 7.4).

Aesthetics and Play

The moment when experienced AAA game developers took over the direction of *Econauts*, art and aesthetics came to the forefront. A pivotal moment early in development occurred when John Karczewski, the project lead, took me aside and asked, "Kurt, do we want to make this *really* a game?"

Figure 7.4
Revamped *Econauts* with characters, story, and tutorials.

"Of course!" I replied. The question surprised me. I thought making games was exactly what we were doing.

"Ehhhh . . . not really," was the reaction I got. Sure, we were "making games," but hitherto, they'd been led by academics. We hadn't put commercial game developers fully in charge of production, with the authority to prioritize features and production schedules.

"Sure, why not?" I thought, as I looked around the center. We hadn't brought together this kind of talent to make educational simulations. For all of the reasons that projects may or may not work, I figured one should live or die on the basis of its being too gamelike. "Let's make a game. I'll push back on learning objectives, but you've got my approval to run with it. You won't get in trouble for making a game."

The biggest differences, in regard to production, between *Econauts* and previous games were (1) an emphasis on art and the play experience; (2) a very close read of the marketplace, including analyses of what kids were playing and how *Econauts* would fit into the market; (3) production streamlined around the core game play loop; and (4) regular internal play sessions. As compared with earlier game designs, we emphasized solidifying a fun, playable core game experience. Regular play sessions enabled the team to play and replay the game to expose shortcomings and add little features—from tweaking art to polishing internal game timers, such as how long it took to perform specific actions.

One emblematic decision was to add animal characters for each role. We became convinced that such characters were necessary to (1) pique interest, (2) quickly communicate roles and play types, and (3) increase identification with each role. Aesthetically, *Econauts* bears a strong resemblance to the Disney movie *Zootopia*, through stylized anthropomorphized characters that walk upright and wear human clothes (see Julius, 2016). Much as seen in *Zootopia*, we developed different personality types for each species (fastidious rabbit farmers and grumpy mining moles). As we had done with previous games, we developed dozens of pages of concept art until we arrived at characters that thrilled kids. We developed male and female characters for each role and connected each to the character class archetype.

Refining game play and creating compelling characters was not new for us, or certainly a learning game. What was new for us, at least, was prioritizing these features. In contrast to *Trails Forward*, for example, we intentionally limited the scope and prioritized adding new art and refining art over adding components to the simulation. Most of game development is about trade-offs, and in educational game development, we rarely prioritize art, aesthetics, or engaging game play over representational fidelity or learning gains. I wanted to try one game, at least, in which the game developers could unapologetically run with making a fun game.

The resulting game, *Econauts*, was a functioning multiplayer game in which players competed to be the first to reach a financial goal (e.g., $10,000). *Econauts* included three unique levels (Madison, Milwaukee, and Trout Lake) and supported about two to three hours of play. *Econauts* featured three roles: farmers and food processing (rabbits), lumber and timber (bears), and mining and manufacturing (moles). Each role combined one resource-gathering profession (farming, lumber, mining), one processing profession (food plant, lumber mill, steel mill) and a consumer-facing (grocery store, home builders, car lots) endgame. The basic progression followed a real-time strategy game logic of building units and upgrading to extract resources more efficiently, but instead of featuring direct combat,

Econauts featured indirect competition over land. Each role was designed to appeal to different play styles; farming appealed to builders and was slower paced, whereas logging was faster paced and involved moving around the map while managing harvesters, and mining was somewhere in between.

Econauts was our most successful mix of aesthetic pleasure and learning. Playing *Econauts* feels like frantically trying to build a business while keeping an eye on an ever-changing environment, all without causing environmental collapse. There is something very personal about playing building games on mobile devices, and watching another player chop down trees or build factories where you'd planned to plant a farm was compelling. Emergent play mixed collaboration and competition as players raced to meet financial goals while competing with one another (indirectly) over space (certain land was inherently valuable) and collaborating with one another where interests aligned (such as preserving buffer strips to improve land value). The emergent aesthetic was something like collaborative competition, wherein players would each try to maximize resources without collapsing ecosystems; the lesson of the game could be expressed as players all trying to maximize land use for their own interests, but if they don't work together to preserve the underlying ecosystem, they will all suffer.

Econauts' pedagogical value was in creating a game situation in which players became emotionally invested in studying the effects of human actions on a simulated ecosystem. Recall that *Econauts* was built on a simulated watershed; this version simulated phosphates, heavy metals, industrial wastes, and algae flowing through the watershed (see figure 7.5). Players "see" these effects on-screen, primarily as algae and fish kills. It took a few iterations, but the nasty algae and fishbones did the trick. We added tools for players to get data from the game so they could run analyses on their simulated systems. We also made these data visible in ending screens through rankings and achievements.

Robert Bohanan, a scientist and educator from the North Temperate Lakes Long Term Ecological Research (LTER) Network, developed a pedagogical model of thinking, playing, and reflecting. Students would play through the game once, observe what transpired, and then have five minutes to develop agreements before they replayed the maps. Many groups developed the idea of planting buffer strips along waterways to minimize the flow of pollutants through waterways. Some groups even created their own subgoals of keeping pollution levels below thresholds. Similarly to

Figure 7.5
Fish kills in *Econauts*.

earlier work with *Civilization*, in which we designed short, replayable scenarios so that students could become fluent on maps (Squire, et al., 2005), we found a natural tendency for students to compare outcomes across game sessions to infer properties of the simulation.

Econauts was the most engaging game that our lab produced. Efforts to tune the experience to be gamelike paid off; the game's art was inviting, the moment-to-moment game play was engaging, and the multiplayer competitive game experience was compelling. It was common for students to immediately ask to play again after their first game. After play-testing *Econauts* at events, it was common for kids to play again at home, as evidenced by our server logs.

At the same time, the game's biggest drawback was the educational value of its moment-to-moment game play. *Econauts* did not offer meaningful simulation of farming, logging, or mining. Although the maps were realistic and indeed students could use them as a source of data, the cognitive work of game play (micromanaging units and managing production) was not inherently educational. Perform a think-aloud protocol of an *Econauts* player and you would not see anything like the thinking of an ecologist.

Scaling Innovations through Entrepreneurship

Whatever its drawbacks as a learning tool, consensus was that *Econauts* was a promising game. Minimally, a multiplayer, cross-platform (Mac, PC, tablet) real-time strategy game was compelling. There was nothing quite like it in entertainment or education. Several key features would be necessary for commercial deployment, including a lobby, matchmaking, and artificial intelligence to take over in case players disconnected. Similarly, we would want to include new ecosystems and maps (such as water usage in southwestern deserts), but the engine itself could support these expansions.

The opportunity to explore these ideas arose in 2014, when *Econauts* was selected to participate in co.lab, an accelerator for digital games located in Silicon Valley. We assembled a team that we hoped could become a company that would take *Econauts* to market. The team included project lead John Karczewski, PhD student and lead programmer Mark Stenerson, creative director Brian Pelletier, and Ira Sockowitz and Peter Stidwell from the Learning Games Network. Mark and Ira moved to the San Francisco Bay Area for a few months, while the rest of the team telecommuted.

Econauts, for all of its strengths, was not ready for investment. The specific reasons, which follow, are instructive for educational game developers and are reframed here as findings more applicable broadly.

(1) Interfaces and user experience need to be optimized for specific markets. The *Econauts* interface and user experience, which had been tested with dozens of students, looked better than any science learning game that we had seen, although we had not yet optimized it for school or home markets. Co.lab's market analysis revealed problems with the interface, which is indicative for academic educational technologists generally; if *Econauts* still needed an overhaul to be ready for market, one further questions whether we were truly exploring the potential of games for learning in our research.

(2) Commercial developers hoping to enter schools need to optimize for the classrooms of today rather than seek to change them. *Econauts* was not optimized for schools (or really the entertainment space) and needed significant reworking to be marketable to schools. Where *Econauts* excelled was in its play aesthetic, which captured a fundamental concept in ecology, built a game around it, and then offered promising avenues for further exploration

Games, Design, Schools, and Markets   129

(such as student-authored scenarios). *Econauts* did *not* solve teachers' most immediate problems, such as reducing lesson planning, grading, or raising test scores (see Cuban, 1986). Making *Econauts* more school friendly would be straightforward: grab a textbook, examine the illustrations, and make gamelike challenges out of those (such as an interactive erosion or glaciation level). In fact, market analysts suggested just these kinds of choices: eliminate multiplayer, reduce divergent outcomes, streamline play more closely around objectives, fit more objectives per level, and so on.

(3) For all the talk around disruptive technologies and risk taking, investors are relatively conservative and are interested in technical solutions to social problems, functioning products with subscribers, and teams with a track record of success. Everyone regarded *Econauts* as an interesting product with potential, but it was not offering a turnkey technological solution to problems (e.g., artificial intelligence to improve expository writing or improve parent communication); it was several iterations away from being deployed at scale; and our team was experienced and excited by it but was not about to quit everything to dedicate our lives to it. To really work, a core group would need to leave GLS and make this our sole focus. We would need to turn *Econauts* into something awful, and for what end? To make investors richer? If we could get *Econauts* working to the point where we had paying customers, why would we need investors at all? Investors would require not just a share the profits but also a voice in the direction of the company, and none of us wanted to give that up. Once we had the right product, we could leverage our own press contacts and distribution networks.

(4) Finally, we should be very wary of applying Silicon Valley investment (or any for-profit) models to our schools. In 2019, we were all familiar with how "moving fast and breaking things" had deleterious effects on journalism, businesses, and communities, as Facebook has harmed local newspapers, Amazon has decimated local retailers, and these combined forces have concentrated wealth away from rural communities and toward urban technology centers. Do we want educational decisions made by these same people and processes? Few, if any, people we encountered understood anything about learning, schools, or pedagogy. Most "experts" were driven by a vague dissatisfaction with their own schooling, a sense that textbooks were ripe for disruption, and a (naive) belief that technologies could modernize school processes, probably through the magic of data. Companies such

as Lightbox and Junyo offered to marry the engaging properties of games with data to systematize learning and engagement in order to revolutionize education.

Sometime around perhaps 2015, the learning games investment bubble burst (although excitement may be inflating again). Games did not turn out to be a magic bullet for education, and algorithms for engagement would not revolutionize education. The major games and learning companies (GlassLab, Junyo, co.lab, Lightbox) receiving investments have pivoted toward data-driven learning and assessment. The lack of a solidified hardware platform for students (such as a mixture of Chromebooks iPads, and Bring Your Own Devices), the failure of key products in the marketplace (*SimCity EDU*, *Use Your Brainz EDU* (a *Plants vs Zombies* mathematics game; see Schute et al., 2016), and, in general, the realization that games are not going to revolutionize education overnight. As Filament's Dan White argues, many investors buy into this simplistic model of investing in games that raise test scores more efficiently than other media, as if raising test scores were somehow a reasonable goal of education (Wan, 2018).

Implicit to this investor- and data-driven vision of games for learning is an all-encompassing game-based learning model in which all learning occurs through the game. The vision is that designers can create encompassing environments in which all activities are logged and tracked. Curricular decisions are made by designers and algorithms, rather than teachers, students, and parents. The learning models embedded in such curricular approaches run counter to everything that situated learning theorists admire about games, such as the ability to try on new identities, explore through transgressive play, and learn through failure.

Game-Based Curricula with *Econauts*

Our curricular models use games as a springboard toward inquiry-based or project-based learning. Taking *Econauts* as an example, our weeklong curriculum followed our play → explore → study → build format.

Day 1: play. Students began by playing *Econauts*. Students completed a brief pre-assessment, which included a mapping activity with watershed, designed to activate prior knowledge, and then played the "Madison" scenario. After playing, Robert led a debrief asking questions such as "What did you observe?," "What accelerated the spread of toxins?," and "What prevented them?" After a five-minute discussion, students replayed the scenario, switching roles and observing what transpired. Conversation around the game was lively, and students negotiated with one another about where to plant farms, place factories, or build homes.

Day 2: explore. Having situated the activity, Robert began day 2 with a brief introduction to watersheds. He then led students through a mapping activity in which they identified and predicted the flows of toxins through similar watersheds. Next, they played another round of *Econauts* but switched roles. They ended the day by posting a strategy for their favorite role to the game's online forum. Much of the debate centered on which career was most profitable.

Day 3: study and build.[3] Robert led a walk around the shoreline of Lake Mendota. The weeklong camp was held at UW–Madison's Memorial Union Terrace, which sits along the shoreline of Lake Mendota, right about where one player wanted to place a logging facility. Using maps and clipboards, they made observations about sources of runoff, ground cover, and industrialization around the lakes (smokestacks from a power plant can be seen just a few blocks from this location). Students then created physical maps based on their observations, using graph paper. Most students privileged interesting game play scenarios over mapping ecological concepts in new biomes; in other words, they were more interested in making an interesting logging/farming/mining map than in exploring a new ecosystem.

Day 4: explore new cases. Students read about watersheds on the LTER website and then played *Citizen Science*, a game about lake ecology in which students role-play as youths engaged in studying the same watershed. *Citizen Science* gives a very different, first-person-type experience of lake science and introduces vocabulary (e.g., algae, phosphates, nitrates, eutrophication) in the context of investigations. *Citizen Science* focuses on evidence and argumentation and strives to inspire players to affiliate with the enterprise of science.

Day 5: play, critique, and reflect. The unit wrapped up with students playing one another's scenarios and discussing proposals of what should be done to the lake. Because the editor was not yet functional, we imported students' maps ourselves between days 3 and 5 and then let them play one another's games, which they mostly enjoyed. Robert presented lake management scenarios, which students debated using the argumentation framework presented in *Citizen Science*. Its "snow globe" simulation was particularly valued by students in this exercise.

This curriculum is a starting point for how games-based learning should look, rather than an empirical assessment of its efficacy toward meeting those goals. I've argued for games as a springboard toward more meaningful activities. Part of their value is in capturing complex systems, letting students play and experiment with ideas, and providing just-in-time practice and feedback, all of which can be difficult to do within the context of inquiry-based or project-based learning. The idea, however, that we would privilege learning in games over these other, more worthwhile activities seems absurd and counter to the very idea of education.

The most important part of this curriculum is the interplay between multiple forms of game play, the physical visit to Lake Mendota, and inquiry-based activities in which students engage in meaningful creation. The role of games in the curriculum should not be to deliver content, or generate data for test scores, but rather to raise interest, provide practice, and prepare students to do something meaningful.

Reflections on Games, Schools, and Markets
Econauts represents the pinnacle of our lab's attempts to make integrated K–12 game-based learning experiences. *Econauts* was designed to do what digital games can do well: raise interest, introduce students to complex systems, create opportunities for student authoring and sharing, and provide opportunities to assess students in complex problem solving. *Econauts* demonstrated (to us, at least) that educational games can be compelling learning experiences *because* they capture the aesthetic play of ideas (in this case, ecological management). However, the trade-offs that go into making a good, polished game that works reliably for its intended audience and meeting the demands of research are real.

Complex assessment in games Most game-based assessments measure students' performance on closed-ended problems, such as how they are completing math problems or reasoning through science concepts (cites). Co.lab advisors were pushing *Econauts* in that direction; imagine tailoring scenarios to specific learning goals, which is basically what they did with *SimCity EDU*. Narrowing the game experience toward "right" and "wrong" solutions works with relatively linear adventure game experiences (see the next chapter) but less well with simulation-based experiences, wherein the joy of the game is in playing and learning in unexpected ways. Capturing and modeling complex thinking in these domains is not impossible. Ben DeVane, Shree Durga, and I (2010) developed one such model for *Civilization* scenarios; in "Ecologists Who Think Like Economists," we developed relatively expert *Civilization* players and then investigated what choices they made in-game so as to create a model of expert *Civilization* play. In contrast, most game-based assessment uses evidence-centered design, which starts with the target domain as the end goal, models game play to match that underlying task domain, and seeks to measure how well game play matches that end state. Good game-based assessment, I argue, will reverse this pattern so that game designers create the kinds of learning that we want to see happen, gather evidence to demonstrate efficacy, and then partner with assessment experts to unpack how that expertise arises.

The most interesting, and untapped, uses of game analytics are for the open-ended processes of real-time collaborative problem solving in changing conditions (e.g., analytics of *Overwatch* teams); learning analytics applied to game designs (e.g., which moves while designing *Econauts* scenarios predict genuine understanding); and measures of teamwork and communication in distributed networks (e.g., what forms of social participation in *Econauts* modding communities predicts scientific understanding later in life). We are not yet generally using analytics techniques to investigate more open-ended complex processes such as game *design* or the sharing of game artifacts. Our lab did begin applying such analytics to games, particularly through our Studio K project, in which we developed automated approaches to characterize game design with Microsoft's Kodu (see Hatfield et al., 2013). The underlying logic here is to create complex, open-ended learning goals (such as designing a good game or a good ecological scenario) and then tracking what steps students take when designing such games so as to better assess their progress. Matthew Berland (2017) has demonstrated this use of learning analytics in constructionist learning environments, which is still a generative, but underexplored, approach to learning analytics in games. Imagine using analytics to map the social life of students' mods, how their social networks expand through participating in a Pro-Am community, or how their discourse evolves over time through participating in a game environment.

Creating genuinely engaging game experiences for research The original vision of *Trails Forward* was to create a multigenerational community of practice around learning games so that students could engage in complex modeling and argumentation in a science game, the way that they do while theorycrafting in *World of Warcraft*. The idea was to create compelling, complex game play in which they would examine game data, argue about underlying causes, and engage in reflective practices around their game play in an online community.

Econauts, and indeed this generation of games, did at time engender robust argumentation, but (as with our earlier work with *Civilization* and Constance Steinkuehler's work with *World of Warcraft*) this reflection occurred almost entirely within the context of game play and rarely, if ever, on forums. We devised all kinds of reflection activities to encourage student reflection and created assignments on game forums, but, almost without exception, they lacked genuine, robust inquiry, argumentation, and debate found on other game forums (see Steinkuehler & Duncan, 2008). I'm reminded, after trying to do this for a few years, just how difficult it is to create open-ended game play capable of sustaining that kind of argumentation, and then how it is even harder to make it about the underlying content. *Econauts* came close to inspiring this kind of argumentation; kids in particular loved to debate which character class was strongest. But this was a far cry from the robust argumentation we hoped to see around science content. I'm also reminded that it's relatively rare even to participate in such forums within games; most players don't visit them. Finally, it seems possible that as a medium, forums were something of an artifact of that era of web technology. Today's arguments about games happen just as often in Discord channels, YouTube comments, and Reddit discussions. Regardless, as designers, our goal is to create experiences that compel learners to talk, to share, and to create.

Games to fit into schools or to transform them? Co.lab advisors' feedback reminds us of the greatest conundrum facing this generation of learning game designers: Do we want to create games that will fit into schools, or do we want games that will transform them? *Econauts* is a prime example of a game that could go in either direction. Advisors wanted us to create scenarios to cover more content. Imagine twenty-five custom-made single-player scenarios around targeted earth science concepts (e.g., erosion, weathering, or glaciers). This approach would leave behind interesting interplay among policy, land use, and the long-term impact of behavior that inspired

Econauts. We, on the other hand, wanted to prioritize more constructionist features (more capacity for user creation tools), tools for extracting data from game play, and tools for facilitating argumentation.

Optimizing for what? Co.lab reminded us that even if *Econauts* was compelling for well-supported classroom or after-school use, it was developed and optimized for research and informal use; it was not developed as a teacher-facing product designed to meet teachers' needs. The problems that *Econauts* tried to solve (people learning the intersection of human and ecological systems) was not one that teachers had asked to be solved. Teachers, I suspect, would ask for a comprehensive curriculum that they could draw from for teaching specific concepts, assign as homework, and use to track students' progress through standards. In fact, the product that teachers want is probably BrainPOP; not surprisingly, our lab's best commercial success was licensing the *Citizen Science* game to BrainPOP, which provided funds for adding features and updating functionality.

Knowledge games for learning A promise of knowledge games is that people might learn while contributing to our understanding of the world. *Econauts* grew out of this vision, and we hoped to foster a distributed game-based learning community consisting of students in schools, kids playing in after-school settings, community leaders, and government officials. We held *Trails Forward* play sessions with each of these groups, and although all of them valued the experience, they also pushed the game in different directions. Recall how loggers insisted that a realistic bidding model would be essential to building a predictive model, whereas teachers wanted us to scale back from the specifics of logging.

In the cases of *Anatomy Pro-Am* and *Trails Forward*, helping learners become sufficiently fluent in the domain that they were able to make meaning from the core game experience and contribute to the underlying science was nontrivial. We saw no evidence to suggest that it was not possible, but the time demands alone were substantial. In both cases, we ended up creating unique interfaces for each population, with a common data infrastructure (ADAGE). In theory, this shared infrastructure would enable the game experience to grow along with students; data could persist across game sessions and students could develop a growing profile. Regardless, participating in a meaningful knowledge game requires interacting with objects in fine-grained level detail that will likely not be applicable for young learners. In short, this finding harkens back to the earlier distinction between idea models and predictive models (or low- and high-fidelity simulations). Generally speaking, idea models are good for learning, whereas predictive models are good for policy. I would be surprised if a good "knowledge game for education" gets made, but my hope is that someone out there can surprise me.

Making impact games for research versus the market Recall that GLS evolved so that it could help ideas, products, and teams overcome the "valley of death" and enter the marketplace. We invested heavily in commercial game talent, art expertise, and knowledge of how game markets function, at times at the expense of a more traditional research focus. Understanding of the contexts of production (such as game development processes) is useful knowledge for games scholars more broadly; I'm certainly a more qualified teacher of game development having led the GLS team. And I felt at the time that this was a defensible move. The majority of academic learning games were criticized for incorporating few of the features or processes associated with commercial games. Recall the pivotal moment in the development of *Econauts* when John Karczewski asked whether we really wanted to develop this like a game and how adopting a gamelike approach involved including characters, choices, much better art, and higher degrees of polish than we had previously undertaken.

There are also opportunity costs to this more applied orientation to research. Every dollar spent on, say, art is not being spent on other features. Teams organized around overcoming the valley of death are more likely to depend on tried-and-true approaches and less likely to push the boundaries of what is possible. In terms of *Econauts*, as learning analytics and machine learning were ascending, one could have imagined prioritizing the implementation of much more artificial intelligence for dynamic difficulty or smarter bots (as was envisioned in *Trails Forward*), but from a game development perspective, it was clear that we could make far more progress with a team of artists, as compared with the cost of one machine learning specialist, particularly if the core issues involved attracting broad audiences in order to sustain a game community. Although one can point to specific features (or lack thereof) that might be indicative of a more research-oriented approach, I think the bigger challenge is simply where one's time is being spent. For better or for worse, much of mine was focused on getting real games to scale.

Having led the GLS team for five years and having seen how academics and game developers operate, I'm reminded that academics really excel at creating halfway functioning demonstrations that exist to probe research questions. Everything from the transient nature of students to the timelines of the academic calendar produce challenges to creating functioning software. Andy Phelps, who directs the Rochester Institute of Technology's MAGIC Spell Studios and has shipped multiple functioning Xbox games, has written about the challenges of developing commercial games in academic contexts. A key difference, perhaps *the* key difference, between academic and commercial game development is timing and polish. In describing the development of *Hack, Slash & Backstab*, Phelps et al. (2020) described how the basics of the game were functioning after about three weeks of development, but refining the game to work as an Xbox game required another year of developing, refining, and cutting features and, in general, a level of iteration and polish that's foreign to academics. Phelps and Consalvo described how in academics, we might have parts of a game that don't work smoothly or are confusing and these need to be ironed out before shipping. This kind of detailed work is expensive and difficult to do in an academic environment.

8 Private-Public Partnerships for Scale

In the summer of 2017, W. W. Norton & Company and Gear Games at the University of Wisconsin–Madison published *At Play in the Cosmos*, an astronomy game for college students, on the iTunes Store. Going from a few developers to a team of more than fifteen making a legitimate game to be used by tens of thousands of students was an accomplishment. This chapter covers transitioning from an independent operation to one that works with partners at scale. How does this change the development process? The chapter provides a detailed behind-the-scenes look at making consumer-ready games, forging partnerships, and doing contract work through universities. It provides a road map for groups tackling similar challenges while using the experience to theorize game design more broadly.

Context: Games, the Market, and Higher Education

Games for impact developers struggle to define their market. Students in schools do not make purchasing decisions; elementary students do not (largely) choose which school they will go to, or much of anything, other than what books to check out from the library or purchase at the book fair. College students choose courses and majors and sometimes instructors but do not choose textbooks or software. Those who make purchasing decisions (administrators) want materials (e.g., games) to solve *their* problems, such as the need for higher test scores, better attendance, or fewer behavioral problems (see Halverson & Collins, 2012). Teachers have relatively low purchasing power but are starting to purchase games that address their needs (e.g., providing middle-class parents with extra homework; easier grading). Parents purchase supplementary materials for their children at home or through PTA-supported site licenses of game-based learning systems such as *ST Math*. This supplemental market is growing and could even disrupt traditional instruction, particularly through subscriptions sold to wealthier parents.

Universities are an interesting market for game-based interventions because teachers and students share more purchasing power. Instructors and sometimes departments choose textbooks and face few implementation barriers. For better or for worse, student satisfaction is a major factor in teacher evaluation, if not *the* major factor, which suggests an opportunity. Specifically, the opportunity is to use games in college introductory science courses that attract nonmajors, where engagement is always a challenge.

Partnerships
In January 2014, W. W. Norton & Company, a midsize, independent, employee-owned publisher based in New York City, reached out to GLS to make an astronomy game. Best known as the publisher of the Norton Anthology series, Norton also publishes trade books and college textbooks. Each Norton textbook is accompanied by digital resources, which frequently include online tutorials, videos, animations, and simulations, developed by a specific digital editor. Norton wanted to make a game for its introductory college textbook *Astronomy: At Play in the Cosmos*, to be authored by Adam Frank, an astrophysics professor at the University of Rochester. Frank proposed that Norton develop simulations and mini-games to accompany the text.

Subject Matter Expert Team
The subject matter expert team, led by Dr. Jeff Bary of Colgate University, also included a national panel of representatives. Richard Townsend (UW–Madison) was helpful for local game developers. Professor Dave Wood (San Antonio College) knew teaching in community colleges. Adam Frank (University of Rochester), the founder of National Public Radio's *13.7: Cosmos and Culture* and a regular contributor to NPR's *All Things Considered* and the *New York Times*, brought expertise in communicating science. Norton also recruited instructor focus groups, play-testers, and classroom testers for the project.

Preproduction

Introductions, Negotiations, and Forming a Partnership (Three Months)
Entering a partnership is exciting but risky. How committed is the partner? How will the partner react when the project faces technical and design

obstacles (e.g., a planned feature doesn't work) or institutional obstacles (e.g., changes in leadership)? Entering a partnership means being a part of one another's professional lives for years.[1]

This partnership appealed to us because Norton is not a typical textbook company. As an employee-owned publisher, Norton is less subject to profit chasing than a publicly traded company would be, and less likely to suffer from changing leadership. The specific partner members were smart, experienced, and sophisticated in the domain. The context (university courses), instructional strategy (using a game for situated understanding of phenomena), and business strategy (using the game to promote an established product) were sound. We also simply liked one another and wanted an excuse to work together.

It took about eighteen months from initial introductions to actually start work, which is typical. Six months were dedicated to exploring the relationship, discussing designs, and scoping a potential project.[2] While GLS scanned the environment for similar games, brainstormed ideas, and formed a proposal, Norton team members generated internal enthusiasm for the project. Two key interrelated questions drove the initial design considerations:

1. What framework (genre, narrative) could tie together wide-ranging content (e.g., internal composition of planets, physics, black holes)?
2. How should we leverage the interactives? The book includes discrete interactives used for teaching. Could we integrate them into the game? Games already existed that depict concepts such as gravity, but we wanted students to apply them to more specific phenomena, such as the gravitational pull of planets.

GLS developed and submitted a framework for the theory, design, and development of a game. We proposed a single game with an overarching narrative. This approach situates learning within roles to understand *why* learning a domain is important while also making a better marketing tool. A story-driven game with characters, quests, and story stands out more than a collection of simulation mini-games. The challenge was scoping. How could we pull off this style of game within a modest game development budget (anticipated to be around $500,000)? Norton invited GLS to submit a high-level document for internal review.

Developing the General Concept (Three Months)

We next had to develop an idea for vetting. We got out astronomy books and developed a high-level ten-page game design document (GDD). Norton commissioned ten written reviews of this GDD by instructors in institutions ranging from two-year colleges to influential state universities. The reviewers were cautiously optimistic, though they could not envision the finished product. They also raised concerns such as the challenges of balancing science and science fiction and avoiding androcentric perspectives. Norton took these reviews and wrote a formal request for proposals (RFP).

Testing the Idea and Formalizing a Partnership (Three Months)

In the fall of 2014, Norton announced the RFP, which created a tricky situation. University centers are not competitive with agile start-ups. Norton had been generous in funding our design work, brought significant expertise in astronomy *and* publishing, and, of course, was funding the project. It was right for Norton to conduct due diligence before awarding a contract. But it left us exposed to losing the bid once we signed over our ideas.

In the end, we needed to trust our partners. A competitive RFP would ensure that the plan was strong. As an academic group, GLS needed to support the best plan rather than our development team's interests. The GLS bid was warmly received in November 2014. Over forty editors and directors discussed the proposal across multiple Norton editorial board meetings. A key to the bid's success was GLS's inclusion of games-based learning researchers, who would help ensure quality. The end result was cautious optimism, but more questions:

- **Look and feel.** Would high-resolution graphics be necessary? Would students raised on AAA games be impressed by our production?
- **Customizability for instructors.** Could instructors customize levels for teaching purposes? Could specific missions be assigned for homework or lab?
- **Ownership.** What model of copyright should we use? How should royalties work? Was GLS an "author"? We weren't work-for-hire contractors.
- **Related versions.** Could we make versions for home use, K–12 use, or other contexts? How were publishing rights in those contexts handled?
- **Schedule, deliverables, and payment.** How should milestones and payments work? Book publishing and game publishing have different models. Game development requires more up-front funding to pay developers.

Private-Public Partnerships for Scale 143

Negotiations continued for three months as a subcommittee of Norton directors and editors tackled these issues. We were a year into the project with no contract and no detailed design document.

Design Jam: Rapid Needs Analysis, Team Building, and Ideation (Two Weeks)

Game design jam In March 2015, GLS hosted a design jam to generate design ideas, uncover tacit assumptions, and generate cohesion among team members, even without the final contract. In contrast with a typical project, in which a subject matter team might understand the content, our team had a deep understanding of the diverse contexts of implementation, which ranged from community colleges to elite private universities. We also had a good grasp of where students excelled and where they struggled in astronomy.

The design jam functioned as a quick and dirty needs analysis and consensus builder, similar to Bichelmeyer and Boling's (1998) collaborative rapid visual prototyping. Rather than conduct analyses to distill functional specifications, we built versions of the game to design our way through problems. We divided into subgroups. Each group included designers, educators, editors, astronomers, market researchers, and product managers. Each team took an hour to mock up a version of the game. We compared features and compiled a list of questions.

A design jam cultivates trust on a team. We break up groups (e.g., developers) and pair them individually with other stakeholder groups right away. As teams develop ideas in competition with other groups, bonds form across disciplines. Trust is especially critical in learning game projects with trade-offs between features (e.g., added assessment features versus improved character models). Teams with shared values are less likely to develop animosities. When teams feel respected and that their goals are accounted for, they can let go of defending their turf. A sign of a good team is when one member misses a meeting and others advocate for the absent member's views.

Game jam results Through the game jam, a sense of team developed. Angst over protracted negotiations was replaced by enthusiasm for the possibilities of this partnership. We defined the following design pillars:

1. Emphasize thinking with evidence over memorization.
2. Promote conceptual understanding of fundamentals (scale, universal nature of physical laws, interaction of light and matter, origin and evolution of structure of the universe).

3. Use the game to illustrate *why* we know what we know.
4. Tie together concepts in the textbook (e.g., how understanding the rate at which stars form factors into frequency of planetary systems).

Jeff developed a detailed three-page content analysis of learning objectives, while GLS translated these ideas into game design patterns. We found little published research about learning astronomy (see Plummer & Krajcik (2010) for a notable exception, as well as Ken Hay's work (Barab et al., 2000), so we worked largely on intuition.

Connecting Quantitative Representations to Qualitative Understandings
A key design goal emerged: building qualitative understandings of astronomy through game play and connecting them to quantitative representations. Mathematical notation is a barrier for students, particularly those who "thought they signed up for an astrology class." Introductory, nonmajor courses focus on conceptual understanding and do not require calculations, which become the dividing line between majors and nonmajors. Perhaps we could help students attach quantitative understandings to these qualitative intuitions (see Ken Forbus's work in qualitative physics; Chang, 2016). We still had not resolved how to connect all four textbook sections (physics, planets, stars and galaxies, universe) in one game, within budget, with a consistent interface, nor developed a coherent narrative framework.

Committing to a Narrative Framework
The winning design was a mission-based role-playing game in which players explore space as contractors. Our inspirations included Han Solo from *Star Wars* and the *Firefly* series. We brainstormed missions: launching a spacecraft, exploring nearby galaxies, and identifying a habitable planet for possible colonization. The core game play loop included asking questions (e.g., Does this section of a galaxy have habitable planetary systems?); collecting data with tools (e.g., a virtual light spectrum analyzer); and confirming or disconfirming results (e.g., traveling to a planet to see if they were right). We hoped that the game would enable students to think scientifically, which is the primary course goal but is difficult to engender through didactic instruction. Missions, such as saving a mining station from a rogue comet or traveling near a black hole, could enable us to integrate topics as well as appeal to multiple interests; for instance, some players might like a rescue mission, while others might prefer exploration. We collectively

Private-Public Partnerships for Scale

committed to a "hard science fiction" approach, whereby the game would embrace plausible futuristic technologies.

Key Issues: Navigation and Scale

Navigation was a key challenge, as follows:

1. How can we represent size and scale on-screen, given how small a ship is in comparison with planets and stars?
2. How will players navigate? Video game flight controls are notoriously difficult to learn. How scientifically plausible do the ship's thrusters need to be?
3. How will players travel to galaxies? Most phenomena are *multiple light years* from Earth. Without hyperwarp, *Cosmos* would involve literally years of sitting in place.

Faster than light (FTL) navigation and Interactive Star Chart Professors Frank and Bary made a persuasive case for plausible faster than light travel. We designed an Interactive Star Chart (see figure 8.1) with three goals in

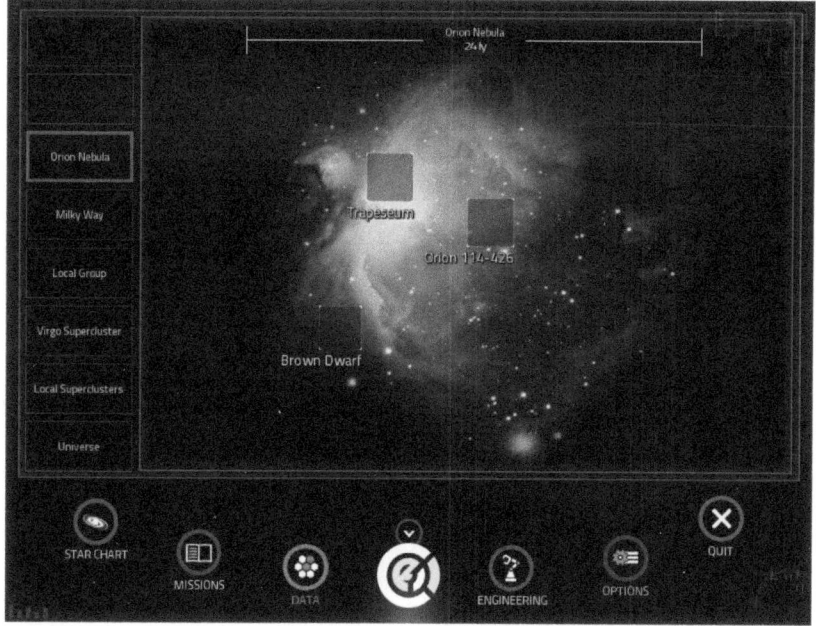

Figure 8.1
Alpha build version of the Interactive Star Chart (fall 2015).

mind: (1) simplify navigation, (2) scaffold students' building of an intuitive sense of structure in the universe, and (3) overcome technical memory limitations associated with rendering the entire universe on a mobile phone. By repeatedly consulting the map, students interact with locations, are introduced to the organization of the universe, and may internalize patterns. Imagine, in contrast, representing the universe as one continuous system with no navigational signposts; students would "fly blind" by setting coordinates but would not see how the universe is organized.

Embedded tools We featured astronomers' tools embedded directly in the game, which is becoming an established educational game design technique (see Gaydos & Squire, 2012). Learners encounter how and why tools are used—a key science learning goal. We identified seven key tools, including the following:

- **Small Angle Tool.** Used to measure the angular sizes of objects; employs the small angle approximation to calculate physical size.
- **Mass Analyzer Tool.** Used to calculate the masses of celestial objects when a smaller object orbits around a much larger object. The player measures the orbital period of the selected system and uses Newton's Version of Kepler's Third Law to calculate the sum of the masses.
- **Spectrum Analyzer Tool.** Used to collect and analyze spectra of celestial objects including stars, supernovae, and nebulae (see figure 8.2).
- **Luminosity Tool.** Used to measure the apparent brightness of a star and use the inverse square law of light to calculate the luminosity of the star.

Making the abstract concrete: Articulating a vertical slice A vertical slice is a functional version of the game experience. Making a vertical slice requires the team to consider the media elements and technical systems required for a functioning system. This slice included (1) a mini-narrative, (2) a mission, (3) an interactive simulation, (4) a Smartwork Demo assignment (consisting of several interactive homework questions based on the book's explanation of mission content), and (5) an e-book demo. We decided to build *Cosmos* in Unity, porting to iOS (iPad 4 and iPhone), PC, Apple, and Android tablets. Data would be stored on Norton's servers, which was important in meeting Family Educational Rights and Privacy Act (FERPA) regulations. The interactives would be stand-alone, HTML 5, and available for offline use but also accessible via game play.

Private-Public Partnerships for Scale

Figure 8.2
Heads-up display mock-up of the spectrometer.

Game design document After completing the design jam and review, we began writing a general design document. Lead designer and project manager Mike Beall spent hundreds of hours reading and talking with astronomers, especially local astronomy professors. The design document grew to twenty-eight pages and included concept art, mock interfaces, and links to detailed subdocuments (e.g., missions, systems engineering planning). Subject matter experts regularly read and returned documents with line-by-line edits within twenty-four hours. The feeling of an integrated team working together, rather than a traditional developer-expert relationship, continued.

The art team gathered research art, sketched images, and developed high-resolution visual materials for external consumption. Led by artist Brian Pelletier, the team developed concept art of the player's ship, its command center, and the look and feel of the world (see figure 8.3). The general aesthetic feel (space) was feasible; plentiful reference art exists for celestial bodies, and most of them are spheres, with particle effects. The team sought a clean, futuristic look that was also functional. Graphic artist Jake

Figure 8.3
Early ship concept art and ship with weathering.

Ruesch researched interfaces and developed mock-ups. Jake drew from the work of Jayse Hansen, the user interface designer behind the heads-up display (HUD) of Iron Man's suit in the Marvel film franchise (see figure 8.2). *Iron Man* made an excellent reference piece because its designers included the controls and data streams one would theoretically need to navigate in an Iron Man suit. Nothing appearing on-screen in the *Iron Man* HUD is gratuitous, meaning that it was a fully functional flight control interface.

Missions: A tool for aligning game play and learning objectives Design occurred through writing missions and aligning them with course content to cover learning objectives. The main four areas of an astronomy course—physics (e.g., gravity, light), planets, stars, and cosmology—involve relatively different scales and, potentially, interfaces. Astronomical processes are . . . astronomically slow in comparison with the human life span, so missions that explore these concepts required some creativity.

We designed a walk-through of one mission (gather helium-3 from the Horsehead Nebula) in detail (see figure 8.4). The mission's learning goals were to understand blackbody radiation and Wien's law. Wien's displacement law involves calculations of the temperature of celestial bodies based on light waves. To add to the dramatic effect, we added a narrative arc in which a rival corporation detects the player and the player must act quickly. This feature gave a hint of a broader world beyond the character and suggested narrative possibilities.

Interactive simulation design Professor Jeff Bary wrote a 143-page design document that articulated forty-nine interactive simulations. Some

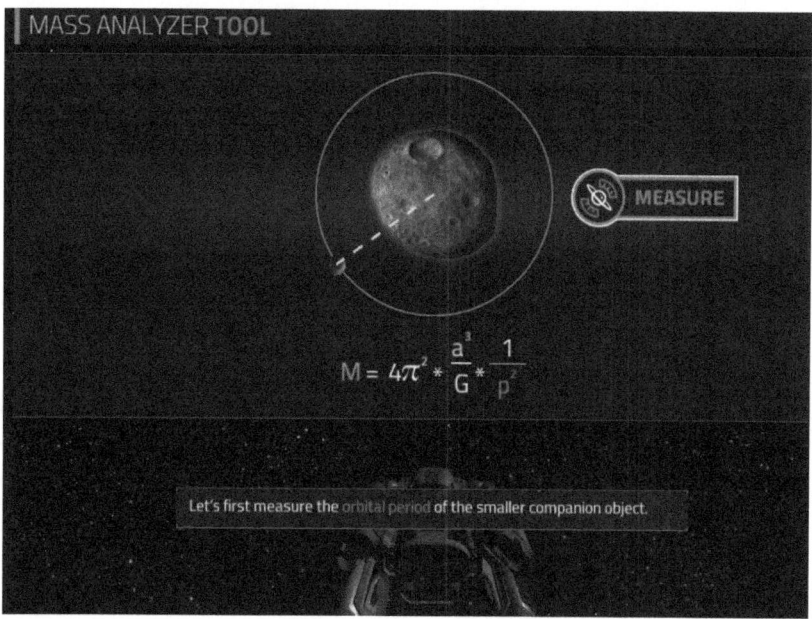

Figure 8.4
Slice of a mission walk-through.

interactives already existed; we were just making them "juicier," meaning more appealing, through features such as amplified input (Juul, 2009; Poole, 2000). Twenty-nine interactives made their way into the game.

This interactive list was a pivotal step in the game's development. A list of concepts translated into interactive systems became the game's master list of verbs. We now had (1) a comprehensive scoping of the domain, (2) descriptions of systems ready translated into game scenarios, and (3) representations for nonastronomers to study. Simply put, if you want to teach a game developer astronomy, a design doc of interactive simulations is a good way to do it. This authoritative list became our design bible.

Production

Getting to Alpha (Five Months)
Finally, in early September 2015, we hosted a formal kickoff to celebrate the start of production. We needed to align the editorial team, the astronomers, and leadership on a final production timeline that defined size and scope. In comparison with previous academic research projects, *At Play in the Cosmos* followed a relatively linear, waterfall-style design. The exceptionally long preproduction period required us to define ideas before committing lines of code and left little time for dead ends. We had to pick a direction, commit, and go. We were now embracing the type of production schedule that Filament Games had used with us, mentioned in the first chapters of this book. In this period, we employed three programmers and two artists.

Two design tensions characterized the project from that point forward: (1) balancing the needs of a guided astrophysics simulation with those of a video game (which requires choices) and (2) communicating conceptual knowledge of physics without intimidating students. The mission structure enabled players to go through specific steps in solving problems, but it also felt like an interactive point-and-click workbook. We imagined, with larger budgets and more time, creating a procedurally generated universe (as in *No Man's Sky*) and letting the player explore it with astronomer's tools. Executing that idea was beyond our scope.

Navigation and controls The most pressing decision was how to create simple, intuitive, but scientifically plausible flight controls. Navigating in

	Sprint 1 - 8/26	Sprint 2 - 9/2	Sprint 3 - 9/9	Sprint 4 - 9/16	Sprint 5 - 9/23	Sprint 6 - 9/30	Sprint 7 - 10/7	Sprint 8 - 10/14	Sprint 9 - 10/21	Sprint 10 - 10/28
				September				October		
General Code			Enemy Ship AI	Star Chart resource images		Mines polish - tracking and explosions	Out of Play Area - warning & guidance back			
Missions		Start Mission 10	Start Mission 9	Start Mission 11		Start Mission 12	Start Mission 13	Start Mission 15	Polish Missions 12-15	Start Mission 16
Missions		Volumetric Unity Functionality—GREG	Volumetric Unity Functionality—GREG		Mission 6 polish	Mission 6 - 11 Polish	Start Mission 14 (Collection) ETA CARINAE			
Tools	reduce delays in small angle tool progression	add more comparison spectra for star types								
Tools	Stop all VO upon exit from tool	Implement drag & drop mechanic for tools								
Tools										
Artwork	Saturn's rings FTL environment	add Proxima b	Shields							
Artwork	Ant Nebula	tbd	Lasers							
Artwork	Comet Artwork	Comet Artwork	concept for in game HR diagram							
Artwork		Upgraded FTL particles	concept for habitable zone pop up							
Artwork			Objects for Missions 9-11 are identified							
Design			Final Progression changes for Missions 9-11			Final Progression changes for Missions 12-14				
Design		Design progression for missions 9-11	Design progression for missions 12-15	Design progression for missions 16-20						
Design		update tool usage checkboxes								
Design		Star Chart slides for Missions 9-11	Tool data for Missions 9-11		Star Chart slides for Missions 12-14	Tool data for Missions 12-14			Star Chart slides for Missions 15-18	Tool data for Missions 15-18
Design								Final Object Selections		

Figure 8.5
Example project timeline and milestones.

true 3D without any floor as a reference point is difficult. The flight controls used in computer flying games confuse novices (see Jenkins et al., 2003). Touch interfaces offer new solutions to these dilemmas. Hundreds of mobile games tackle this problem, from traditional flight sims to bird flight simulator games, and mobile touch flying controls have evolved considerably.[3] We mined these games for ideas.

After multiple design iterations, we landed on a "tap to determine direction" interface. An early prototype featured the iPad accelerometer so that players moved by positioning the iPad, but this approach was shelved because it would not cross platforms. The final version, which came after twelve iterations and three hundred user testers, was a HUD with a crosshairs that indicates direction. Tapping anywhere on-screen adjusts the ship's orientation in that direction. On the lower right corner of the screen (near the thumb), the player moves thrusters in forward or reverse. This design gives experts more control and enables novices to set course, coast most of the time, and stop by selecting neutral.

Flight-based game play   The "gameness" occurs within missions. Players fly within regions to interact with representations of celestial bodies. Mission mechanics employ flying and racing game tropes, wherein players collect objects, navigate obstacle courses, or avoid traps.

Allowing the player to fly through debris fields, asteroid belts, planets, and even nebulae posed a unique problem: how could we display these in real time, given the differences in scale between a spaceship and celestial bodies? The difference between the size of celestial objects and the player's ship is so large that the numbers are difficult for a computer to represent. In a 3D game, the position of any object is represented by x, y, and z values, and each of those values is limited to seven decimal places. Missions in which players flew through asteroid fields broke because the player's ship became a rounding error in comparison with large objects. Developer Greg Vaughan invented a rendering approach in which the player's ship is proxied in a scaled-down environment, which allows large objects to be rendered separately and overlaid in the play space while maintaining appropriate parallax movement. This creates the illusion of flying toward the large object and having that object scale and move as expected.

Building a vertical slice   We decided to build a vertical slice demonstration for the American Astronomical Society's annual meeting in January 2016.

Private-Public Partnerships for Scale

A real deadline only four months away could galvanize the team and focus our work. We created an eighteen-step storyboard including steps such as the following:

Walk-through

1. Splash screen
11. UI shows the density formula and a close-up view of binary asteroids
    a. As part of the formula is highlighted, the corresponding visual element is highlighted to show the relationship
    b. UI now shows the density value on asteroids
    c. Player taps [next] button?
12. UI shows auto calculations being done for remaining two sets of binary asteroids
13. UI shows three sets of binary asteroids to choose from
    a. Player taps to select a set of binary asteroids (based on displayed information)

This vertical slice required a player log-in system, a user interface, integrated tools, navigation, in-game animations, and a mission tracking system. If these functions worked within three months, the risk of failure would go down. We could then play with designs to get a feeling for what worked.

Similarly to agile software development, we started a process of regular, playable builds to evaluate progress and maintain stakeholder alignment. The first playable build was done on October 21, 2015, about six weeks after the project kickoff. Major updates occurred biweekly.

Art tests The design team used reference art gleaned from NASA and elsewhere, but we verified all designs with experts. We leveraged play squads (frequent, informal play-testing through groups touring the lab on field trips) for feedback. Questions in this phase included "What feelings does this conjure?" and "Who is the game for?" Students wanted a fast, scientifically accurate vessel that could also defend itself. Jacques Cousteau (in addition to *Firefly*) became an inspiration. We eventually designed multiple unlockable ships.

The benefits of having a professional art staff (as opposed to someone who could make 3D models) are apparent. Figure 8.3 shows a ship rendering, which includes weathering, an effect that gives the ship a sense of history and depth. In most academic projects there are, at most, one or two artists, who fight for their survival or spend their time communicating with nonartists. In contrast, our team had up to six artists at any time who were constantly trading designs, critiquing one another's work, and sharing work with one another that inspired them.

Negotiating depictions, accuracy, and game play The editorial team kept the game on track, particularly in regard to product needs. In this exchange, the developers asked scientists for information but were pulled back before they collectively went down a rabbit hole of detailed information. Recall the rabbit holes we collectively burrowed on *Trails Forward* as we geeked out on Northern Wisconsin logging. The following exchange was one part of a multi-threaded conversation that occurred around the November build. Developer Mike Beall asked:

> Can you give us detailed info (fictional but plausible) for 3 sets of binary asteroids (assuming they are mostly spherical)? We need Mass, Diameter, and Distance from ship to asteroids in kilograms/kilometers. Example: Mass = 100,000 kg, Diameter = 67 km, Distance = 350,000 km.

Jeff Bary offered the following vignette in response:

> The goal of this mission is to have students learn and recognize which observable characteristics of the binary asteroids allow them to determine the masses and sizes of the asteroids. Then, they need to recognize that the mass and size allows them to calculate the density. Density allows them to determine the composition of the asteroids and thus determine which one or ones are most suitable for mining.
>
> 1. Choose a density for the asteroid or asteroids
> 2. Choose a radius/diameter.
> 3. Use #1 and #2 to calculate masses for the asteroids and note the ratio of the masses.
> 4. Choose a separation or total semi-major axis. (Separation will be a property that students will measure.)
> 5. Use semi-major axis and sum of the masses to find the period of the orbit. (Period will be a property that students will measure.)
> 6. Make up a distance to the asteroids. Reasonable distances will be on the order of millions to 2 or 3 hundred million kilometers
> 7. Use the small angular formula, which relates the physical size and distance to the object, to calculate the angular size of the asteroids. (Angular size will be a quantity students will measure in the game.)

Private-Public Partnerships for Scale 155

Rob, a Norton editor, responded:

> The calculations required in this workflow make me nervous. In the book, all math is optional (covered in Going Further boxes) because we know how few instructors require calculations as part of the course. In fact, only 10 of the 45 problems at the end of each chapter require calculations.
>
> **My worry is that this workflow reads a bit more like a script for a quantitative online lab as opposed to a game where students learn intuitively through play** [emphasis added]. If the first mission we review with the market has the AI walking students through multiple calculations, the audience might not think this is a game at all. I am curious to see whether instructors have that perception tomorrow.

Erik Fahlgren, an editor and vice president at Norton, echoed Rob's comments:

> I want to echo what Rob is saying. The vast majority of this market does not teach or expect students to use ANY math. Ratios (if this is twice as large, how much faster will it go) is the extent of math used at most schools.
>
> Asking students to DO math in the game would be an astronomical mistake.

In addition to offering witty puns, editors functioned as proxy user experts for the team.

Scaffolding mathematical representations The team liked the idea of connecting properties of celestial bodies with their variables in formulas so that players "make" connections. Astronomer Adam Frank commented:

> I am digging the new build and the ability to see just the equation with variables or with #'s but it leads to a super important killer question which, if we get it right, might really let us break through: How to let students get a "feel" for the behavior embodied in an equation?
>
> For example, consider an inverse law: $Y = 1/X$
>
> I would be so happy if my students really understood that as X gets bigger, Y gets smaller and vice versa. This issue will come up for every interactive with an equation and if we get it right we will be heroes.

Through interactions such as these, the team continued to focus on the interplay between quantitative and qualitative understandings. The resulting mission, in which players search for iron deposits inside asteroids, is included to give the reader a feel for the game flow. In this third mission, players attempt to repair their ship and use the mass analyzer tool to identify an iron-rich asteroid. Players are presented with questions ("Does that asteroid have iron?") and use a variety of tools to answer them. Later missions require combining skills and choosing from tools.

Focus groups In addition to art focus groups and regular user testing, we conducted a focus group with thirty-five students in October 2015. Such sessions can be led by graduate students, teachers, or developers, but in this case developers ran the focus group so that they could observe students' reactions.[4] The majority of students chose to be independent contractors completing rescue operations. Popular themes included exploring the unknown and saving the human race. Military themes were less interesting. Preferences coalesced around sleek, fast ships. Students wanted the ship's "computer" to have a distinct personality.

CORI in game narration to address nongaming, nonscience majors Designing for nongaming, nonscience majors remained important. Project lead Mike Beall advocated for an in-game narrator (like Jarvis in *Iron Man*) to guide players. Mike was excited by the opportunity to recruit David Simkins, a game design professor at the Rochester Institute of Technology, who has a deep, reassuring voice, to narrate. Interface designer Jake Ruesch turned this idea into the Cosmic Operations Research Interface (CORI), which eventually became the game's UI system and a critical design feature.

January Play-Test (Five Months)
In early January, Norton presented the vertical slice to the publisher's directors and astronomers. Consensus was as follows:

1. *The visuals looked great.* The game sparked people's imaginations for what an astronomy game could be. The production quality was impressive. Participants were eager to see the game published.
2. *The game was too didactic.* The missions, based on the "workflow" provided by professors, resulted in game play that felt like formulaic labs.

This feedback echoed the team's concerns, although we were comfortable with the game's status. If the core game play was regarded as sufficiently academic, we could increase engagement through narrative, choices, and polish (Schell, 2008).

The road to beta The core game ideas, missions, and systems were functioning. Now, to finalize the narrative, we needed to build out missions, create art assets, develop and integrate interactives, and create systems to report game play data into Norton's learning management system.

Fleshing out missions Theoretically, the design was set to go after the alpha tests; we confirmed learning objectives, a HUD, controls, lists of missions, and

Private-Public Partnerships for Scale 157

design details for interactives. Each mission required a detailed walk-through, art assets, text for voice-over narrations, and specifications for data to be tracked in the mission. For example, Mission 4 contained the following description:

> While the Ion Thruster tanks are full of Xenon, the Helium-3 tanks needed to power FTL Drive are nearly depleted. CORI suggests traveling to a nearby, Wolf-Rayet star, a massive, dying star that produces a fast-moving stellar wind, rich in Helium-3. Using the correct tool, the Players must first confirm that the target CORI has selected is indeed a Wolf-Rayet star. Players can then FTL to the Wolf-Rayet. Players are challenged to fly close to the star while sustaining damage from the high energy photons and the strength of the hyperactive stellar wind.

- Zoom to M1–67 Nebula & WR 124
- Use Spectrum Analyzer to confirm WR 124 is a Wolf-Rayet star
- FTL to WR 124
- Learn to collect He 3 from solar winds
- End of Mission

Programmers used these key events to develop missions. The designer notes from this phase look like an astronomy student's notes, as the following Protoplanetary disk notes illustrate:

> **PPD's**—mention wavelength of image—infrared
> - Must be in a nebula
> - Determine star type—spectral class—not fusing hydrogen
>   - Debris disk—Oldest—planets and rings instead of clouds
>   - Epsilon Eridani
>   - Vega
>   - Fomalhaut
>   - Beta Pictoris
>   - HR8799

Each mission went through a thorough vetting, including twenty different variables, ranging from 3D artwork to final subject matter expert sign-off, managed through spreadsheets.

Final art started appearing in the engine in 2016, which brought momentum to the project. Seeing working images of spaceships and celestial bodies inspired team members (who frequently shared excited comments over email) and made the project feel much closer to a reality. This phenomenon is common.

Project management Our project management process is somewhat typical for modern game design. Regular play-tests drove production. They focused the team, ensured that production was on track, and guided the evolution of the controls and interface. Developers had daily stand-up meetings, weekly teamwide check-ins, and biweekly builds pushed out to partners. Communication was mediated through email over fifty planning and management documents. A sprint schedule from the fall of 2015 depicts typical production tasks.

Crafting system. A crafting system, in which players could collect materials while on missions and use them to upgrade their ship, arose as a way to expand game play. We hoped that the crafting system would reinforce that the universe is made of elements that can be broken down, used, and processed and that future space exploration may rely on such activities. Aesthetically, the crafting system was designed to deepen the player's bond with the spacecraft, enhance a sense of independence and adventure, and drive forward missions narratively. A spreadsheet tracked which elements could be useful and where they are found in the universe. The ship crafting interface was inspired by the award-winning *Faster Than Light*.

Spring play-test PhD student Jennifer Dalson conducted a play-test with thirty-three students in the spring of 2016. Results were positive (they liked the game, wanted a glossary), but after observing the session, we decided to enhance CORI for a more unified game experience.

Glossary We prioritized implementing the in-game glossary (called the database) that provides just-in-time information on 222 phenomena encountered in-game. Players can also access 29 interactives that illustrate concepts. If part of what games do is pique curiosity and situate information, robust in-game repositories are critical.

Data integration The game itself is a free download, but players purchase the game through Norton's site or gain a log-in with the textbook to unlock the game. Once connected, the game saves data offline and uploads it to Norton's learning management system. The game captures and records variables including log-ins, missions played and completed, and achievements unlocked. These data are recorded and presented to instructors.

The road to gold The original goal was to ship in the fall of 2016 (which was admittedly aggressive). Between the late start and changes in project velocity, we pushed the soft launch back to the spring of 2017 and the full launch to the fall of 2017. For the first versions, we targeted touch interfaces (phones and tablets, both Android and iOS), although *Cosmos* worked on PCs throughout development.

Final development production goals By the fall of 2016, *At Play in the Cosmos* was a recognizable game, with the major systems intact. The remaining development tasks, listed here, primarily were polishing and refining (although future updates were anticipated).

1. *Refine the tool progression* so that missions build upon one another logically. The game features seven tools, interspersed across missions so that players are introduced to them gradually, do not use them repetitively, and eventually use them in combination.
2. *Add gas and particle collection systems* for flying missions. Flying missions required systems for setting targets on-screen, helping players who become stuck, tracking progress, and collecting, storing, and reporting data.
3. *Refine the log-in flow.* These systems worked but needed to be airtight for use at scale.
4. *Finalize data collection and reporting* to work with Norton's learning management system.
5. *Finalizing narration script.* Changes in mission text required rerecording voice-overs (as opposed to editing text files), so creation of the final narration script was treated reverentially.

Fall Play-Test

We conducted a final play-test with all eight missions and seven tools. Astronomy professors at the University of Wisconsin–Madison and Colgate University enacted *Cosmos* in their courses however they saw fit (e.g., required activity or extra credit). A total of 184 students (164 Wisconsin, 20 Colgate) participated in the study; 660 students interacted with the game, including in class lectures.

Overall perceptions of game experience This user study confirmed that the game was on the right track. Students reported enjoying the game and felt that it helped them think about astronomy. Professors regularly used interactives for demonstrations, which students recalled and valued. Most students were reticent to see the game required as a part of the class. They preferred it offered as extra credit, a supplemental guide, or lab discussions.

Perceptions of game play Missions were still too didactic, and students wanted more free-form exploration. This version had a free-form exploration mode, but few found it. It was too late to change the overall design, but these findings increased our concern with balancing missions well, adding in missions where players could navigate ships, and calling out the open exploration mode through achievements.

Formulas and equations At the University of Wisconsin, students were introduced to equations via a single PowerPoint slide during lecture. This PowerPoint slide was intended to introduce astronomy concepts. The beta version of *Cosmos* displayed equations, and then players would instruct CORI to calculate the equation. Students could click on parts of the equation to see how it was constructed, but they were not required to calculate values, manipulate components, or answer questions to move forward.

The equations lacked interaction. Students appreciated the visual representations, but many believed the game could create investment by requiring them to demonstrate understanding. Some students wanted to calculate values, while others anticipated that it would be too stressful. Suggested solutions included clicking and dragging components.

Final Steps and Polish

In the final months of 2016, the following major features were added:

1. **Interactive tools and equations.** The tools were revamped with drag-and-drop functionality so that players select numerical values and drag them into equations. They can move and interact with equations without doing calculations. This feature could be further improved upon by future developers.
2. **Missions.** The eight beta missions were expanded to twenty missions that include new visualizations. A time travel feature was added to enable players to visit the universe as it existed 13.7 billion years ago.
3. **Storyline/text.** The final narrative involves the Corporation using alien artifacts to maintain a stranglehold on resources required for human expansion into the cosmos. The missions follow the mythological archetype of Joseph Campbell's hero's journey.
4. **Voice-overs.** We recorded more than six hundred lines of in-game dialogue, with voice-overs and sound effects added. Ideally, we'd record scratch vocals earlier and then focus the final run-up on polishing, quality assurance testing, and small tweaks.

Roads Not Taken

We still had lists of dream features and adaptations:

1. **More open-ended play outside of missions.** We imagined the game being more open-ended and discovery oriented so that, for example, players might explore the universe via the star map and visit celestial systems freely. We did not prioritize these features because generating the universe (as was done in *No Man's Sky*) is nontrivial and is not guaranteed to interest players. Still, we wanted a more sandboxy feel within our framework. Advanced game play could support emergent quests (such as obtaining more helium-3) so that players could use their understanding of which stars have helium in order to locate and collect it. The universe could be the players' game board.

2. **Opportunities to interact with stars and planets.** Missions occur near planets but outside of their atmosphere. Issues with gravity, relative size and scale, and floating point calculations all eliminated missions in which the player could interact with planets or stars. One could imagine landing missions (such as a lunar lander) or roving missions on planets. We could also explore physics through takeoffs, landings, and projectiles. These ideas were cut because they did not target new learning objectives and required new game systems.

3. **More complex mission structure.** *Cosmos* includes a relatively linear set of twenty missions, which came together in the final months. Minimally, we wanted side missions and quests that would increase player choice and agency. Ideally, missions would tie to different factions (perhaps one mining for profit, one seeking a universal world order). Shaping the future of the universe would be an appealing narrative context.

Reflections

Cross-Institutional Team Building

A successful cross-institutional team results from personal working styles, project parameters, timing, or even luck. Academics, publishers, and game developers come from different professions with different values. Many readers will have experienced projects mired by game developers who obfuscate their expertise, academics who overapply knowledge from their domain (without understanding real-world constraints), or publishers who insist on features based on whatever market scan, report, or random game title has floated across their desk. These problems usually arise from insecurity and defensiveness and are best combated by parties taking one another's roles seriously.

Everyone on this project saw its success as an important professional opportunity, which could lead to more opportunities, including personal advancement. You would think that aligning a project's success with all team members' personal success would be commonplace, but it isn't always the case. It is common for game managers to pit teams against one another or place them in competition for resources. Groups defend turf and personal and professional reputation at the expense of the project. Minimally, they incentivize people to put their heads down and do their job rather than raise issues that threaten a project's success.

Team leaders' primary job is to align teams around shared values to create collective responsibility for a project (and then resource them and get out of the way). Team members thrive when they see how a successful project will benefit them. This means nipping individualistic behavior in the bud before it spreads, having no tolerance of toxic or undermining behavior—such as team members spreading gossip—and asking all team members to understand the values and skills of other team members.

Academics are often likely to be bad team members. In academia, an individualistic culture rewards stars instead of teams. Faculty are incentivized to evoke an aura of mystique and to critique rather than build. Graduate students and postdocs, as aspirants into that system, are incentivized to take ownership of projects and carve out areas as their own. Academia rewards performance in one's domain along narrow metrics, such as publications. Shifting the goal to making impact requires explicit attention to these issues.

Genuine curiosity about others' work Curiosity is a key requirement for successful partnerships. It is a good sign when team members query one another about their fields or areas of expertise (such as textbook publishers' views on digital publishing or astronomers' thoughts on intergalactic space travel). A rule of thumb that guides our team is that *on a good team, members understand not only what other team members do but also their personal and professional goals, so as to support them.* We made a point of learning what would make the project a success for each organization and individual. We cultivated a spirit of making one another look good.

Managing for momentum To highlight an effective practice, recall the pivotal point when astronomer Jeff Bary developed the list of interactives. Bary's representing astronomy through the lens of interactive design was inspiring. By contributing to the design in tangible ways, subject matter experts added project momentum, which Aleckson & Ralston-Berg (2011) concluded is a key attribute for game-based learning teams. Building on the work of Bacharach (2006), Aleckson argued that the most critical variable to a project is momentum (an agile concept), which arises by passionate team members who beget more passion (and momentum). A challenge for faculty doing game design is that momentum requires regular, sustained face-to-face interaction and real hands-on contributions.

Educational Game Design in a University Science Course

Designing a college game to cover an entire course differs from previous examples in this book in three key ways:

1. **The game had to capture more than one or two interesting interactions.** In many learning games, designers find a sweet spot where "there is a game in the content" and then design experiences around it. The rest is left to other resources. In this case, the game needed to carry an entire course, including phenomena at different scales and perspectives.
2. **As part of a textbook, the game had increased pressures for accuracy.** Any learning game must bear fidelity to the subject matter, and accuracy colors all learning game design. However, each decision needed to be vetted by editors, reviewers, and the field at large. Every scientific representation involves simplifications and trade-offs; few images of the solar system, for example, capture the distance between planets while also showing relative scale. Graphic designers always make choices in perspective, color, scale, and foreground that have ramifications for learning.
3. **The game needed to be comprehensive but focused.** While *Cosmos* had to cover the majority of the course content, it also had to stay close to course content. Anything the player does that is not related to learning goals is extra cognitive work, which has been hypothesized as an impediment to using games at scale (Kirschner, Sweller, & Clark, 2006)). Our response to this challenge was to build game scenarios in which players thought with the game content. The resulting game was a little "schoolish," which may be endemic to the design context.

Design Walk-Throughs, Game Play, and Innovation

The art of educational game production involves understanding one's capacities, risks, and dimensions by which one hopes to innovate. *At Play at the Cosmos* sought to innovate along the dimension of creating *a high-production game that captured thinking in astronomy delivered at scale*. It succeeded mostly. It works less well as a stand-alone game or a presentation of ideas. We are now studying how *Cosmos* is used in courses and suspect that it will be best used (1) as an introductory experience before each unit and (2) as practice and application before comprehensive exams. Because game design occurred through design vignettes, or workflows, the resulting game play was true to the domain but somewhat linear.[5] Educational game designers should be mindful of how the format of design documents (vignettes versus rules) shapes the game play we produce.

Situating design processes We often think of design models as idealized routines that exist outside of material and institutional contexts. Design patterns, institutional processes, and team constraints constitute design. In *Cosmos*, the new, risky partnership led to extensive preproduction, which then created a more linear, waterfall approach. This pattern was further reinforced by publishing realities; publishers minimize risk by defining products carefully, bringing products into focus through progressively realized designs, and conducting extensive user testing. All of these steps were good, but they also locked down the product form early. An agile, prototyping approach would place a ship in space and play around until ideas came to mind, but letting the project emerge through cycles of building and testing would not have worked in this context.

The resultant design process also shared features with agile development. Development was built around sprints. These sprints brought the project into progressive focus through removing design obstacles. Substantial design work did occur later, particularly implementing flying mechanics, but because each game iteration was shared with dozens, if not hundreds, of students, we had a good awareness at all times of where the game was working and where it was not. We also knew, with some degree of confidence, how it would be used in classes.

Despite whatever frustrations or misgivings we may have, we would not change this process. Innovation comes over the course of several games and projects. *Cosmos* built on our team's prior successes and borrowed from existing designs. We hope that other teams will borrow from it too, so that educational games five or ten years from now will have the open-ended sandbox play that we wanted. Much as Filament Games has developed, tinkered with, and improved tools in its games (such as the argumentation tool; see Squire & Gaydos, 2012), GLS/Gear will continue to build code libraries and design solutions that can be improved upon for future learning games. As such, we should always be wary of those seeking summative judgments on whether any one game (let alone the medium) is effective.

9 Conclusions

Between 2000 and 2020, games for impact grew from a fringe idea to an established discipline. Every day, millions of kids play games such as *ST Math* at school, play games made by other kids at home through *Roblox*, or learn about ancient Egypt with their parents through *Assassin's Creed: Origins Discovery Tour*. Research on the efficacy of games has grown as well. We now know that games can be an effective technique for supporting learning, often better than other methods, and we can demonstrate how specific features, such as cooperative game play, improve learning. Game play can even have an impact on neurological functions. This chapter is an attempt to summarize what we know about making games and to suggest future directions.

Models for Educational Game Design

The previous chapter ended with reticence to prescribe one method for developing impact games, but commonalities across projects exist. Most projects flow from preproduction to prototyping to production to polishing to services and support, although academic projects rarely make it past prototyping. As educators, we don't do nearly enough to help students understand real production, polishing, or support (Phelps, Egert, & Consalvo, 2021). The next section highlights the basic tasks in each phase. Factors such as time durations are listed as percentages of effort and time and are spiritual numbers, not to be taken literally.

1. Preproduction (10 Percent)

Staffing, Time, and Results
The order of the following steps is not important. Staffing includes one (mostly) full-time design lead, with small percentages of other staff members.

The results are a ten- to fifteen-page game design document (GDD) and, often, a grant document. This phase commonly lasts three to six weeks, depending on other commitments.

1a. Find inspiration Preproduction begins the moment you have an idea. Ideas can come from anywhere. My first book, *Video Games and Learning*, covered idea generation in some detail. Games can start from genres (real-time strategy for environmental management), from existing games (what if *Pokémon GO!* were an exercise game?), from content (physics is hard to learn), or from market opportunities (kindergarten is the new first grade). The key challenge in this phase is to identify players' verbs—the actions that players do—and how they align with project goals.

1b. Develop the idea The goal is to articulate a fuzzy idea so as to improve it. Often a single lead designer develops the idea; at other times it is done by committee. Sketches, particularly for user interfaces, are important. Follow brainstorming guidelines: there are no dumb ideas; prioritize quantity over quality; learn to say, "Yes, and . . . ," and so on (see IDEO U, n.d.). Ideas change, so don't worry about perfection.

1c. Identify stakeholders and partners Who needs to help the game succeed? A single person might make a self-funded entertainment game (think *Plague Inc.*, *Minecraft*), but working in institutions such as schools complicates things. A working theory of the *problem* (e.g., climate change, attention deficit hyperactivity disorder), a hypothesized *solution* (e.g., awareness raising, attention training), and a theory of *change* (e.g., how your game will change practice) are required. Partners guide development, validate underlying models, and evangelize products to press and consumers.

1d. Create a paper-based prototype in a design jam Design jams achieve several goals. They (1) break down a team's disciplinary barriers, (2) get obvious ideas out of the way, (3) uncover constraints, and (4) transition the team toward *playable* ideas rather than presentations of content. This last point is important. We are conditioned to conflate education with content exposure, whereas game design is creating systems of interaction, and teams often struggle to make this transition. Assemble a team for a design jam, usually by the third meeting. Quickly create a paper-based prototype *that other groups will play*. Teams work for a single session (forty-five to ninety minutes usually works) and then play one another's games. Afterward, compare features. Take pictures of the work. Usually a lead designer

Conclusions

will emerge, and this person will own the main design document. Combine these notes before the day is over (before going to bed).

1e. Conduct a strategic analysis Analyze *internal* assets (team skills, values, and goals) and *external* market, cultural, and technical trends. As captured in table 2.1, developers should examine how their goals, values, and interests in a project align with the broader environment (such as a strengths, weaknesses, opportunities, and threats analysis; Dess et al., 2018). Understanding the external context does *not* mean following trends. If the market is trending in one direction (e.g., toward large, high-resolution story-based games), going the opposite way (e.g., a pixelated construction game written in Java) can work (it did for Notch with *Minecraft*!). The key is to be *mindful* of decisions.

1f. Form a team; identify a project lead and a design lead Soon, if not already, a point person needs to maintain focus on moving parts. A good project manager (who is probably also the design lead) is curious, a good communicator, and good at thinking with systems and leading teams of people. A separate design lead may emerge, however. Critically, project managers need to manage relationships, define roles and responsibilities, set expectations, and build momentum.

1g. Write a game design document The goal of a design document is to *communicate* an idea (Librande, 2010). I recommend a visual one-page design document with user experience (UX) flows; see chapter 2. A lot is written about GDDs, templates can be found online, and they mostly share key features. The National STEM Video Game Challenge format is fine. It includes the *target audience*, the *platform*, the *genre*, the *core game play*, the *visual style*, and the *characters* and *story line* (E-Line Media, 2017). Designers articulate the design pillars, or guiding aesthetic philosophy. They may include specific technical specifications, market opportunities, and findings from strategic analyses. Conduct a preliminary content and needs analysis: interview stakeholders, shadow experts, learn about the domain, consult syllabi and textbooks, and consult research on *project goals* (e.g., learning, behavioral change) in the target domain. Designers aren't becoming experts in the topic but are skimming for key ideas. Expert partners can keep designers on track. In this phase, consult a lot of prior art, games in the target genre or genres, instructional videos, and children's books in the domain. Designers should talk about the idea and the domain as much as possible.

Design is its own discipline, but in short, designers spend time inside the head of the players. Why do they want to play? What do they encounter? The game will change a lot between now and the end, but the moment-to-moment user experience should be thought out. Many design documents contain user stories or vignettes (see Patton, 2014). Designers should have fun and go down rabbit holes in this phase. Be sure that the document represents the thinking of each domain in game design, including artists, programmers, educators, and subject matter experts.

Less Talk, More Rock

We pause to introduce the concept of "less talk, more rock" (Superbrothers A/V & Boyer, n.d.). The concept is simple. The creative process begins with (1) inspiration. Designers next (2) talk about the idea—do all of the steps discussed in the previous section but in even greater detail. The bigger the organization, the more talking is required to explain, justify, or defend ideas. For academics, this talking is grant writing. Finally, much later, designers (3) actually make the thing. "Less talk, more rock" says skip the talking (step 2) and get to rocking as fast as possible. Make a version of the game early, whether it is a toy to play with or even a mockup. Paraphrasing developer Jordan Mechner, Superbrothers A/V & Boyer (n.d.) wrote:

> Go right from the inspiration—the vision—to actually making it. Don't think it through. Don't talk about it. Don't plan it. Dive in and start making it happen. If you do that—if you can start rocking—you'll get some momentum, and when you have some momentum then the project has a chance, because now you're into it. It's going somewhere, it's tangible. Sure, you'll still run up against problems to solve and decisions to make, but you'll approach these in the moment and solve them in the moment. You'll solve them so you can keep moving.

These experiences match mine. Anyone who wants to start with inspiration, skip the analysis, and just start making has my blessing. Showing a prototype to partners for feedback can often work better than talking about an idea anyway.

2. Prototyping (25 Percent)

Start building. The more prototyping-inclined (less talk, more rock) may have started already. We can divide prototyping into two broad approaches:

(1) developing a toy and (2) designing a vertical slice. Each approach has strengths and limitations (roughly mapping to a prototyping versus waterfall approach), which are determined by skills and context. Teams building toys might get away with a programmer or a programmer-artist, whereas teams building a vertical slice need to cover art, programming, subject matter expertise, pedagogy, sound and possibly user analytics, assessment, and web integration.

Those inclined toward prototyping will design a *playable toy*. Taking a toy-driven approach entails developing small, playable versions of the game and putting them in front of as many people as possible. Programmers will usually opt to make toys. This approach is best explicated by Colleen Macklin and John Sharp in *Games, Design, and Play* (2016). In *Fair Play*, our virtual lab prototype was a toy that helped us understand that people wanted to play with individuals' stories rather than the lab as a whole. The key to toys is to build them quickly to get data and be ready to throw them away. Building the wrong toy can cause problems if stakeholders confuse it for the final direction.

Large institutional contexts with funders usually require a *vertical slice*. A vertical slice, best explicated in the example of *At Play in the Cosmos*, is a playable version of one full aspect of the game system, such as a mission. A vertical slice can uncover the full pipeline of production tasks, which is helpful in understanding all of the development challenges early. In the *Cosmos* case, the vertical slice included player log-in systems, data management and integration, the mission, promotional media, game play videos, teacher tools, and assessment tools. Developing a master development list of early tasks can be critical for scoping an impact game and ensuring that project funding milestones are met and funders reassured.

Art Pipeline

Many academic teams use placeholder art (or ignore art altogether), and I hope this book has convinced readers of art's importance. Art in game design is its own discipline and beyond the scope of this chapter. However, much as in game design more broadly, there is a rough process in determining an art direction, developing high-resolution concept art, testing art with core audiences, refining art, working with the technology team to define art specifications and technology requirements, developing art for in-game use, polishing, play-testing, and refining with feedback. Our projects featured extensive art testing, and we liked to test art with dozens, if not hundreds, of youths in the target audience throughout production.

The prototyping and play-testing phase will reveal layers of interactions among game play, art, design, and user experience. Recall how in *Econauts* we engaged in several iterations of artwork to communicate pollution to players. Much work goes into ensuring that players can infer meaning from game animations (e.g., is that character sad in *Crystals of Kaydor*?). Developers cannot make these judgments; we are too familiar with the game to see it from the eyes of a new player.

Programmers

As programmers prototype, a tension emerges between developing serviceable code for demos to answer questions versus developing enduring, robust systems. If you are prototyping, *all of the code will be thrown away*. It is best to make this decision explicitly.

In my nonscientific experience, there are roughly two types of developers: those who excel at quick and dirty prototyping, especially kludging together prototypes that are good enough for testing (or research), and those who make scalable systems. It is critical to cast the right kind of programmer in the right role at the right time. Regardless, everyone needs to understand project goals, which phase production is in, and then where people's skills are best utilized.

Key production tasks for programmers in this phase are to tackle technological unknowns (can we sufficiently render facial animations in *Crystals of Kaydor*?), uncover technical limitations and challenges (such as the floating point issue in *At Play in the Cosmos*), understand and define technical specifications for designers and artists, and map out technical systems and requirements, which are critical when operating in institutional contexts. These include but are not limited to defining player log-ins, data tracking, achievements, and integration with other systems, such as learning management systems. Versions of each of these systems, even kludgy ones, will be put in place during prototyping.

Designers and Researchers

Educational and level designers spend their lives in documents and conducting field tests during the prototyping phase. Designers write levels, text for characters, and missions and integrate learning goals with game play.

Researchers study learners' playing to see what thinking emerges from game play. Simple game play sessions—with both students and experts—help validate that (1) game play captures disciplinary thinking and (2) students think more like experts in desired domains through game play (see Squire & Gaydos, 2012). Researchers develop and pilot instruments. Researchers and designers should work closely (or be the same graduate student) to scour the research literature, consider which data would constitute good evidence for completing project goals, and engineer game play moments to elicit those data (working with a data team). At the end, someone should conduct a pilot study with the vertical slice. This study need not be published research if that is not the goal; it could be a friends-and-family release to gather impressions.

Team Meeting Patterns

Developers work together closely, usually co-present. Developing games in this phase on academic calendars becomes tricky. Daily stand-up meetings and weekly play-tests maintain momentum. Project management techniques may differ, but most map backward from the final deliverable date, planning milestones along the way, including 20–30 percent extra for unanticipated events. The game developer Valve's design cabal framework is a great model for game developers in this phase (using a prototype-driven model, see Birdwell, 1999).

Outputs include vertical slices of working game play and evidence of desired impact occurring through play. Most games in this book were taken to this point.

3. Production (50 Percent)

Full-on production mode differs significantly by genre and project type. Of the games discussed in this book, only *Fair Play* and *At Play in the Cosmos* entered full production, and the chapter on *Cosmos* provides a feel for game production.[1] Team sizes and patterns differ by genre but can include artists, programmers, subject matter experts, and some mix of researchers and data scientists, depending on the project. Meeting schedules and teams are similar to the prototyping phase, although teams building a working toy will need to backtrack and create data systems and final art assets as needed. Here, game design might feel like paint by numbers: the prototype specifies what needs to be built. Success in this phase relies on good skills in game and project management, which is its own discipline. Since I started writing this book, films and documentaries on game development have exploded; learning game developers should become familiar with them (see Allgeier, 2017; Daglow, 2018; Schreier, 2017; Spaulding, 2009).

Prepare for Plot Twists

Learning games face unique challenges, and most learning games face at least one major turning point at which it seems that the game is not working. In *Fair Play*, bias events were not sufficiently clear, and game play needed to be more exciting. In *Cosmos*, game play was too linear. In *Citizen Science*, the story felt flat and we introduced a plot twist involving a pet muskrat trying to foil players. In most of our projects, there were "two games wrestling with each other" in this phase. My advice is to find the game that is most authentically tied to the impact goals and emphasize that, even if other ideas seem more fun. During production, developers and producers examine the game critically and address these needs as they arise. Development timelines and budgets need to leave cycles open for these changes. The best game companies "don't ship games until they are ready," which is not a luxury that most learning games specialists enjoy.

User Testing

User testing goes from focused testing in controlled, well-supported conditions to open, hands-off tests conducted in authentic contexts. By the time a game is in production, the team should be recruiting volunteer strangers. I prefer biweekly tests in controlled settings to keep developers in the habit of developing and testing features. In the Apple iWatch version of *Tenacity*, for example, we have given the devices to youths to take home and play with for a few weeks so that we can test core features, verify the basic hypothesis, detect patterns in play, and add final features as necessary. These tests are real deadlines that focus production and attune a team to an ethos of developing and testing.

Introducing learning tools based on user studies Untapped opportunities exist to build new learning mechanics based on observations of play. Most projects test after production is complete, for obvious reasons, but researchers uncover user patterns that might suggest new learning mechanics. In the *Progenitor X* example (chapter 5), I described how we identified opportunities to embed assessment questions in dialogue during play. In *Fair Play*, we found that embedding interactive quiz mini-games directly in the main story arc to reinforce experiences was engaging, relevant, and effective. Teams might explicitly save development cycles for integrating such features later in development.

Plan for polish Polish, one of the most important but least understood phases in game development, refers to making minor changes to the game that improve the user experience. In *Econauts*, for example, we changed the timing of producing units to quicken pacing, and we intensified the art so that pollution *felt* gross. Others commonly polish by tweaking audio and animations to create the right feel. Game feel, another critical concept, is brilliantly described by Steve Swink in *Game Feel: A Game Designer's Guide to Virtual Sensation*, also mandatory reading for game developers. In "The Art of Game Polish: Developers Speak," game developers reported preserving 10–20 percent of development time *beyond* buffers for overruns for polish (Zoss, 2009).

Most games run out of time, money, or both. Teams face difficult decisions about which features to keep and cut. Scoping conservatively enough to preserve time for polish is critical.

4. Service and Maintenance

Games, like any software, require maintenance and updates. Upgrades to operating systems, security patches, and upgrades to underlying frameworks, such as Flash or Unity, can render software outdated. The earliest developed games described in this book are now obsolete. Without ongoing revenue streams for updating, games go bad. Most development contracts contain some form of an ongoing service contract. Once digital platforms supplant or augment print ones, opportunities for games for impact should grow.

Designing monetization schemes is a critical part of contemporary game design, and commercial video games are pioneering new game business models worth attending to. The traditional distribution model, in which consumers purchase games from a store, is declining in importance, whereas subscription-based games, collectible card games, and now games with in-game purchases for extra downloadable content are increasing in influence. In 2018, *Fortnite*, a free game, generated $2.4 billion in revenue from in-game purchases (mostly player skins), and now even "traditional" console games (such as *Madden NFL*) offer in-game purchases. Publishers are experimenting with subscription services that enable unlimited play, similar to the way Netflix works. There are few good financial models of games for impact, but we should soon see integrated donation buttons. Examples could include donating inside *Econauts* and receiving a new level, with proceeds going to fund a research lab, or donating to a meditation app and receiving new content.

Subscriptions to learning games may someday be driven by learning analytics and personalized content. Imagine playing a learning game for free and then subscribing to a service that reveals your strengths and weaknesses as a learner, as well as offering custom-tailored learning experiences. The next section explores further these market considerations.

The Games for Impact Market

Subscriptions are a key opportunity for games for impact to supplant traditional publishing. Over the past few years, investors made the largest investments in history on educational technology, which will be used as a placeholder for the field more broadly. In 2020, global investments in learning technologies reportedly reached over $16 billion, which is over 32 times higher than the financial investments in 2010, and surging compared to recent record breaking years such as 2016 ($7.33 billion) and 2013 ($6.54 billion) (HolonIQ, 2021). Just which product or industry model transitions to digital is not certain. It could be a textbook company such as W. W. Norton & Company or a classroom management provider such as Canvas that publishes games. Perhaps Khan Academy will become a de facto textbook. An educational game developer such as Filament Games could combine its games with analytic tools and generate sufficient market capitalization to buy out a textbook company, as Riverdeep did in the early 2000s.

At least six factors contribute to these investments:

1. The proliferation of broadband-enabled mobile devices that constitute a stable distribution platform
2. New content delivery formats and genres, such as video on demand and digital learning games that are well suited for learning

3. Learning analytics that track users' behavior in games to measure learning
4. The emergence of global markets, most notably China and India, which can be served by digital delivery systems that leapfrog paper-based ones
5. A vacuum created by educational publishers' slow transition to digital publishing
6. New monetization models (e.g., sponsorship, advertising, or subscription)

To illustrate the potential disruption in educational publishing, consider that Khan Academy (largely funded by the Bill & Melinda Gates Foundation) has almost an entire K–16 curriculum over two thousand online videos that are chunked, sequenced, and organized for self-paced instruction across math, science, language, history, economics, and finance, in a free system. Khan Academy is an instructionist system (based on content delivery), but it resets the baseline for classroom instruction because it frees teachers from content delivery (Bonk et al., 2016; Wiley & Gurrell, 2009).

What is the role of games in this? A games for impact template can be found in *Ender's Game* or in *Ready Player One*. In these novels and films, learners tackle open-ended problem-solving missions (like a more open-ended version of *At Play in the Cosmos*) combined with focused skill-building activities as in *Progenitor X* or *Virulent*. The games discussed in this book are nowhere near the production level of *Ready Player One*, but the seeds are there. Consider combining the open-endedness of *Minecraft: Education Edition*, *Discovery Tour by Assassin's Creed: Ancient Egypt*, or *Plague Inc.* with gamified practice problems in something like Khan Academy or *ST Math*. Imagine if games assessed students as accurately as tests *and* assessed other dimensions, such as grit and collaborative problem solving.

The cost of developing games is an issue, but that equation will change as hardware platforms emerge. Right now, most educational materials, including textbooks, workbooks, and tests, are purchased by districts, at a cost of about $250 per student per year.[2] A company could give away an entry-level tablet (currently priced at $250, and assume a three-year life span) for an annual subscription rate that comes under this price point. My sixth-grade son currently carries fifteen pounds of textbooks and notebooks to school every day and would love this.[3] Google's Stadia, an up and coming cloud-based gaming service, is one way educational games could be a reality—especially if it flops in the entertainment space and Google seeks to repurpose it.

New platforms will combine digital materials, real-time tutoring, coaching and feedback (by machines or humans), and dynamic assessments. Outstanding questions exist:

- Could cheap games and videos disrupt publishing? Disruptive technologies evolve from cheap solutions and supplant traditional technologies (Christensen, 2009). Could a low-cost technology, such as Khan Academy, *ST Math*, or Virtual High Schools supplant textbooks?
- Does technology investment belong in education at all? Technology investors pour money into a company, gain market share, and then figure out a business model. As is the case with Amazon, Uber, and, famously, MoviePass, they disrupt first and worry about details later. Do we want to expose our educational system to this sort of capitalism?
- Do we trust big technology to make good curricular decisions—to build learning experiences around important, meaningful ideas? Do we trust our children's data in the hands of an industry with the mantra "Move fast and break things"? Do we trust tools of "surveillance assessment"? Approaches championed by technology companies may be instructionist and impervious to teacher input.

None of these questions will be settled as long as there is disagreement about end user hardware platforms. As long as schools oscillate between Chromebooks (which are quite poor for gaming) and tablets, we won't see much movement in K–12 publishing. The chief alternative, which is the right model for most academic projects, is open educational resources.

Open Educational Resources and Games for Impact

Open educational resources (OER) have similar goals, with perhaps more noble intentions. Open education is often taken to mean "free and online," but open education is better described as an intellectual movement (Grodecka & Sliwowski, 2014; Wiley & Gurrell, 2009). Open educational resources are anything made available under open licenses, meaning that anyone can use, reuse, and distribute them. Most online resources, such as Coursera and Khan Academy, are *currently* free, but they are not *open*; they are not shareable and reserve the right to alter the conditions of their availability, such as the ability to charge fees later. Further, "free" products aren't free to produce, distribute, or maintain. Downes (2006) outlined several models and examples under which open educational resources are sustained, including endowments (Stanford Encyclopedia of Philosophy), membership fees (the Sakai Educational Partners Program), donations (Wikipedia), conversion to pay (Linux), corporate sponsorship, government funding (Canada's SchoolNet), and institutional commitment and support (MIT OpenCourseWare). Many projects, notably MIT's OpenCourseWare, combine facets of each funding model within a single project.

Academics often default to open for the following reasons:

Open educational resources are promotional materials for universities and consistent with their mission to educate the public, particularly for public universities. If public universities have information (lectures, teaching materials), why not make them available to currently enrolled students? (See Wiley, 2008.) Why not alumni, or the state that supports them? Shouldn't the public have access?

Funders often require learning materials (e.g., syllabi, tutorials, videos, games) to be open and free. Mission-driven agencies, government and private, often fund universities to produce information for the public, such as curricula for teaching data sciences to elementary school students. Many grants exist to intercede where the market has not (e.g., no one has built a computer science curriculum for elementary school), so they *require* information to be in the public domain.

Open-access materials are often required for large-scale collaborative, multidisciplinary research tackling big problems. Much university activity is driven by tackling big problems (alternative energy, systemic racism, academic achievement) that generate educational materials. These usually require open access.

Faculty like to share information and benefit from public sharing of information. Faculty are evaluated in part through impact. Keeping research and teaching materials behind firewalls makes one irrelevant. Success in quantified metrics (such as the h-index) and qualitative ones (expert judgment) is increased by having one's work available.

Knowledge generation is ultimately an open enterprise. The most straightforward example of the benefits of open publishing may be academic conversations around syllabi. Sharing syllabi online enables instructors to share ideas, keep current, and improve teaching. Academics, particularly when advancing theoretical and social agendas, are incentivized to publish as openly as possible. Taken together, these point to a robust ecology of open materials, including free learning experiences.

Games in Open and Closed Systems

Software ecosystems are poised to divide into (1) an open, close-to-free system used in academics and (2) a closed, for-profit one used more broadly. Many scholars are queasy about closed data systems that hide their algorithms. Data-driven systems are only as good as the data that go into them and must account for social issues such as parents' income. Good systems also need to be transparent and include methods for correction when they are wrong (O'Neil, 2017).

Like many educational technologists, I got into this field in the hope that game-based technologies could be a vehicle for progressive pedagogy. The hope was to leverage educators' interest in technology to engage youths in meaningful problem solving, collaborative work, and creative expression. Much of my career has been built around the idea that we can ride the wave of enthusiasm for computers (later the internet and mobile devices) to channel the energy "going into technology" toward something progressive. Or, restated, if there is going to be technology investment, we can at least help ensure that it is used well. To not try to shape these movements is, to rephrase retired Stanford professor Robert Kozma, to be stuck standing on the sidelines of our own game.

A key lesson from this wave of work (see the discussion of *Econauts* in chapter 7) is that by the time a game or any technology goes through the steps required to secure funding, it starts to resemble the system that it enters more than something transforming it. In order to appeal to investors, a tool would need to work seamlessly within that system, including with existing assessment regimes, rather than transform them. Tools will need to be demonstrated to work in classrooms as they are; those requiring multiple age groups or community partnerships are going to get cut. Similarly, tools that seek to change *what* is taught will be redirected to teach old goals better. It is an open question as to whether any technology could transform schools, and it seems that schools are poised to change in response to laptops, mobile devices, and the internet, but the best bet for making change may be to work through personalized learning or data-driven decisions, which are frameworks that currently have purchase in schools (Halverson, 2019).

Game developers should also be wary of investors. Investors often want games, like *Econauts*, to be so fleshed out that it is not clear what investors would bring. We were asked to finish game levels, expand the game across the curriculum, generate research results (ideally demonstrating how it outperforms other methods) and a base of paying customers; at that point, why would we need investors? Successful, highly valued curricular reforms can go for *years* without achieving findings of this sort, because of the importance of teachers, student interest, or socioeconomic status as mediating variables (see Dynarski et al., 2007). Most investors have little experience with education, and how long do you think they would go before turning games into interactive worksheets? Would they be willing to forgo easy profits to have higher-quality curricula? Having watched Filament Games, the Learning Games Network, and other companies meet with investors, I am only more inclined to question the role of for-profit institutions in education.

Finally, we need to ask whether efforts to create high-quality, data-driven digital learning experiences will ultimately help or hinder good educational practices. Will quality games give teachers more autonomy, creativity, and flexibility, or will they continue their deprofessionalization? Our approach has to been to create flexibly adaptive materials that teachers use to engage youths in authentic learning experiences. Ideally, game play comprised about 20 percent of learning experiences, as in the play → explore → study → build cycle described for *Econauts*. The culmination of a curriculum should usually be *making or doing* something, ideally something that works in the world. My enthusiasm for games for impact has been an attempt to leverage their collaborative, constructionist, and transgressive qualities as models for enacting participatory learning models (see Squire, 2003). Now that games for impact are no longer novel, we may need to re-center these to more enduring values.

I would love for my own kids to learn microbiology by being a virus, health by trying to cure cancer, or astronomy by leading a team deep into space. I want them to be curious, active learners who are fully emotionally engaged at school, which they are not through memorization and worksheets. At the same time, if we outsource curricular decisions to data-driven processes, curricular control moves further away from learners' interests. My own concerns as a parent of two school-aged children are less about their academic achievement and more that schools, especially high-performing suburban schools, crush their curiosity, reduce learning goals to memorization, force them to conform to narrow learning experiences defined by technocrats, and offer no opportunities to pursue passions (or even decide what they want to learn) until they leave public education.

Conclusions: Games for Impact in Institutions Such as Schools

If the games discussed in this book, and games made more broadly, are so good, then why haven't we seen more of them? Why do we have *Plague Inc.*, *Minecraft*, and *Assassin's Creed: Origins Discovery Tour* but not educational versions of *Virulent*, *Anatomy Pro-Am*, *Econauts*, or *At Play in the Cosmos*? Why have these products not gone to market, or, stated more broadly, why have games for impact largely remained hobbyist activities and failed to permeate formal institutions such as schools?

Efforts to promote the adoption of games in institutions such as schools have struggled because of (1) inconsistent and insufficient hardware platforms, (2) inadequate purchasing and distribution platforms, (3) economic moats, and, most important, (4) contradictions between games and schools. The first three factors are relatively straightforward and do not need much explication. In the mid-2010s, schools adopted Chromebooks rather than iPads or Windows machines, and Chromebooks are horrible gaming devices. Critically, just as Unity gathered steam as a powerful game development platform, schools invested in machines incapable of doing much with 3D games.

The more important challenge for educators is how these technologies fit within the social organization of institutions such as schools. The hope of progressives has been that games-based approaches would empower learners (or patients in health care) to have greater autonomy. Learning would be oriented toward problem solving, collaboration, and creativity (Squire, 2002). The attraction of games, as articulated by Gee (2004), was how they embodied the values of situated pedagogy and could be models for instruction. Assessment would be ongoing and formative, and students would have a greater say in making claims over their own competency, just as personalized health care seeks to empower patients to make better decisions.

We are reminded, however, that reforming schools is a perennial challenge. Schools exist, to no small extent, to sort kids into tracks for social classes (Domina et al., 2017). An increasingly hypercompetitive society drives middle-class parents toward high-performing schools as defined by such metrics, which increases pressure on teachers and administrators. Websites such as greatschools.org compound this pressure as property values become tied to test scores. As a result, teachers and principals are under

Conclusions

enormous pressure to meet quantified metrics such as increased test scores, in some cases with teachers' pay being tied to test scores (Shifrer et al., 2017). Games do nothing to reinforce this sorting function, and in fact they probably run counter to them.

Middle-class parents, especially those in technical fields, are aware of these limitations and are enrolling students in after-school and summer programs in increasing numbers. If I were to bet on the future of learning games, it would be in an open-ended gaming and modding community that featured something like our play → explore → study → build model being implemented in informal settings. One can imagine a game like *Econauts*, particularly if it supported scripting as a way to teach programming, as an effective way to drive interest in learning outside of school.

Coda: Making Impact in Universities

Games for impact programs are often cutting-edge experiments for the university. They are how universities experiment with online learning, digital content development, or private-public partnerships. Games programs are not the *only* site where innovation occurs, and in fact engineering faculty are often ahead of us. But as a young field, we have emerged through new mechanisms, such as transdisciplinary institutes or cost recovery programs, and fought for space and legitimacy. Further, many of us are not satisfied with laboratory studies that suggest impact; we want to make it through research, products, or even companies that take these ideas to scale.

This chapter reflects on what institutional innovations might teach us about the future of the university more broadly. It touches briefly on academic capitalism and the modern university, describes how projects are funded and staffed, and shares some lessons learned from doing this work. I try to capture "the stuff no one tells you," particularly the ins and outs of issues that students ask about most often.

Academic Capitalism

The modern university is changing. We are moving from an era of exploding enrollments, expansive public funding, and stable costs to one of stabilizing enrollments, shrinking public funding, and soaring costs.

External Factors
The good news is that the alarm bells that permeated education in the mid-2010s have subsided. Enrollments are at historic highs, and higher education remains a crucial path toward social and material advancement. In

the United States, 20.5 million students are enrolled in higher education, which is a huge increase over my generation (13.5 million enrolled in 1990; Hussar & Bailey, 2018). Society regards a prestigious college degree as a form of social and cultural capital, as evidenced by the college admissions bribery scandals that emerged in 2019. Parents across income brackets see participation in college as an important part of personal fulfillment. Employers use higher education as a sorting mechanism, for better or for worse, as indeed does society as a whole.

The public is slowly turning its back on higher education, through declines first in state support and then in federal research support (Newfield, 2016; Slaughter & Leslie, 1997). The declining state support for education in the United States is well documented elsewhere and primarily creates rising tuition.[1] Increased tuition also makes funding of research more expensive, since grants pay students' tuition.

More important, federally funded research is nowhere near the national priority it was after World War II. Government funding for academic research was seen as a security issue because it helped establish US dominance during the cold war. Higher education is no longer seen as the front line of the cold war, and as a result fiscal and social conservatives see higher education as an easy target. Research has fallen from about 25 percent of discretionary federal spending to around 10 percent today, at the same time that research in health care and technology has exploded (Newfield, 2010).

Activity-Based Budget Models
Universities have reacted by changing their internal structures to be more adaptable. They have moved from historical budgeting (you get the same budget as last year plus or minus some) to budgets based on metrics. Internal resources are increasingly allocated through internal metrics (such as credit hours or federal grant dollars; see Rhoades & Slaughter, 2009). University leaders hope that people further down in the organizational hierarchy will be empowered to initiate change. In theory, this method (also called activity-based budgeting) displaces budgeting authority from the top (in historical budgeting, all decisions flow from senior administration) and toward faculty (Gallagher, 2011; Slaughter & Rhoades 2004). Faculty are empowered to form centers and fundraise around efforts that they regard as important, start new initiatives where they can find demand, and dissolve

efforts that are no longer useful, which bureaucracies somewhat famously struggle to do.

Most games scholars have run into the limits of historical budgeting: academic departments coalesce around the ideas of previous generations so that innovative questions (like games) that sit between fields are falling between the cracks. For a long time, games researchers weren't hired at all because they were not really computer scientists, nor psychologists, nor humanities scholars.

Unfortunately, activity-based budgeting exacerbates the widening gap between the haves and have-nots (see Hearn et al., 2006). "Hot" areas that attract students or grant dollars (such as games) are resourced, while traditional areas suffer. Universities risk overinvesting for short-term gains at the expense of areas of enduring importance, such as philosophy. The humanities in particular wrestle with these issues, at a time when we need deep thinking about the purposes of education, learning, and what it means to be human (Gee, 2020).

Funding

These pressures all intersect to increase pressure for external funding. Competition for federal grants is especially fierce because federal grants also add prestige. Not only do they fund graduate students; they also contribute to multiple components of national rankings, such as federal grant dollars brought in, research expenditures, and number of funded graduate students.[2] Faculty are evaluated by their record in winning grants and their potential to earn new ones, which has a series of cascading effects. The short-term response of faculty is increased time spent writing and administering grants, fundraising with private donors, and engaging in "entrepreneurial activities," such as forging partnerships with industry or starting cost-recovery programs.

The result is a death spiraling effect on faculty whereby they spend more time writing grants. The more that faculty compete for grants, the more the demand for research dollars increases (while the supply of research dollars holds steady, if not shrinks; AAAS, 2017). Researchers report declines in grant success rates across fields, and in some social science fields, the success rate for National Science Foundation (NSF) grants is below 5 percent (Gallup & Svare, 2016). This competition creates more uncertainty for faculty competing for grants, which means more competition for grants or a search for new revenue streams altogether, such as private contracts, licensing of intellectual property, or cost recovery programs.

Could private contracts offset cuts in public funding? Might there be blue ocean scenarios in which if the lab sells a product, it funds a generation of students? These are in part the motivations for researchers to embrace new models.

Spanning Discovery to Delivery

Although the gold rush for impact games has subsided, the future of games for impact looks healthy. Games for impact programs attract students, grant dollars, and headlines. And as long as faculty are required to teach game development, universities will be incentivized to study how game development techniques are applied to social problems (e.g., learning, health, or the environment). I expect the next wave of innovations to come from these programs. A small team of undergraduates can do in a capstone class what once took several full-time staff members months to do. If even a percentage of ten thousand students in game programs shows interest in games for impact, an explosion of games can occur. Game students using Unity and Steam could match the explosion of documentary films supported by cheap digital cameras and video editing and digital distribution (Netflix, Vimeo, Hulu, YouTube).

I'm personally betting on the *Minecraft* generation making games for me to play through my retirement, so get on it.

Faculty and graduate students often ask specific questions about how centers are funded and staffed, which this section fleshes out. Funded projects typically fit into one of five categories (see below, detailed in the table that follows):

1. *Government grants (e.g., NSF)* are awarded through competitive review. Lengthy timelines, paperwork, and reimbursement spending models challenge small organizations. These are the tentpole projects that should drive an academic center.
2. *Private foundation grants* are driven by the lab's reputation and sponsor's priorities.
3. *Government contracts* (e.g., through DARPA, the Defense Advanced Research Projects Agency) are competitive responses to agency requests.

They require institutional capacity, knowledge of agencies, and significant oversight.

4. *Private contracts* are initiated by private groups. They want a university's expertise and reputation but balk at university costs and timelines.
5. *Local partnerships.* Companies, individuals, and agencies (often alumni) partner with universities to tackle local problems. Projects are smaller in size but often rewarding.

The different funding models cover different parts of the research spectrum (basic, applied, translational, outreach and dissemination). *Basic research* is funded largely by federal grants. *Applied* research can be funded

Revenue source	Primary focus	Life cycle phase	Good for	Limitations
Government grants	Areas of established scientific concern	Researching ideas already developed, large-scale research	Empirical research on valued problems	Difficult to fund art and design
Private foundation grants	High-risk research, social impact	Early spadework, late dissemination	Funding students, unusual expenses (travel), public-facing work	Smaller amounts, difficult for large-scale technology development
Government contracts	Applying technologies to solve problems	Implementation of research and scaling	Scaling impact, researching interventions in contexts	Require infrastructure, administrative oversight, reputation, logistics, and planning
Private contracts	Developing products at scale that work in the world	Toward the end of a project once it has demonstrated impact or efficacy	Funding specialized talent (art, design) or technological infrastructure	Require investment of time in nurturing partners, legal overhead; often will not cover research costs
Local partnerships	Leveraging university expertise to solve problems	Dissemination	Outreach and dissemination	Little money; won't cover base costs

by federal grants as well as by mission-driven government agencies and sometimes industry. *Translational* research (applying techniques to solve real problems) is similarly funded by agencies but also can be funded by local partners. *Outreach and dissemination* are usually funded by local partners but occasionally by grants.

Becoming an Entrepreneurial Center

Federal grants and local partnerships flow naturally from academic activities, but executing private contracts is usually beyond what universities do well. Contracts require resources to generate publicity, engage the public, monitor practitioner problems, and network. In my experience, universities do not address the following issues, and anyone seeking to be entrepreneurial within the university must do so.

1. *Business development does not exist.* Game groups need to attend industry meetings, maintain visibility, and visit partners to generate business and monitor the landscape, which requires basic travel funds.
2. *Client work requires dedicated communications.* Communication specialists sharpen messaging, manage social media presence, work with the press, and identify new opportunities. Timely communications are crucial with funders that expect immediate responses and same-day meetings (which are not practical for faculty).
3. *Financial management is geared toward federal grant reporting, not project planning.* Universities struggle to support fine-grained staff allocations and expenditure tracking required by contract or for forecasting. Managing multiple projects with different spending rules, start and end dates, and staff allocations is consuming.
4. *Purchasing processes are designed to ensure responsible use of public funds, not agile software development.* Universities (particularly public universities) adopt spending rules for responsible stewardship of public funds. Purchases of game equipment, awards of subcontracts to consultants, and travel to nice locations can look suspicious. However, private funders expect teams to purchase games and subscriptions, hire outside help, and attend meetings as needs arise, regardless of what an original budget proposed.
5. *Human resource processes are not geared to a creative or technical industry.* Universities' job designations and policies do not align with those of

game staff. Most obviously, talented artists might not have advanced degrees, and programmers cannot be paid market rates (even if funders would pay them). More subtly, game teams evolve rapidly and are hired, promoted, retrained, and laid off in ways unusual to universities.

These challenges can be addressed by administrative support, but university leadership must see these problems as worth solving. Even the most supportive leaders (as we had) can be surprised by these entrenched roadblocks. A popular backup plan is to start a private nonprofit with the explicit purpose of supporting the game lab's research.

Core services to games for impact Making games for impact (or any entrepreneurial activity) requires building core services beyond traditional research, in the following five areas:

(1) *Branding and web services.* Working with clients requires graphic and web design capacities on par with the private sector. We used them extensively for meeting materials, project websites, and conferences, and soon our team was in high demand across campus. A modern web team can pay for itself at most universities.

(2) *Outreach specialist and teacher liaison.* Outreach specialists are the primary point of contact for teachers, students, and educators and are the face of the organization to service providers. An outreach coordinator to manage all outreach experiences (which we called PlaySquads) was invaluable. Our PlaySquad teams were composed of five to seven undergraduates and three to four graduate students, and they created learning materials, supported curricular enactments, collected data, and supported researchers conducting studies. Outreach specialists also helped game developers find participants for user tests. An outreach specialist can be a former teacher, but our best ones had (a) completed advanced graduate study in education, (b) regional recognition as innovative teachers, and (3) an entrepreneurial orientation.

(3) *Outreach database.* A database of all outreach activities helps coordinate fieldwork across multiple investigators and projects. Included in this database are all teacher demonstrations, teacher training materials, open house events, and direct student contact through play sessions and train-the-trainer sessions. Codirector Richard Halverson left the GLS Center to create a collaborative learning network to support research collaborations. Modern games groups should create lifelong learning networks so that all

citizens (but especially students and teachers) partner with the university to further their education and training. Games groups are well poised to house such efforts because they often have professional staff in-house in areas from 3D art to web programming to hardware hacking.

(4) *Learning analytics specialists.* A data management specialist coordinates data infrastructure across projects. Within our lab, this role managed ADAGE (Assessment Data Aggregator for Game Environments), our framework for capturing, storing, and analyzing data. Ideally a permanent research scientist, the data management specialist develops and maintains research instruments and is the point person on data gathering across games. The learning analytics specialist enables researchers to deploy surveys to students in-game or to mine player clickstream data (see Ramirez, 2016).

(5) *Institutional Review Board (IRB) specialists.* An IRB is an institutional review board that provides assurances that researchers are engaging in research ethically. A dedicated IRB specialist is essential for achieving a useful economy of scale. Thematic research centers can run twenty-five simultaneous active IRBs, and a designated specialist can coordinate research instruments so that faculty and students can respond to emerging opportunities. For example, a graduate student researching an emerging phenomenon (such as *Pokémon GO!*) might work through the IRB coordinator to amend an existing IRB and get into the field quickly. Partners often contact the center about an opportunity to study something on a quick turnaround, such as running a game design program on a school holiday. An IRB coordinator also helps coordinate across school districts, each of which has its own rules.

Making games for impact within a university is a challenge but is possible. The biggest hurdle is overcoming a culture that rewards individual achievements rather than making impact. Making impact requires courtesy meetings, classroom site visits, and countless administrative meetings of all sorts. We often prioritized making a real impact in the world (making playable games, visiting classrooms, supporting teachers with our materials) over traditional research, probably to our detriment. Other academic groups focused on impact reported similar experiences.

Becoming an Internal Change Agent

Institutions invest in a games for impact center as a strategy to adapt to the digital age. Maybe the imaginative, subversive nature of our community also reminds aging administrators of an earlier time when they had dreams. Anyway, for the time being, games for impact leaders are in the middle of institutional innovation. Innovation sounds exciting enough; what's not to like about changing things? The reality is that innovation means confronting policy because, in the words of Carmen Medina, a former director of the Center for the Study of Intelligence at the Central Intelligence Agency, "innovation is the opposite of policy." As Medina (2019) wrote:

> Policy incorporates what the past has told us about the best way to do something—and let me just say that the "best way" incorporates a whole set of assumptions that merit examination. For example, organizations often think that smooth operations are the **BEST** operations; the desire for smoothness, however, can trample over other good things such as diversity of thought and trying out new ideas.

Convincing people to change operations is hard, and these challenges persist across government agencies, textbook publishers, and software publishers. Most of us realize too late that our real job is as an organizational change manager. We have already failed to nurture relationships with administrators, understand institutional pressures, or cultivate goodwill across the organization.

Making games for impact requires alignment with (and management of) institutional leadership. Game development attracts many people who view authority, at best, with skepticism. This attitude, which is cultivated in many areas of academics, is a hindrance to making change. The first job of a change agent is to "understand your boss and gain credibility" (Kelly et al., 2014). In *Rebels at Work*, Medina and colleagues (Kelly et al., 2014) lay out two foundational tasks for change agents: "1. Understand what most worries your boss and find ways to ease those worries, and 2. Build credibility and trust with your boss." Few academics think of "managing bosses" (or even having them), but successful innovation within an institution requires support from and alignment with institutional leaders (deans, center directors).

Innovation requires partnering with administrative staff. Administrative staff enact policy in most institutions. Academic *leadership* (chancellors, deans) know little about business processes and regulations, have little discretionary budgetary power, and, crucially, are impermanent. Administrative staff maintain organizational compliance, interpret written policies, translate regulations for leaders, and safeguard institutional memory. The same is true in government, where elected leaders and political appointees come and go. Change agents must embrace working closely with administrators to learn the dark arts of bureaucratic jiujitsu (see Kelly et al., 2014). Tackling challenges is our job.

Making games for impact (or doing entrepreneurial research) within a large organization benefits from unrestricted funding and may not be possible without it. Unrestricted funding allows investment in new areas, bridging across grants, and seed money for travel or other business development activities. Running a research and development lab is like running a small business within a larger parent company (which is also like an investor). It requires attention to business functions such as cash flow, liquidity, market analysis, and short-term, midterm, and long-term projections. Having resources to invest in emerging areas is enormously beneficial; hype cycles drive funding.

Making games for impact requires attending to changing, often conflicting metrics of success, attuning staff to any changes. Competing priorities (research results versus broad impact, different target markets) are challenging and stressful to staff. Further, artists, programmers, educators, evaluators, experimental psychologists, ethnographers, and teacher coordinators have different value sets and priorities. In any academic capitalist milieu, the environment changes rapidly, and attuning teams to shifting priorities is critical.

Managing change within a team means balancing needs for a consistent core staff with new skills and fresh ideas. A consistent team is valuable when delivering products on deadline. Development practices become routinized. Pipelines and conventions are established. A culture and way of working emerges. Research labs, in contrast, are driven by transient people (students and postdocs) who are recruited for specific expertise or serendipity. Fresh combinations of people lead to innovation. Researchers need to be mindful of tensions between staff committed for the long term (who live locally and build careers through the center) and transient people. Graceful entrances and exits need to be planned.

Entrepreneurial teams should pay extra *attention to traditional academic metrics (competitive research grants, peer-reviewed publications, and students attracted, graduated, and placed in the academy).* Development teams attracting significant outside resources are particularly subject to critique. Some criticism is driven by envy and cannot be avoided, but it is also easy to let production deadlines supplant conference proposals or other academic deadlines (particularly if it means laying off key staff). We hoped that veteran developers could manage business development, but nonacademics generated few business opportunities. It may be that running such a lab requires institutional support for business development to be sustainable.

The Future of Making Games for Impact in the Entrepreneurial University

As the context for academics changes, we may no longer have a choice but to forge new partnerships. Academic funding is changing, and the students we graduate face a different world. In most fields, the vast majority of graduate students will not occupy academic positions. There is more competition for fewer positions, and there are even higher expectations to raise external funds. An integrated research and development context is invaluable for anyone working as a researcher. Students gain experiences working in cross-functional teams and contributing to products with real deadlines. Indeed, we may be *obligated* to prepare students for this entrepreneurial world, in which they will respond to emerging trends and changing landscapes.

It is tempting to imagine that games for impact programs will thrive at universities because they can attract students, generate revenue, or place students in industry, but none of those factors really supports the main purpose of the university, which is to accrue social capital (creating and perpetuating class for its members; see Bourdieu, 1996). Games for impact centers and their next-generation equivalents cannot simply rely on internal metrics because they do not, fundamentally, solve institutional problems, unless the school is struggling for students. In an age of competitive college enrollments, universities themselves will have students; attracting students across majors is a zero-sum game within the institution. Likewise, raising external contract funds is great for the center but does not affect metrics by which universities are ranked. In fact, raising millions in contracts mostly just creates risk and adds extra work for administrators.[3] It is far better for these activities to leave the university by being "spun out," which, in today's environment that values (or fetishizes) entrepreneurship, is an important source of social and political capital. Creating jobs to bolster the local economy is in most states an important social and political point. Still, as most entrepreneurial academics will tell you, creating local jobs is not *really* valued.

We are reminded that universities exist to generate knowledge, but more than that, they exist to amplify social and cultural capital for the institution as a whole. To succeed, a games for impact initiative needs to reinforce this core function of raising prestige. If done correctly, games that truly create impact *can* reinforce social capital. They can spread the impact of a university and help its brand. Framing the value in terms of adding to social capital adds even more pressure, however, to ensure that games for impact are of high quality. It means doubling down to ensure that the struggles described here—hiring good artists, doing good science, and attending to teachers' needs—are not ignored. Most likely, the value for such centers will truly be realized years later as the ideas and students developed through such programs make their way into the world.

Examples such as the relationship of the Harvard Graduate School of Education with the *Sesame Street* franchise suggest paths forward for impact games. The future of games for impact in the university is in reconciling the local need to secure resources (e.g., liberal arts programs co-opting games to thrive in a competitive landscape) with the university's purpose to generate social and cultural capital. For universities not located in major technological hubs, such centers might create social capital by being a link to the modern world and economy. As someone who has recently relocated to California after decades in the midwestern United States, the differences between the "flyover states" and coastal centers of wealth are striking. For many institutions, simply putting students in conversation with the modern technology world will be valuable. Other institutions may value patents, start-ups, or even celebrity.

Games for impact is now an established enterprise, so much so that some of these lessons may no longer be necessary. The next wave of media and technology for impact, whether it be artificial intelligence learning assistants or brain-computer interfaces, will fit similar patterns, though. My hope is that this volume contributes to our understanding of both making games for impact and making impact from the university more generally. As computational technologies invade more and more of our lives, it is not enough for academics to be theoreticians or even critics; I argue that we need to lead by helping shape the realities that we want to see. In the progressive tradition of John Dewey, we have an obligation to test our theories by seeing how they work in the world. Computational technologies will further shape how we think, learn, and interact, to the point at which transhumanism is an inevitability (and perhaps it is already here; see Harari, 2017).

I suspect, however, that games for impact will continue to play a decisive role in these discussions. At their core, games are simulated systems that structure interactions, and as such, they are powerful metaphors for understanding technological systems for humans. The ideas that we understand as game designers, creating engagement, shaping emotional reactions, structuring social interaction, are enduring. Similarly, the flip side of that question—How do we gather scientists, teachers, artists, and programmers to invent new kinds of experiences in reticent institutions?—resonates across technologies.

Acknowledgments and Dedication

This book is dedicated to everyone who collaborated on this work. I hope that I've represented your experiences and the work fairly. We shared the vision of making learning more engaging and meaningful for kids, and at times we succeeded. In some places, we fell short. This opportunity to work with you was the culmination of a longtime dream to assemble the team(s) that we did, and I want to thank you. Writing this book helped me better understand how much we did accomplish, and I hope that it gives you some amount of pride as well. This book really is the result of all of our work, not just my own, so these acknowledgments will read a little like the credits from a mid-1980s Metallica record. My apologies. As proud as I am of the work we did together, I'm even more proud of the work that everyone is doing now.

First, thanks to Doug Sery at MIT Press for taking on this project, help in shaping the vision, and insights throughout the process. I hope that we can work together again soon. Thank you Patricia Harris at WPS and everyone at MIT Press for the careful editing and patience pulling this together!

I need to acknowledge that the bulk of the work described here was done in close collaboration with Rich Halverson, who also deserves credit for whatever we accomplished. Everything in this book was the result of a shared vision that you helped inspire and create – from the nuts and bolts (directing *Virulent* and ADAGE), to helping create the vision for the GLS Center and teaching me about how organizations work. Much of what is in this book is the result of your thinking, and whatever parts aren't, are possible only because of your selfless support. More important, you were and are a great friend. Thank you.

Erica, thanks for supporting us. The energy, ideas, and people you brought to GLS helped make it what it was, not to mention everything you've taught me about studio-based education. I can't wait to read your book. We both miss you both.

Thanks go to Andy Phelps and Jaksa Cvitanic for feedback on early drafts. I need to also thank Andy for his friendship and guidance as a fellow traveler. I've learned so much from you about how any of this is done and wouldn't be where I am today without you. Thanks. I'd like to thank Ben Sawyer for his thoughts, edits, and friendship, which gave me the confidence to finish this over the pandemic, as well as sharing parenting advice and bringing Izzy along for adventures. Thank you Dan Jacobsohn for sharing late night chats, early morning runs, and wisdom on innovation and organizations, and you had the right idea getting out of this racket. Maybe I'll join you soon. I'd like to thank Jon Roketenetz, David Simutis, Adrian Martin, and Mike Beam for insights on everything.

I'd like to thank the folks at Filament Games for their help and collaboration, especially in the early phases of this work. I've learned so much about game design from all of you (Dan Norton, Dan White, and Alex Stone, but also Monica Marlo and others), and I hope the chapters describing our collaboration do it justice. I continue to learn from you all and find inspiration in your work, and I hope to game again with you soon, Mr. Norton. I miss you.

Thank you to Sangtae Kim and Susan Millar for inviting Rich Halverson and me to become a part of the Morgridge Institute for Research. Sang your investments in us made this book possible. You extended my horizons of what was even possible. You were tireless advocates for us and taught me to dream big and think beyond traditional methods of impact. In short, you ruined me, so thank you. You, too, Rock Mackie. You also ruined me. Susan, you and Terry were like a second family to us during stressful times, and we will always remember it. You are good people.

David Krakauer was equally ruinous, having transmitted the virus of a biologically grounded, nonreductionist social science for studying complex information flows in naturally occurring environments. David, you invested far more time in meetings about parking and human resources policies than any one person should have to in a lifetime. Thanks for your investment in us. With this book now behind me, I look forward to a pilgrimage to SFI and doing real work.

Thank you, Julie Underwood, a tireless, but more important, incredibly *effective* leader who not only understood our vision but also enabled our

Acknowledgments and Dedication

work to continue in our times of need. I will never forget what you did for us, particularly you calling us in Germany having sorted out another mess. You are a star. The last two-thirds of this book happened because of you. Thank you.

I'd like to thank Richard Davidson, Molly Carnes, Michael Ferris, and Steve Carpenter at UW-Madison for being exceptional collaborators who not only shaped this intellectual work, but taught me how to be a professor in the world. Richie, you in particular went to bat for us when we needed it, which we will always be grateful for. You are all excellent people who have helped make Madison a special place, and I hope that I take some of your spirit with me.

Thanks to Matthew Berland for collaborating on *Virulent*, Studio K, the table projects (which were largely your creation), and everything computer science and data related. You helped make GLS what it was in the last few years, and your expertise in data analytics, procedural literacy, and computational thinking made much of this work possible. Thanks also for getting me to try cyclo-cross. Let's collaborate on something!

None of this would have been remotely possible without the guidance of James Paul Gee. Jim laid the foundation for our group, and this work was in many ways the realization of his vision. Thank you, Jim, for continuing to be a wonderful mentor and friend. I lean on things you've taught me almost every day.

I need to thank our partners and funders who made this work possible. Elizabeth VanderPutten at the National Science Foundation has been a longtime funder and advocate for this work, for which I'm deeply grateful. Jan Kolodner and Chris Hoadley supported the latter phases of this work, and the last few chapters were inspired by Jan's criticisms and thoughts. I hope that I've been able to capture the real things that we learned from this work, beyond the story normally written.

Eric Bauman, Alex Games, Doug Russell, and Rob Bellinger were all incredibly important partners, and without your support this book could not have been written. Your trust and support for GLS made this all something interesting beyond the typical research lab. Eric and Alex, it was a real treat to work with you as colleagues as well as former students, and I look forward to when our professional paths cross again. Rob, let's bike together some day.

I like to thank my current students, Maria Anderson Coto, Max Collins, Francis Persa, Richard Martinez, Lika Liu, and Rose O'Leary for your work on Tenacity, misinformation, and ideas, contributions, and commitment to this generation of GLS. Thanks to Richie Poon, Dishanth Shankar, Caleb Chu, Jackson Greaves, and Zach Cloutier for your exceptional work on Tenacity. Richie and Dish—you guys really knocked it out of the park. With this book behind me, I can't wait to see what we do!

The heart and soul of this book is, of course, the graduate students and staff who really did the work. In roughly chronological order, I'd like to start by thanking Nathan Patterson and Ben Shapiro, who led *Virulent* and *Anatomy Pro-Am*, respectively, and really made those projects go. Nathan, your fearless leadership in those early days got this off the ground. I'd like to thank the *Virulent* team of Terra Lauterbach, Mike Beall, Kevin Harris, Matthew Gaydos, Moses Wolfenstein, Terra Javier Corredor, and Heinrich Soebke for creating the proof of concept with very little road map, as well as John Yin for welcoming the collaboration. I'd like to thank Erin Robinson for coming to work with us, and teaching me by example what an exceptional game designer does. The *Anatomy Pro-Am* team of Rock Mackie, Dr. Lonie Salkowski, Greg Vaughan, Shannon Harris, Ben Shapiro, David van Leeuwen, and Katja Halverson, and Filament Games, similarly did amazing work with remarkably few resources and insufficient guidance on my part. Ben also led *Trails Forward* and was instrumental in our vision for crowdsourced science, and he has more good ideas go by in a semester than most people have in a career. Ben, I look back and see that my best and most fun work came from riffing ideas with you. You're brilliant, and I hope that we can work together again soon, perhaps I'll work for you some day.

The bulk of the games in the book were created by an era of students—Meagan Rothschild, Liz Owen, David Hatfield, Sarah Chu, Breanne Litt, Amanda Ochsner, Shannon Harris, Caro Williams, Wade Berger, Ryan Martinez, Rex Beaber, Amanda Barany, Dennis Paiz-Ramirez, Clem Samson-Samuel, Sean Seyler, Mark Stenerson, Adam Mechtley, Jonathan Elmergreen, and Gabriella Anton—which was among the favorite of my career. You all handled the chaos and roller-coaster ride exceptionally well, again with minimal guidance. Thank you for forming and making the community that you did, which was the engine for this work. I want to thank Meagan and Dennis in particular for leading (1) our teacher community and (2) cognitive bias games. Both of you took on WAY more than you ever should have been allowed to. It's no surprise that you are both stars now. Perhaps I would gladly come work for you some day.

Acknowledgments and Dedication

Thanks to Mark Stenerson, Craig Anderson, Jennifer Dalsen, Steffan Slater, Emily Mabie, and Keari Bell-Gawne for work on *Virulent*, *Econauts*, *Trails Forward*, and *At Play in the Cosmos*. Thanks to Steffan, who pretty much ran the data analytics effort for a while as an undergraduate. I'd love to collaborate some day. Thanks to Jennifer, Emily, and Keari for your enthusiasm and for stepping up and running with projects amid the chaos. Craig and Mark, I think of you as running the anchor leg of GLS, stepping up to keep things going over the home stretch. Mark, *Econauts* would never have happened without you as glue. You raised the quality of work around you, and I realize now more than ever what you contributed to that project and the lab as a whole, and I want to thank you for your tireless creative problem solving. Craig led many of the late-stage efforts around *Virulent* as well as basically functioning as a postdoc while I wrote this book, and I want to thank you for your positive organizing energy across the life of this book.

Thanks to Jonathan Elmergreen for managing GLS and Constance's life, which is by extension mine as well. I miss you. This is also a good place to thank Katie Friedl, Megan Rothschild, and Lizzie Smith for helping raise our kids. None of this is possible without you.

Speaking of which, thanks to Walter and Warner Squire for listening to me discuss drafts and putting up with crankiness between edits.

Thanks to Eric Klopfer, Scot Osterweil, and Ira Sockowitz for your support and work with the Learning Games Network. Thank you, Ira, for your countless hours of time and effort helping us right the ship. Thanks to Eric and Scot for riding the LGN chapters out together. I'd gladly share a foxhole with either of you. In case I haven't said it enough, though, in addition to being incredibly smart and savvy, Eric, you are a role model for how to be a good colleague and academic. Scot, you are possibly the best learning game designer I've met.

I really have to thank the developer team that was the heart and soul of the second half of this saga and who showed infinite patience with constant organizational reshuffling. Working with you all was a personal and professional highlight for me, and through writing this book I've come to terms with the fact that I'll likely not get another chance like this. I learned so much from all of you; there's no way that I could have written this book, or teach in the position I am in now, without you. Brian Pelletier—I learned a great deal about game design, game production, and working with people from you. Your kind spirit and sense of humanity were centering for all of us, as was your inspirational work. Watching you work was a real treat. Thanks to you, Aaron Bahr, Kevin Alford, and Devon Klompmaker, for your professional developer chops, and special thanks to Allison Salmon and Isaac Goodin. Both of you stood up and learned to do whatever was needed, including creating Studio K, our community platform, and our data infrastructure, making up most of it as we went. I wish we could have done more to leverage your *design* talents, but at least I get to play your games now. Thank you both.

Thank you, Greg Vaughan, for building an exceptional team of programmers and leading our team through waves of technology and personnel changes with a calm and steady hand. You are a real gem, and any organization would be lucky to have you directing its center. Thanks to Terra Lauterbach for giving your design talents to our team. There was more than one occasion on *Progenitor X* and *Econauts* when I stood back in awe watching you create and polish designs. You are a star. Thanks to John Kurschewski for your even calmer, and just as steady, hand in programming and designing; you are a joy to work with, and I learned a lot by watching you lead *Econauts*.

I'd like to thank the art team, Mike Beall, Jacob Reusch, Jason Palmer, Sarah Aken, and Adam Wiens. Working with you all was just a lot of fun, and I consider it a privilege to have been able to do so. Jake, I wish I had just a fraction of your getting-things-done energy. You are an inspiration, and not a week goes by where I don't miss working with you. Jason and Sarah, you are some of the most hilarious and fun people I've worked with. Keep it going. Adam, you are clearly the smartest of any of us; thanks for hanging with us as long as you did.

And then there's Mike. Thanks for stepping up those last years and making everything—but particularly the Norton project—run. From the moment I changed Warner's diapers forward, you committed everything to making this team work. I could not be more proud of the work you've done and are continuing to do.

Thank you, Becky Torrisi, for joining us on this adventure and making everything work. Your "there has to be a way to do this" spirit, combined with an ability to read the fine print of every government or university manual and rule and find the one possible solution to bureaucratic problems, is a gift. I'm happy that you're back to working on actually fun things. I hope you come visit us in the desert.

I want to thank my colleagues both in curriculum and instruction at the University of Wisconsin–Madison and in informatics at the University of California, Irvine, who have shaped my thinking. There are too many to name at either place, but I want to specifically thank Tom Popkewitz, Michael Apple, Gloria Ladson-Billings, and Carl Grant at UW–Madison for their inspiration and help. As I move into this next phase of my career, I lean heavily on the examples that you set. I want to thank André van der Hoek and everyone at UC Irvine for their support in creating a platform for these next phases of work, and Mimi Ito for her vision and leadership in the Connected Learning Lab. I look forward to the next phases of this work with all of you.

Finally, thanks to Constance Steinkuehler for your support as partner, spouse, and collaborator. I've learned more from you than you know. None of this would have happened without your boundless energy, enthusiasm, and light that inspired me to dream, and none of it would have gotten done without your encouragement, support, and care. You are a brilliant collaborator. The best parts of this book are colored by your spirit and intellect, and I don't know where my ideas begin and yours leave off. I want to thank you for your faith in and bottomless well of support for me. I can't wait to find out what we do next, whether it's research, gaming, surfing, raising two boys, or making art in the desert. The best is yet to come.

Notes

Chapter 1

1. A. S. Khan, "*Plague Inc.*," Public Health Matters Blog, Centers for Disease Control and Prevention, https://blogs.cdc.gov/publichealthmatters/tag/plague-inc/.

2. This section could have been written about Scratch, a programming platform that has been used by millions of people to create games and other media, and which has been described extensively elsewhere (see Kafai & Burke, 2015; Resnick, 2017).

Chapter 2

1. AAA game is an informal designation used within the games industry to connote a big budget game that is expected to be a top selling title, appealing to a large audience.

2. GlassLab ("Glass" stood for "games, learning, assessment") brought together academics (Katie Salen), game developers (Michael John), and psychometricians (Robert Mislevy) on the Electronic Arts campus. Arizona State University's Center for Games and Impact also partnered academics (James Paul Gee and Sasha Barab), with industry leaders such as Alan Gershenfeld (Activision) to publish *Never Alone*, one of the best successes in this domain. Carnegie Mellon University professor Jesse Schell's Schell Games company (which currently employs about one hundred people) evolved out of its Entertainment Technology Center. Tracy Fullerton's Game Innovation Lab recently developed a virtual reality installation of Henry David Thoreau's Walden Pond (in addition to having launched world-class development teams such as thatgamecompany). Robin Hunicke at the University of California, Santa Cruz, spun out Funomena games.

3. Based on a talk titled "T4 Culture at Blizzard," given at the University of California, Irvine, on May 21, 2019. Seth is currently working this into a book. His earlier book, *Team Leadership in the Games Industry*, is mandatory reading for anyone but especially for academics leading game development teams.

4. Aaron Cammarata and Raph Koster's work on the Trust Spectrum, which is fundamentally about trust in game play, can also help game managers understand trust in teams.

5. This was probably an example of Miller's (1956) classic "seven plus or minus two" limitations of short-term memory. Miller, G. A. (1956). "The magical number seven, plus or minus two: Some limits on our capacity for processing information." *Psychological Review* 63 (2): 81–97. CiteSeerX 10.1.1.308.8071.

Chapter 3

1. See http://www.gamesandcrowds.tips/ for more resources on crowdsourced games.

2. This decision, which is anathematic to most researchers, is all too common in design-based research, in which researchers constantly make trade-offs among the needs of students, teachers, and researchers.

Chapter 4

1. Without getting into the details, Gamergate was a reactionary movement against progressives who questioned sexism in the games industry, masquerading as concerns for ethics in games journalism.

2. There are one-person design "teams," particularly in the indie genre, who do all of the art, programming, level design, sound, and back-end data infrastructure themselves. But these rare projects are the exception that proves the rule. They take years to complete, target niche audiences, and rarely are 3D or include industry-standard artwork. They would not, for example, meet the demands of *Fair Play*.

3. This arrangement was made possible by the support of UW–Wisconsin's dean of the School of Education, Julie Underwood; WID director, David Krakauer; and senior university legal counsel, Ben Griffiths, to whom I am indebted.

Chapter 5

1. "Truly Functional Arterial Cells Reportedly Created for the First Time," *Genetic Engineering and Biotechnology News*, July 11, 2017, https://www.genengnews.com/topics/omics/truly-functional-arterial-cells-reportedly-created-for-the-first-time/.

2. This section leans heavily on the dissertation work of Liz Owen (2014).

Chapter 7

1. Honestly, the idea developed in part because Ferris, who had been part of this group for a few years, felt that the group (like most academic groups) was having

Notes

a hard time getting beyond the phase of discussing articles and ideas and toward operationalizable research projects.

2. K. Faster, "How Vilas County Is Trying to Reinvest Its Economy," WisCONTEXT, March 16, 2017, https://www.wiscontext.org/how-vilas-county-trying-reinvent-its-economy.

3. Normally, we would enact the build phase on day 4, but we needed an extra day or two to import students' designs into the game engine.

Chapter 8

1. I recommend that anyone entering a partnership read Raymond W. Merritt's *The Partnership Handbook* (1986).

2. We often use a dating metaphor (introduced to me by Alex Chisholm at Learning Games Network) and seek to formalize the partnership after the third meeting (or date).

3. Bird flying games are among my favorite new game subgenres enabled by Unity and cheap online distribution. If you haven't gone down the rabbit hole of mobile game subgenres recently, it is highly recommended.

4. In cross-functional teams, the choice of leaders for focus groups can be consequential. They have power in shaping how questions are framed, results are interpreted, and messages are conveyed to the design team. Those with user data usually win arguments about development priorities.

5. *Full Spectrum Warrior* (which is quite similar to *Cosmos*) also wrestled with mission-driven tutorials and open-ended experimentation, and at times it felt like a tutorial for a game that didn't exist.

Chapter 9

1. *Citizen Science*, mentioned earlier, was fully developed and maintained by Filament Games.

2. C. Zook, "Infographic: Textbook Costs Skyrocket 812% in 35 Years," Applied Educational Systems, September 7, 2017, https://www.aeseducation.com/blog/infographic-the-skyrocketing-cost-of-textbooks-for-schools-students.

3. The average high schooler carries twenty pounds of books every day, which is kind of difficult if you bicycle to school. As much as we worry about screen time in schools, I often wonder if heavy backpacks aren't a bigger issue. See, for example, S. Dong, "Text Heavy: The Hidden Weight of Our Paper Textbook Use," Redwood Bark, February 10, 2021, https://redwoodbark.org/29130/opinion/text-heavy-hidden-weight-paper-textbook-use/.

Coda

1. It's worth recognizing that the rapidly rising costs of higher education are also caused by increased competition for students, a lack of price controls, and increased regulatory pressures.

2. Almost half of the metrics in ranking systems such as those published by *U.S. News & World Report* are pegged to federal grants, including funded students, grant expenditures, and federal grants awarded. Ironically, universities conduct federal research at a loss, by the time faculty start-up packages, graduate student subsidies, and administrative overhead are considered. As a result, universities also look for other ways to monetize faculty research, such as patenting inventions (Newfield, 2016).

3. As an example, the Wisconsin Center for Education Research (WCER) spun out WIDA (World Class Instructional Design and Assessment). WIDA develops language materials and tests, which once brought tens of millions to WCER. One might think a university would never let such a group go, but in reality, running the group internally ran into the problems described here, and ultimately WCER decided it made more sense to spin out the group. Whether this decision was the "right" one is not the issue; the key is that readers might anticipate that in a time of budget cuts, a university would never let tens of millions of dollars walk out, but there are fewer reasons to keep these activities internal than one would think.

References

Adams, C. M., & Wilson, T. D. (2011). Virtual cerebral ventricular system: An MR-based three-dimensional computer model. *Anatomical Sciences Education*, *4*(6), 340–347. https://doi.org/10.1002/ase.256.

Aleckson, J. D., & Ralston-Berg, P. (2011). *MindMeld: Micro-collaboration between elearning designers and instructor experts*. Madison, WI: Atwood.

American Association for the Advancement of Science (AAAS). (2017). *R&D at colleges and universities*. Retrieved March 20, 2021, from https://www.aaas.org/programs/r-d-budget-and-policy/rd-colleges-and-universities.

Anderson, C. G., Binzak, J. V., Dalsen, J., Saucerman, J., Jordan-Douglass, A., Kumar, V., Turker, A., Berland, M., Squire, K., & Steinkuehler, C. (2016). Situating deep multimodal data on game-based STEM learning. In C. K. Looi, J. L. Polman, U. Cress, and P. Reimann (Eds.), *Transforming learning, empowering learners: The International Conference of the Learning Sciences (ICLS) 2016* (Vol. 2). Singapore: International Society of the Learning Sciences.

Bacharach, S. B. (2006). *Keep them on your side: Leading and managing for momentum*. Avon, MA: Platinum Press.

Baio, J., Wiggins, L., Christensen, D. L., Maenner, M. J., Daniels, J., Warren, Z., Kurzius-Spencer, M., Zahorodny, W., Rosenberg, C. R., White, T., Durkin, M. S., Imm, P., Nikolaou, L., Yeargin-Allsopp, M., Lee, L.-C., Harrington, R., Lopez, M., Fitzgerald, R. T., Hewitt, A., . . . Dowling, N. F. (2018). Prevalence of autism spectrum disorder among children aged 8 years—Autism and Developmental Disabilities Monitoring Network, 11 sites, United States, 2014. *Morbidity and Mortality Weekly Report Surveillance Summaries*, *67*(6), 1–23. https://doi.org/10.15585/mmwr.ss6706a1.

Barab, S., & Dede, C. (2007). Games and immersive participatory simulations for science education: An emerging type of curricula. *Journal of Science Education and Technology*, *16*(1–3). https://doi.org/10.1007/s10956-007-9043-9.

Barab, S. A., Hay, K. E., Barnett, M., & Keating, T. (2000). Virtual solar system project: Building understanding through model building. *Journal of Research in Science Teaching, 37*(7), 719–756. https://doi.org/10.1002/1098-2736(200009)37:7<719::AID-TEA6>3.0.CO;2-V.

Baranowski, T., Blumberg, F., Buday, R., DeSmet, A., Fiellin, L. E., Green, C. S., Kato, P. M., Lu, A. S., Maloney, A. E., Mellecker, R., Morrill, B. A., Peng, W., Shegog, R., Simons, M., Staiano, A. E., Thompson, D., & Young, K. (2016). Games for health for children: Current status and needed research. *Games for Health Journal, 5*(1), 1–12. https://doi.org/10.1089/g4h.2015.0026.

Barnett, S. M., & Ceci, S. J. (2002). When and where do we apply what we learn? A taxonomy for far transfer. *Psychological Bulletin, 128*(4), 612–637. https://doi.org/10.1037/0033-2909.128.4.612.

Bartle, R. A. (2003). *Designing virtual worlds*. Berkeley, CA: New Riders Group.

Bary, J., & Frank, A. (2017). *At play in the cosmos*. New York: Norton.

Bauman, E. B. (2016). Games, virtual environments, mobile applications and a futurist's crystal ball. *Clinical Simulation in Nursing, 12*(14), 109–114. https://doi.org/10.1016/j.ecns.2016.02.002.

Bauman, E. B., Adams, R. A., Pederson, D., Vaughan, G., Klompmaker, D., Wiens, A., Beall, M., Ruesch, J., Rosu, E., Schilder, K., & Squire, K. (2015). Building a better donkey: A game-based layered learning approach to veterinary medical education. In A. Ochsner, J. Dietmeier, C. C. Williams, & C. Steinkuehler (Eds.), *Proceedings, GLS 10, Games+Learning+Society Conference, Madison, WI* (pp. 372–375). Pittsburgh, PA: ETC Press.

Bavelier, D., Achtman, R. L., Mani, M., & Föcker, J. (2012). Neural bases of selective attention in action video game players. *Vision Research, 61*, 132–143. https://doi.org/10.1016/j.visres.2011.08.007.

Beall, M., Davidson, R. J., Farajian, R., Flook, L., Freeman, A., Harty, C., Kral, T., Levinson, D., Owen, V. E., Salmon, A., Slater, S., Smith, A., Solis, E., Steinkuehler, C., & Vaughan, G. (2013, June). *Games for mindfulness and pro-social behavior: The Tenacity project collaboration* [Conference presentation]. GLS 9.0, Games+Learning+Society Conference, Madison, WI.

Belkin, D. (2018, February 19). U.S. colleges are separating into winners and losers. *Wall Street Journal*. https://www.wsj.com/articles/after-decades-of-growth-colleges-find-its-survival-of-the-fittest-1519209001.

Berland, M. (2017). Constructivist analytics: Using data to enable deeper museum experiences for more visitors—lessons from the learning sciences. *Visitor Studies, 20*(1), 3–9. https://doi.org/10.1080/10645578.2017.1297116.

Bichelmeyer, B., & Boling, E. (1998). *Filling the gap: Rapid prototyping as visualization in the ISD process* [Conference presentation]. Annual meeting of the Association for Educational Communications and Technology, St. Louis, MO.

References

Binzak, J., Beall, M., Anderson, C. G., Azari, D., Wielgus, L., Dalsen, J., Squire, K., & Steinkuehler, C. (2015). Designing tenacity. In K. E. H. Caldwell, S. Seyler, A. Ochsner, & C. Steinkuehler (Eds.), *Proceedings, GLS 11, Games + Learning + Society Conference, Madison, WI* (pp. 374–378). Pittsburgh, PA: ETC Press.

Birdwell, K. (1999, December 10). *The cabal: Valve's design process for creating Half-Life.* Gamasutra. https://www.gamasutra.com/view/feature/131815/the_cabal_valves_design _process_.php.

Bliss, T. J., Robinson, T. J., Hilton, J., & Wiley, D. A. (2013). An OER COUP: College teacher and student perceptions of open educational resources. *Journal of Interactive Media in Education, 2013*(1), p.Art. 4. https://doi.org/10.5334/2013-04.

Blume, B. D., Ford, J. K., Baldwin, T. T., & Huang, J. L. (2009). Transfer of training: A meta-analytic review. *Journal of Management, 36*(4), 1065–1105. https://doi.org/10 .1177/0149206309352880.

Boeker, M., Andel, P., Vach, W., & Frankenschmidt, A. (2013). Game-based e-learning is more effective than a conventional instructional method: A randomized controlled trial with third-year medical students. *PLoS One, 8*(12), Article e82328. https://doi.org /10.1371/journal.pone.0082328.

Bogost, I. (2007). *Persuasive games: The expressive power of videogames.* Cambridge, MA: MIT Press.

Bonk, C. J., Lee, M. M., Reeves, T. C., & Reynolds, T. H. (2018). The emergence and design of massive open online courses. In R. A. Reiser & J. V. Dempsey (Eds.), *Trends and issues in instructional design and technology* (4th ed., pp. 250–258). New York: Pearson.

Bonnechère, B., Jansen, B., Omelina, L., & Van Sint Jan, S. (2016). The use of commercial video games in rehabilitation: A systematic review. *International Journal of Rehabilitation Research, 39*(4), 277–290. https://doi.org/10.1097/MRR.0000000000000190.

Bourdieu, P. (1996). *The state nobility: Elite schools in the field of power.* Stanford, CA: Stanford University Press.

Bransford, J. D., & Schwartz, D. L. (1999). Rethinking transfer: A simple proposal with multiple implications. *Review of Research in Education, 24*(1), 61–100. https:// doi.org/10.3102/0091732X024001061.

Brown, J. S., Collins, A., & Duguid, P. (1989). Situated cognition and the culture of learning. *Educational Researcher, 18*(1), 32–42. https://doi.org/10.3102/0013189X018001032.

Caldwell, B. (2011, February 15). *Jonathan Blow interview: Do you believe social games are evil? "Yes. Absolutely."* PC Gamer. https://www.pcgamer.com/jonathan-blow-inter view-social-game-designers-goal-is-to-degrade-the-players-quality-of-life.

Cammarata, A., & Koster, R. (2018). *The trust spectrum* [Conference presentation]. Game Developers Conference 2018, San Francisco, CA. https://www.raphkoster.com /2018/03/16/the-trust-spectrum/.

Carpenter, S. R., Caraco, N. F., Correll, D. L., Howarth, R. W., Sharpley, A. N., & Smith, V. H. (1998). Nonpoint pollution of surface waters with phosphorus and nitrogen. *Ecological Applications*, *8*(3), 559–568. https://doi.org/10.2307/2641247.

Chang, M. D. (2016). *Capturing qualitative science knowledge with multimodal instructional analogies* [Unpublished doctoral dissertation]. Northwestern University, Department of Electrical Engineering and Computer Science.

Charlier, N., Zupancic, N., Fieuws, S., Denhauerynck, K., Zaman, B., & Moons, P. (2016). Serious games for improving knowledge and self-management in young people with chronic conditions: A systematic review and meta-analysis. *Journal of the American Medical Informatics Association*, *23*(1), 230–239. https://doi.org/10.1093/jamia/ocv100.

Chislock, M. F., Doster, E., Zitomer, R. A., & Wilson, A. E. (2013). Eutrophication: Causes, consequences, and controls in aquatic ecosystems. *Nature Education Knowledge*, *4*(4), 10. http://www.nature.com/scitable/knowledge/library/eutrophication-causes-consequences-and-controls-in-aquatic-102364466.

Christensen, C. M., Horn, M. B., & Johnson, C. W. (2008). *Disrupting class: How disruptive innovation will change the way the world learns*. New York: McGraw-Hill.

Clark, D. B., Tanner-Smith, E. E., & Killingsworth, S. S. (2016). Digital games, design, and learning: A systematic review and meta-analysis. *Review of Educational Research*, *86*(1), 79–122. https://doi.org/10.3102/0034654315582065.

Clark, R. E. (1983). Reconsidering research on learning from media. *Review of Educational Research*, *53*(4), 445–459. https://doi.org/10.3102%2F00346543053004445.

Code, J., Clarke-Midura, J., Zap, N., & Dede, C. (2013). The utility of using immersive virtual environments for the assessment of science inquiry learning. *Journal of Interactive Learning Research*, *24*(4), 371–396. https://www.learntechlib.org/primary/p/41534/.

Cohen, D. K., & Loewenberg Ball, D. (1999, June). *Instruction, capacity, and improvement*. CPRE Research Report Series RR-43. Consortium for Policy Research in Education, University of Pennsylvania Graduate School of Education. https://www.cpre.org/sites/default/files/researchreport/783_rr43.pdf.

Cole, M. (2006). *The fifth dimension: An after-school program built on diversity*. New York: Sage.

Collins, A. (1992). Toward a design science of education. In E. Scanlon & T. O'Shea (Eds.), *New directions in educational technology* (pp. 15–22). Berlin: Springer.

Collins, A., & Halverson, R. (2009). *Rethinking education in the age of technology: The digital revolution and schooling in America*. New York: Teachers College Press.

Conditt, J. (2017, July 22). *Hobbyist developers will make $30 million via "Roblox" this year*. Engadget. Retrieved June 4, 2019, from https://www.engadget.com/2017/07/22/roblox-30-million-pay-out-developers-2017-how/.

References

Congressional Research Service. (2011, September 8). *Forest certification programs*. Report No. R41992. https://crsreports.congress.gov/product/details?prodcode=R41992.

Cooper, S., Khatib, F., Treuille, A., Barbero, J., Lee, J., Beenen, M., Leaver-Fay, A., Baker, D., Popović, Z., & Foldit players. (2010). Predicting protein structures with a multiplayer online game. *Nature, 466*(7307), 756–760. https://doi.org/10.1038/nature09304.

Corredor, J. (2011, June). *Bio-gaming: Videogames as tools to teach cell biology* [Conference presentation]. Games+Learning+Society Conference, Madison, WI.

Corredor, J., Gaydos, M., & Squire, K. (2014). Seeing change in time: Video games to teach about temporal change in scientific phenomena. *Journal of Science Education and Technology, 23*, 324–343. https://doi.org/10.1007/s10956-013-9466-4.

Crowston, K., Mitchell, E., & Østerlund, C. (2019). Coordinating advanced crowd work: Extending citizen science. *Citizen Science: Theory and Practice, 4*(1), 16. https://doi.org/10.5334/cstp.166.

Cuban, L. (1986). *Teachers and machines: The classroom use of technology since 1920*. New York: Teachers College Press.

Dahn, M., Enyedy, N., & Danish, J. (2018). How teachers use instructional improvisation to organize science discourse and learning in a mixed reality environment. In J. Kay and R. Luckin (Eds.), *Rethinking learning in the digital age: Making the learning sciences count, 13th International Conference of the Learning Sciences (ICLS) 2018* (Vol. 1). London: International Society of the Learning Sciences.

Dalsen, J., Anderson, C. G., Squire, K., & Steinkuehler, C. (2017). Situating big data. In M. F. Young & S. T. Slota (Eds.), *Exploding the castle: Rethinking how video games and game mechanics can shape the future of education* (pp. 221–252). Charlotte, NC: Information Age.

Danielak, B. A., Mechtley, A., Berland, M., Lyons, L., & Eydt, R. (2014). MakeScape lite: A prototype learning environment for making and design. In *IDC '14: Proceedings of the 2014 conference on interaction design and children* (pp. 229–232). New York: Association for Computing Machinery. https://doi.org/10.1145/2593968.2610459.

Data USA. (2020). *Vilas County, WI*. Retrieved April 26, 2020, from https://datausa.io/profile/geo/vilas-county-wi/.

Davidovitch, M., Koren, G., Fund, N., Shrem, M., & Porath, A. (2017). Challenges in defining the rates of ADHD diagnosis and treatment: Trends over the last decade. *BMC Pediatrics, 17*(1), 218. https://doi.org/10.1186/s12887-017-0971-0.

DeSmet, A., Van Ryckeghem, D., Compernolle, S., Baranowski, T., Thompson, D., Crombez, G., Poels, K., Van Lippevelde, W., Bastiaensens, S., Van Cleemput, K., Vandebosch, H., & De Bourdeaudhuij, I. (2014). A meta-analysis of serious digital games for healthy lifestyle promotion. *Preventive Medicine, 69*, 95–107. https://doi.org/10.1016/j.ypmed.2014.08.026.

Dess, G. G., McNamara, G., & Eisner, A. B. (2018). *Strategic management* (9th ed.). New York: McGraw-Hill.

DeVane, B., Durga, S., & Squire, K. (2010). "Economists who think like ecologists": Reframing systems thinking in games for learning. *E-Learning and Digital Media, 7*(1), 3–20. https://doi.org/10.2304/elea.2010.7.1.3.

Dezuanni, M., O'Mara, J., & Beavis, C. (2015). "Redstone is like electricity": Children's performative representations in and around *Minecraft*. *E-Learning and Digital Media, 12*(2), 147–163. https://doi.org/10.1177/2042753014568176.

Dhungana, S. (n.d.). *Paper sector.* Wisconsin Department of Natural Resources. Retrieved April 26, 2020, from https://dnr.wisconsin.gov/topic/Sectors/Paper.html.

Dibbell, J. (2006). *Play money: Or, how I quit my day job and made millions trading virtual loot.* New York: Basic Books.

Domina, T., Penner, A., & Penner, E. (2017). Categorical inequality: Schools as sorting machines. *Annual Review of Sociology, 43*, 311–330. https://doi.org/10.1146/annurev-soc-060116-053354.

Dourish, P. (2017). *The stuff of bits: An essay on the materialities of information.* Cambridge, MA: MIT Press.

Downes, S. (2006, January 29). *Models for sustainable open educational resources.* National Research Council of Canada. https://www.oecd.org/dataoecd/3/5/36781698.pdf.

Dynarski, M., Agodini, R., Heaviside, S., Novak, T., Carey, N., Campuzano, L., Means, B., Murphy, R., Penuel, W., Javitz, H., Emery, D., & Sussex, W. (2007). *Effectiveness of reading and mathematics software products: Findings from the first student cohort.* Institute of Education Sciences, US Department of Education. https://ies.ed.gov/ncee/pdf/20074005.pdf.

Eadicicco, L. (2016, December 7). These are the most popular iPhone apps of 2016. *Time.* http://time.com/4592864/most-popular-iphone-apps-2016/.

E-Line Media. (2017). *Game design documents.* Retrieved August 9, 2019, from https://stemchallenge.org/resources/game-design-documents/.

Etzkowitz, H. (2004). The evolution of the entrepreneurial university. *International Journal of Technology and Globalisation, 1*(1). https://doi.org/10.1504/IJTG.2004.004551.

Evans, J., & Benefield, P. (2001). Systematic reviews of educational research: Does the medical model fit? *British Educational Research Journal, 27*(5), 527–541. https://doi.org/10.1080/01411920120095717.

Faster, K. (2017). *How Vilas County is trying to reinvent its economy.* PBS Wisconsin. Retrieved April 26, 2020, from https://www.wiscontext.org/how-vilas-county-trying-reinvent-its-economy.

References

Fertig, S. (2019, May 1). *Review: At Play in the Cosmos*. Eyepiece. Retrieved March 11, 2021, from http://eyepiece.aaa.org/review-at-play-in-the-cosmos/.

Feurzeig, W., & Roberts, N. (2013). *Modeling and simulation in science and mathematics education*. New York: Springer.

Flesch, R. (1948). A new readability yardstick. *Journal of Applied Psychology, 32*(3), 221–233. https://doi.org/10.1037/h0057532.

Gallup, G. G. Jr., & Svare, B. B. (2016, July 25). *Hijacked by an external funding mentality*. Inside Higher Education. https://www.insidehighered.com/views/2016/07/25/undesirable-consequences-growing-pressure-faculty-get-grants-essay.

Games-to-Teach Research Team. (2003). Design principles of next-generation digital gaming for education. *Educational Technology, 43*(5), 17–23. https://www.jstor.org/stable/44429456.

Gardner, M. (1970). Mathematical games: The fantastic combinations of John Conway's new solitaire game "Life." *Scientific American, 223*(4), 120–123. https://www.jstor.org/stable/24927642.

Gaydos, M. J., & Squire, K. D. (2012). Role playing games for scientific citizenship. *Cultural Studies of Science Education, 7*(4), 821–844. https://doi.org/10.1007/s11422-012-9414-2.

Gee, J. P. (2003). *What video games have to teach us about learning and literacy*. Cham, Switzerland: Palgrave Macmillan.

Gee, J. P. (2004). *Situated language and learning: A critique of traditional schooling*. London: Routledge.

Gee, J. P. (2016, March 9). Ramblings of an old academic: Unconfident advice for end-times academics. *Education Review, 23*. https://doi.org/10.14507/er.v23.2041.

Gee, J. P. (2020). *What is a human? Language, mind, and culture*. Cham, Switzerland: Palgrave Macmillan.

Gray, R. (2017, July 11). *Galaxy Zoo: Citizen science trailblazer marks tenth birthday*. BBC News. https://www.bbc.com/news/science-environment-40558759.

Green, C. S., & Bavelier, D. (2003). Action video game modifies visual selective attention. *Nature, 423*(6939), 534–537. https://doi.org/10.1038/nature01647.

Greene, M. J., Kim, J. S., Seung, H. S., & the EyeWirers. (2016). Analogous convergence of sustained and transient inputs in parallel on and off pathways for retinal motion computation. *Cell Reports, 14*(8), 1892–1900. https://doi.org/10.1016/j.celrep.2016.02.001.

Gutierrez, B., Kaatz, A., Chu, S., Ramirez, D., Samson-Samuel, C., & Carnes, M. (2014). "Fair Play": A videogame designed to address implicit race bias through active perspective taking. *Games for Health Journal, 3*(6), 371–378. https://doi.org/10.1089/g4h.2013.0071.

Habgood, M. P. J., and Ainsworth, S. E. (2011). Motivating children to learn effectively: Exploring the value of intrinsic integration in educational games. *Journal of the Learning Sciences, 20*(2), 169–206. https://doi.org/10.1080/10508406.2010.508029.

Hall, M., Frank, E., Holmes, G., Pfahringer, B., Reutemann, P., & Witten, I. H. (2009). The WEKA data mining software: An update. *ACM SIGKDD Explorations Newsletter, 11*(1), 10–18. https://doi.org/10.1145/1656274.1656278.

Halverson, R. (2019, August 11). *What I learned when I studied six Chicago schools transforming to personalized learning environments.* Getting Smart. https://www.gettingsmart.com/2019/08/what-i-learned-when-i-studied-six-chicago-schools-transforming-to-personalized-learning-environments/.

Halverson, R., & Owen, V. E. (2014). Game-based assessment: An integrated model for capturing evidence of learning in play. *International Journal of Learning Technology* [Special issue on game-based learning], *9*(2), 111–138. https://doi.org/10.1504/IJLT.2014.064489.

Harari, Y. N. (2017). *Homo deus: A brief history of tomorrow.* London: Vintage.

Hatfield, D., Anton, G., Ochsner, A., Squire, K., Shapiro, R. B., & Games, A. (2013). *Studio K*: Tools for game design and computational thinking. In N. Rummel, M. Kapur, M. Nathan, & S. Puntambekar (Eds.), *Proceedings of the 10th international conference on computer-supported collaborative learning, University of Wisconsin–Madison* (Vol. 2, pp. 400–403). International Society of the Learning Sciences.

Hawks, J. (2018). *MOOCs after five years.* John Hawks Weblog. Retrieved August 9, 2019, from http://johnhawks.net/weblog/reviews/teaching/moocs-five-years-later-2018.html.

Hearn, J. C., Lewis, D. R., Kallsen, L., Holdsworth, J. M., & Jones, L. M. (2006). "Incentives for managed growth": A case study of incentives-based planning and budgeting in a large public research university. *Journal of Higher Education, 77*(2), 286–316. https://doi.org/10.1080/00221546.2006.11778927.

Hinshaw, S. P., & Scheffler, R. M. (2015). *The ADHD explosion: Myths, medication, money, and today's push for performance.* New York: Oxford University Press.

HolonIQ. (2021, January 5). *$16.1B of global edtech venture capital in 2020.* https://www.holoniq.com/notes/16.1b-of-global-edtech-venture-capital-in-2020/.

Hong, E. (2015). *MOOCs: Coursera tests out its business model with major companies.* http://www.atelier.net/en/trends/articles/moocs-coursera-tests-out-its-business-model-major-companies_434324.

Hussar, W. J., and Bailey, T. M. (2018). *Projections of education statistics to 2026.* NCES 2018-019. Washington, DC: National Center for Education Statistics. https://nces.ed.gov/pubs2018/2018019.pdf.

IDEO U. (n.d.). *Brainstorming.* Retrieved August 8, 2019, from https://www.ideou.com/pages/brainstorming.

Ito, M., & Okabe, D. (2005). Technosocial situations: Emergent structuring of mobile e-mail use. In M. Ito, D. Okabe, & M. Matsuda (Eds.), *Personal, portable, pedestrian: Mobile phones in Japanese life* (pp. 257–276). Cambridge, MA: MIT Press.

James, W. (1890). *The principles of psychology*, p. 463. Retrieved from https://psychclassics.yorku.ca/James/Principles/prin11.htm.

Jenkins, H., Squire, K., & Tan, P. (2003). You can't bring that game to school! In B. Laurel (Ed.), *Design research: Methods and perspectives* (pp. 244–252). Cambridge, MA: MIT Press.

Johansen, J., & Wiley, D. (2010). A sustainable model for OpenCourseWare development. *Educational Technology Research and Development, 59*, 369–382. https://doi.org/10.1007/s11423-010-9160-7.

Johnson, C. (2015, February 20). *Understanding the culture of no* [Keynote address to local, state, and federal officials of Mexico]. Retrieved January 13, 2018, from https://www.dobt.co/blog/culture-of-no/.

Johnson, D., Deterding, S., Kuhn, K.-A., Staneva, A., Stoyanov, S., & Hides, L. (2016). Gamification for health and wellbeing: A systematic review of the literature. *Internet Interventions, 6*, 89–106. https://doi.org/10.1016/j.invent.2016.10.002.

Johnson, S. (2012). Theme is not meaning: Who decides what a game is about? In C. Steinkuehler, K. Squire, & S. Barab (Eds.), *Games, learning, and society: Learning and meaning in the digital age* (pp. 32–39). New York: Cambridge University Press.

Julius, J. (2016). *The art of Zootopia*. San Francisco: Chronicle Books.

Juul, J. (2009). *A casual revolution: Reinventing video games and their players*. Cambridge, MA: MIT Press.

Kaatz, A., Carnes, M., Gutierrez, B., Savoy, J., Samuel, C., Filut, A., & Pribbenow, C. M. (2017). Fair play: A study of scientific workforce trainers' experience playing an educational video game about racial bias. *CBE—Life Sciences Education, 16*(ar27), 1–18. https://doi.org/10.1187/cbe.15-06-0140.

Kafai, Y. B., & Burke, Q. (2015). Constructionist gaming: Understanding the benefits of making games for learning. *Educational Psychologist, 50*(4), 313–334. https://doi.org/10.1080/00461520.2015.1124022.

Keasar, C., McGuffin, L. J., Wallner, B., Chopra, G., Adhikari, B., Bhattacharya, D., Blake, L., Bortot, L. O., Cao, R., Dhanasekaran, B. K., Dimas, I., Faccioli, R. A., Faraggi, E., Ganzynkowicz, R., Ghosh, S., Ghosh, S., Giełdoń, A., Golon, L., He, Y., . . . & Crivelli, S. N. (2018). An analysis and evaluation of the WeFold collaborative for protein structure prediction and its pipelines in CASP11 and CASP12. *Scientific Reports, 8*, 9939. https://doi.org/10.1038/s41598-018-26812-8.

Keller, J. M. (2009). *Motivational design for learning and performance: The ARCS model approach*. New York: Springer.

Kelly, L., & Medina, C. (2014). *Rebels at work: A handbook for leading change from within*. Sebastopol, CA: O'Reilly Media.

Khaled, R., & Vasalou, A. (2014). Bridging serious games and participatory design. *International Journal of Child-Computer Interaction*, 2(2), 93–100. https://doi.org/10.1016/j.ijcci.2014.03.001.

Khatib, F., DiMaio, F., Foldit Contenders Group, Foldit Void Crushers Group, Cooper, S., Kazmierczyk, M., Gilski, M., Krzywda, S., Zábranská, H., Pichová, I., Thompson, J., Popović, Z., Jaskolski, M., & Baker, D. (2011). Crystal structure of a monomeric retroviral protease solved by protein folding game players. *Nature Structural & Molecular Biology*, 18, 1175–1177. https://doi.org/10.1038/nsmb.2119.

Kirschner, P. A., Sweller, J., & Clark, R. E. (2006). Why minimal guidance during instruction does not work: An analysis of the failure of constructivist, discovery, problem-based, experiential, and inquiry-based teaching. *Educational Psychologist*, 41(2), 75–86. https://doi.org/10.1207/s15326985ep4102_1.

Kirsh, D., & Maglio, P. (1994). On distinguishing epistemic from pragmatic action. *Cognitive Science*, 18(4), 513–549. https://doi.org/10.1016/0364-0213(94)90007-8.

Klopfer, E. (2008). *Augmented learning: Research and design of mobile educational games*. Cambridge, MA: MIT Press.

Koster, R. (2018). *Postmortems: Selected essays, volume one*. San Diego, CA: Altered Tuning Press.

Kozma, R. (2000). Reflections on the state of educational technology research and development. *Educational Technology Research and Development*, 48, 5–15. https://doi.org/10.1007/BF02313481.

Krakauer, J. W., & Cortés, J. C. (2018). A non-task-oriented approach based on high-dose playful movement exploration for rehabilitation of the upper limb early after stroke: A proposal. *NeuroRehabilitation*, 43(1), 31–40. https://doi.org/10.3233/NRE-172411.

Kral, T. R. A., Stodola, D. E., Birn, R. M., Mumford, J. A., Solis, E., Flook, L., Patsenko, E. G., Anderson, C. G., Steinkuehler, C., & Davidson, R. J. (2018). Neural correlates of video game empathy training in adolescents: A randomized trial. *npj Science of Learning*, 3, 13. https://doi.org/10.1038/s41539-018-0029-6.

Levinson, D. B., Stoll, E. L., Kindy, S. D., Merry, H. L., & Davidson, R. J. (2014). A mind you can count on: Validating breath counting as a behavioral measure of mindfulness. *Frontiers in Psychology*, 5, 1202. https://doi.org/10.3389/fpsyg.2014.01202.

Librande, S. (2010). *One-page designs*. GDC Vault. https://www.gdcvault.com/play/1012356/One-Page.

Lohse, K., Shirzad, N., Verster, A., Hodges, N., & Machiel Van der Loos, H. (2013). Video games and rehabilitation: Using design principles to enhance engagement in physical therapy. *Journal of Neurologic Physical Therapy, 37*(4), 166–175. https://doi.org/10.1097/NPT.0000000000000017.

Macklin, C., & Sharp, J. (2016). *Games, design, and play: A detailed approach to iterative game design*. Boston, MA: Addison-Wesley.

Malone, T. W. (1981). Toward a theory of intrinsically motivating instruction. *Cognitive Science, 5*(4), 333–369. https://doi.org/10.1016/S0364-0213(81)80017-1.

Malone, T. W., & Lepper, M. R. (1987). Making learning fun: A taxonomic model of intrinsic motivations for learning. In R. E. Snow & M. J. Farr (Eds.), *Aptitude, learning, and instruction* (Vol. 3, pp. 223–253). Hillsdale, NJ: Lawrence Erlbaum Associates.

Marshall, S. J., Gorely, T., & Biddle S. J. H. (2006). A descriptive epidemiology of screen-based media use in youth: A review and critique. *Journal of Adolescence, 29*(3), 333–349. https://doi.org/10.1016/j.adolescence.2005.08.016.

Matheson, C. (2008). The educational value and effectiveness of lectures. *Clinical Teacher, 5*(4), 218–221. https://doi.org/10.1111/j.1743-498X.2008.00238.x.

Mazurek, M. O., & Engelhardt, C. R. (2013a). Video game use and problem behaviors in boys with autism spectrum disorders. *Research in Autism Spectrum Disorders, 7*(2), 316–324. https://doi.org/10.1016/j.rasd.2012.09.008.

Mazurek, M. O., & Engelhardt, C. R. (2013b). Video game use in boys with autism spectrum disorder, ADHD, or typical development. *Pediatrics, 132*(2), 260–266. https://doi.org/10.1542/peds.2012-3956.

McCall, J. (2011). *Gaming the past: Using video games to teach secondary history*. New York: Routledge.

Mead, C. (2013). *War play: Video games and the future of armed conflict*. New York: Houghton Mifflin Harcourt.

Medina, C. (2014). *Stop the worrying: Manage your boss*. Rebels at Work. Retrieved August 9, 2019, from https://www.rebelsatwork.com/blog/2015/03/06/stop-the-worrying-manage-your-boss.

Medina, C. (2015). *Rebel dangers: When your boss leaves*. Rebels at Work. Retrieved August 9, 2019, from https://www.rebelsatwork.com/blog/2014/12/11/rebel-dangers-when-your-boss-leaves.

Medina, C. (2019). *Innovation is the opposite of policy*. Rebels at Work. Retrieved March 20, 2021, from https://www.rebelsatwork.com/blog/2019/2/13/innovation-is-the-opposite-of-policy.

Miller, G. A. (1956). The magical number seven, plus or minus two: Some limits on our capacity for processing information. *Psychological Review, 63*(2), 81–97. https://doi.org/10.1037/h0043158.

Mislevy, R. J., Oranje, A., Bauer, M. I., von Davier, A. A., Hao, J., Corrigan, S., Hoffman, E., DiCerbo, K., & John, M. (2014). *Psychometric considerations in game-based assessment* [White paper]. GlassLab Research, Institute of Play. https://www.ets.org/research/policy_research_reports/publications/white_paper/2014/jrrx.

Mohan, D., Fischhoff, B., Angus, D. C., Rosengart, M. R., Wallace, D. J., Yealy, D. M., Farris, C., Chang, C.-C. H., Kerti, S., & Barnato, A. E. (2018). Serious games may improve physician heuristics in trauma triage. *Proceedings of the National Academy of Sciences, 115*(37), 9204–9209. https://doi.org/10.1073/pnas.1805450115.

Moss-Racusin, C. A., Dovidio, J. F., Brescoll, V. L., Graham, M. J., & Handelsman, J. (2012). Science faculty's subtle gender biases favor male students. *Proceedings of the National Academy of Sciences, 109*(41), 16474–16479. https://doi.org/10.1073/pnas.1211286109.

Nadella, S., Shaw, G., & Nichols, J. T. (2017). *Hit refresh: The quest to rediscover Microsoft's soul and imagine a better future for everyone.* New York: HarperCollins.

National Research Council. (2011). *Learning science through computer games and simulations.* Washington, DC: National Academies Press.

Newfield, C. (2016). *The great mistake: How we wrecked public universities and how we can fix them.* Baltimore, MD: Johns Hopkins University Press.

Online Learning Consortium. (2015). *Online report card—Tracking online education in the United States.* https://onlinelearningconsortium.org/read/online-report-card-tracking-online-education-united-states-2015/.

Owen, L. (2014). *Capturing in-game learner trajectories with ADAGE (Assessment Data Aggregator for Game Environments): A cross-method analysis* [Unpublished doctoral dissertation]. University of Wisconsin–Madison.

Owen, V. E., Anton, G., & Baker, R. (2016). Modeling user exploration and boundary testing in digital learning games. In *UMAP '16: Proceedings of the 2016 conference on user modeling, adaptation, and personalization, Halifax, Nova Scotia, Canada* (pp. 301–302). New York: Association for Computing Machinery. https://doi.org/10.1145/2930238.2930271.

Owen, V. E., & Baker, R. S. (2018). Fueling prediction of player decisions: Foundations of feature engineering for optimized behavior modeling in serious games. *Technology, Knowledge and Learning, 25,* 225–250. https://doi.org/10.1007/s10758-018-9393-9.

Owen, V. E., Ramirez, D., Salmon, A., & Halverson, R. (2014). *Capturing learner trajectories in educational games through ADAGE (Assessment Data Aggregator for Game Environments). A click-stream data framework for assessment of learning in play* [Conference presentation]. Annual meeting of the American Educational Research Association, Philadelphia, PA.

Paiz-Ramirez, D. (2016). *How player movement data improves educational game assessments* [Unpublished doctoral dissertation]. University of Wisconsin–Madison.

Paiz-Ramirez, D., Chu, S., Salmon, A., & Gutierrez, B. (2011). Designing games for non-gamers: Rapid prototyping as a design methodology. *User Experience Magazine, 10*(4). http://uxpamagazine.org/gamesfornongamers/.

Patsenko, E. G., Adluru, N., Birn, R. M., Stodola, D. E., Kral, T. R. A., Farajian, R., Flook, L., Burghy, C. A., Steinkuehler, C., & Davidson, R. J. (2019). Mindfulness video game improves connectivity of the fronto-parietal attentional network in adolescents: A multi-modal imaging study. *Scientific Reports, 9*, 18667. https://doi.org/10.1038/s41598-019-53393-x.

Perry, C. H. (2014). *Forests of Wisconsin, 2013*. Resource Update FS-6. Newtown Square, PA: US Department of Agriculture, Forest Service, Northern Research Station.

Peterson, G. D., Cumming, G. S., & Carpenter, S. R. (2003). Scenario planning: A tool for conservation in an uncertain world. *Conservation Biology, 17*(2), 358–366. https://doi.org/10.1046/j.1523-1739.2003.01491.x.

Phelps, A. M., Egert, C. A, & Consalvo, M. (2021). *Hack, Slash & Backstab*: A postmortem of university game development at scale. *International Journal of Designs for Learning 12*(1), 16–33. https://doi.org/10.14434/ijdl.v12i1.31263.

Plummer, J. D., & Krajcik, J. (2010). Building a learning progression for celestial motion: Elementary levels from an Earth-based perspective. *Journal of Research in Science Teaching, 47*(7), 768–787. https://doi.org/10.1002/tea.20355.

Poole, S. (2000). *Trigger happy: Videogames and the entertainment revolution*. New York: Arcade.

Reagan, R. (1983, March 8). *Remarks during a visit to Walt Disney World's EPCOT Center Near Orlando, Florida*. Ronald Reagan Presidential Library and Museum. Retrieved August 9, 2019, from https://www.reaganlibrary.gov/research/speeches/30883a.

Reich, J. (2015, May 10). In *China, where everything is a MOOC*. Education Week. http://blogs.edweek.org/edweek/edtechresearcher/2015/05/in_china_where_everything_is_a_mooc.html?r=284759497.

Reich, J., & Ruipérez-Valiente, J. A. (2019). The MOOC pivot. *Science, 363*(6423), 130–131. https://doi.org/10.1126/science.aav7958.

Resnick, M. (2017). *Lifelong kindergarten: Cultivating creativity through projects, passion, peers, and play*. Cambridge, MA: MIT Press.

Sabelli, N., & Dede, C. (2001, July). *Integrating educational research practice: Reconceptualizing goals and policies: How to make what works, work for us?* SRI International. https://www.sri.com/publication/integrating-educational-research-practice-reconceptualizing-goals-and-policies-how-to-make-what-works-work-for-us-2/.

Salen Tekinbas, K., Gresalfi, M., Peppler, K., & Santo, R. (2014). *Gaming the system: Designing with Gamestar Mechanic*. Cambridge, MA: MIT Press.

Salkowski, L. R. (2017). *Designing and using simulation to study expert-novice differences in correlating medical imaging with the physical exam* (Publication No. 10289234) [Doctoral dissertation, University of Wisconsin–Madison]. ProQuest Dissertations Publishing. https://www.proquest.com/docview/2266992807.

Saveri, A., & Chwierut, M. (2011, August 9). *The future of learning agents and disruptive innovation*. KnowledgeWorks Foundation and Institute for the Future. https://knowledgeworks.org/wp-content/uploads/2018/01/learning-agents-disruptive-innovation.pdf.

Schell, J. (2008). *The art of game design: A book of lenses*. Burlington, MA: Morgan Kaufmann.

Schrier, K. (2016). *Knowledge games: How playing games can solve problems, create insight, and make change*. Baltimore, MD: Johns Hopkins University Press.

Selzer, J. (2015, July 30). *The market for education technology is booming and fueling a wave of learning innovation!* ArcheMedX. Retrieved January 6, 2018, from http://www.archemedx.com/blog/the-market-for-education-technology-is-booming-and-fueling-a-wave-of-learning-innovation/#.Vtc6tZMrJE4.

Shaffer, D. W. (2007). *How computer games help children learn*. New York: Palgrave Macmillan.

Shapiro, R. B., & Squire, K. D. (2011). Games for participatory science: A paradigm for game-based learning for promoting science literacy. *Educational Technology*, *51*(6), pp. 34–41. http://www.jstor.org/stable/44429969.

Sheehan, Q., Ritter, R., & Scholl, C. (2014). Vilas County Land & Water Conservation Department Chris Stark. Vilas County UW-Extension Community Resource Development Adam Grassl, Vilas County Mapping (2014. AQUATIC HABITATS AND ECONOMY OF VILAS COUNTY.

Shifrer, D., Turley, R. T., & Heard, H. (2017). Do teacher financial awards improve teacher retention and student achievement in an urban disadvantaged school district? *American Educational Research Journal*, *54*(6), 1117–1153. https://doi.org/10.3102/0002831217716540.

Shute, V. J., Wang, L., Greiff, S., Zhao, W., & Moore, G. (2016). Measuring problem solving skills via stealth assessment in an engaging video game. *Computers in Human Behavior*, *63*, 106–117. https://doi.org/10.1016/j.chb.2016.05.047.

The SIGJ2 Writing Collective. (2012). What can we do? The challenge of being new academics in neoliberal universities. *Antipode*, *44*(4), 1055–1058. https://doi.org/10.1111/j.1467-8330.2012.01011.x.

References

Simon, H. A. (1988). Designing the immaterial society. *Design Issues, 4*(1/2), 67–82. https://www.jstor.org/stable/i267276.

Slater, S., and Harris, S. (2013). Using video games to trigger interest emergence and task engagement in science classrooms. In C. C. Williams, A. Ochsner, J. Dietmeier, & C. Steinkuehler (Eds.), *Proceedings, GLS 9.0, Games + Learning + Society Conference, Madison, WI, June 12–14, 2013* (pp. 292–295). Pittsburgh, PA: ETC Press.

Slaughter, S., and Leslie, L. L. (1997). *Academic capitalism: Politics, policies, and the entrepreneurial university*. Baltimore, MD: Johns Hopkins University Press.

Slaughter, S., & Rhoades, G. (2009). *Academic capitalism and the new economy: Markets, state, and higher education*. Baltimore, MD: Johns Hopkins University Press.

Söbke, H., Corredor, J. A., & Kornadt, O. (2013). Learning, reasoning, and modeling in social gaming. In Z. Pan, A. D. Cheok, W. Müller, I. Iurgel, P. Petta, & B. Urban (Eds.), *Lecture notes in computer science, Vol. 7775: Transactions on edutainment X* (pp. 243–258). Berlin: Springer. https://doi.org/10.1007/978-3-642-37919-2_15.

Spaulding, S. (2009). *Team leadership in the game industry*. Boston, MA: Cengage Learning.

Spaulding, S. (2019). *T4 stuff* [Presentation to the undergraduate Multiplayer Games class, University of California, Irvine].

Squire, K. D. (2008). Video games and education: Designing learning systems for an interactive age. *Educational Technology, 48*(2), 17–26. https://www.jstor.org/stable/44429558.

Squire, K. D. (2011). *Video games and learning: Teaching and participatory culture in the digital age*. New York: Teachers College Press.

Squire, K., Gaydos, M., & DeVane, B. (2016). Introduction to special issue on Games + Learning + Society. *Educational Technology, 56*(3), 3–5. https://www.learntechlib.org/p/175756/.

Squire, K., Giovanetto, L., DeVane, B., & Durga, S. (2005). From users to designers: Building a self-organizing game-based learning environment. *TechTrends, 49*(5), 34–42. https://doi.org/10.1007/BF02763688.

Squire, K. D., & Jan, M. (2007). *Mad City Mystery*: Developing scientific argumentation skills with a place-based augmented reality game on handheld computers. *Journal of Science Education and Technology, 16*, 5–29. https://doi.org/10.1007/s10956-006-9037-z.

Squire, K. D., Jan, M., Matthews, J., Wagler, M., Martin, J., DeVane, B., & Holden, C. (2007). Wherever you go, there you are: Place-based augmented reality games for learning. In B. E. Shelton & D. A. Wiley (Eds.), *The design and use of simulation computer games in education* (pp. 273–304). Rotterdam: Sense.

Steinkuehler, C. (2015, March 4). *Next generation assessment: The power of games* [Keynote speech]. Association of Testing Publishers (ATP) Conference, Palm Springs, CA.

Steinkuehler, C., & Duncan, S. (2008). Scientific habits of mind in virtual worlds. *Journal of Science Education and Technology*, *17*, 530–543. https://doi.org/10.1007/s10956-008-9120-8.

Steinkuehler, C. A., & Squire, K. D. 2014. Videogames and learning. In R. K. Sawyer (Ed.), *The Cambridge handbook of the learning sciences* (pp. 377–394). Cambridge, UK: Cambridge University Press.

Stenerson, M. E., Salmon, A., Berland, M., & Squire, K. (2014, October). ADAGE: An open API for data collection in educational games. In *CHI PLAY '14: Proceedings of the first ACM SIGCHI annual symposium on computer-human interaction in play* (pp. 437–438). New York: Association for Computing Machinery. https://doi.org/10.1145/2658537.2661325.

Superbrothers A/V & Boyer, B. (n.d.). *Less talk, more rock.* Boing Boing. Retrieved August 6, 2019, from https://boingboing.net/features/morerock.html.

Taddeo, S. (2017, November 24). Where the jobs are in Rochester. *Democrat and Chronicle* (Rochester, NY). https://www.democratandchronicle.com/story/money/2017/11/24/where-jobs-rochester/885054001/.

Thiagarajan, S. (1998). The myths and realities of simulations in performance technology. *Educational Technology*, *38*(5), 35–41. https://www.jstor.org/stable/44428481.

Tobias, S., & Fletcher, J. D. (Eds.). (2011). *Computer games and instruction.* Charlotte, NC: Information Age.

Todd, A. R., Galinsky, A. D., & Bodenhausen, G. V. (2012). Perspective taking undermines stereotype maintenance processes: Evidence from social memory, behavior explanation, and information solicitation. *Social Cognition*, *30*(1), 94–108. https://doi.org/10.1521/soco.2012.30.1.94.

Tuckman, B. W. (1965). Developmental sequence in small groups. *Psychological Bulletin*, *63*(6), 384–399. https://doi.org/10.1037/h0022100.

Vacca, R. (2017). Bicultural: Examining teenage Latinas' perspectives on technologies for emotional support. In *IDC '17: Proceedings of the 2017 Conference on Interaction Design and Children, Stanford, CA*. New York: Association for Computing Machinery.

Veletsianos, G. (2015, May 27). *The invisible learners taking MOOCs.* Inside Higher Education. https://www.insidehighered.com/blogs/higher-ed-gamma/invisible-learners-taking-moocs.

Veletsianos, G., Collier, A., & Schneider, E. (2015). Digging deeper into learners' experience in MOOCs: Participation in social networks outside of MOOCs, notetaking, and contexts surrounding content consumption. *British Journal of Educational Technology*, *46*(3), 570–587. https://doi.org/10.1111/bjet.12297.

von Stumm, S., Hell, B., & Chamorro-Premuzic, T. (2011). The hungry mind: Intellectual curiosity is the third pillar of academic performance. *Perspectives on Psychological Science, 6*(6), 574–588. https://doi.org/10.1177/1745691611421204.

Wan, T. (2018, December 12). *GlassLab set out to prove games could assess learning. Now it's shutting down*. EdSurge. Retrieved August 8, 2019, from https://www.edsurge.com/news/2018-12-12-glasslab-set-out-to-prove-games-could-assess-learning-now-it-s-shutting-down.

Wang, P., Zhu, X.-T., Liu, H.-H., Zhang, Y.-W., Hu, Y., Li, H.-J., & Zuo, X.-N. (2017). Age-related cognitive effects of videogame playing across the adult life span. *Games for Health Journal, 6*(4), 237–248. https://doi.org/10.1089/g4h.2017.0005.

Wangen, S. R., Shapiro, B., & Ferris, M. C. (2012, August 7). *Crowdsourcing ecological research: Using the Trails Forward simulation platform and video game to address conservation issues* [Conference presentation]. 97th annual meeting of the Ecological Society of America, Portland, OR.

Weinberger, M. (2017, July 25). *A video game you've never heard of has turned three teens into multimillionaires—and it's just getting started*. Business Insider. https://www.businessinsider.com/roblox-how-teenage-developers-are-making-millions-2017-7.

Weiss, E., Richter, S., Krauss, T., Metzelthin, S. I., Hille, A., Pradier, O., Siekmeyer, B., Vorwerk, H., & Hess, C. F. (2003). Conformal radiotherapy planning of cervix carcinoma: Differences in the delineation of the clinical target volume. A comparison between gynaecologic and radiation oncologists. *Radiotherapy & Oncology, 67*(1), 87–95. https://doi.org/10.1016/s0167-8140(02)00373-0.

Wentworth, D. R., & Lewis, D. R. (1973). A review of research on instructional games and simulations in social studies education. *Social Education, 37*(5), 432–440.

Wexler, E. (2015, October 19). *MOOCs are still rising, at least in numbers*. Chronicle of Higher Education. https://www.chronicle.com/blogs/wiredcampus/moocs-are-still-rising-at-least-in-numbers.

Wieman, C. (2007). Why not try a scientific approach to science education? *Change: The Magazine of Higher Learning, 39*(5), 9–15. https://doi.org/10.3200/CHNG.39.5.9-15.

Wildavsky, B., Kelly, A. P., & Carey, K. (Eds.). (2011). *Reinventing higher education: The promise of innovation*. Cambridge, MA: Harvard Education Press.

Wiley, D. (2005, November 4). *Content is infrastructure*. Open Content. http://opencontent.org/blog/archives/215.

Wiley, D. (2013, March 1). *Where I've been; where I'm going*. Open Content. http://opencontent.org/blog/archives/2723.

Wiley, D. (2015). The MOOC misstep and the open education infrastructure. In C. J. Bonk, M. M. Lee, T. C. Reeves, & T. H. Reynolds (Eds.), *MOOCs and open education around the world* (pp. 3–11). New York: Routledge.

Wiley, D., & Gurrell, S. (2009). A decade of development . . . *Open Learning: The Journal of Open, Distance, and e-Learning, 24*(1), 11–21. https://doi.org/10.1080/02680510802627746.

Winskell, K., Sabben, G., Akelo, V., Ondeng'e, K., Obong'o, C., Stephenson, R., Warhol, D., & Mudhune, V. (2018). A smartphone game-based intervention (*Tumaini*) to prevent HIV among young Africans: Pilot randomized controlled trial. *JMIR Mhealth Uhealth, 6*(8), e10482. https://doi.org/10.2196/10482.

Wisconsin County Forests Association. (2013). Wisconsin County forests acres. Retrieved from https://www.wisconsincountyforests.com/forest-resources/forest-acres/.

Wisconsin Department of Natural Resources. (2020). *Wisconsin's private woodlands*. Retrieved April 26, 2020, from https://dnr.wi.gov/topic/ForestLandowners/private.html.

Wisconsin Economic Development Corporation. (2020). *A protected economical resource*. Retrieved April 26, 2020, from https://inwisconsin.com/key-industries-in-wisconsin/forest-products/.

Woodhouse, K. (2015, September 28). *Closures to triple*. Inside Higher Education. https://www.insidehighered.com/news/2015/09/28/moodys-predicts-college-closures-triple-2017.

Woodworth, R. S., & Thorndike, E. L. (1901). The influence of improvement in one mental function upon the efficiency of other functions. *Psychological Review, 8*(3), 247–261. https://doi.org/10.1037/h0074898.

World Health Organization. (2018). *International classification of diseases for mortality and morbidity statistics (11th revision)*. Retrieved from https://icd.who.int/browse11/l-m/en.

Wouters, P., van Nimwegen, C., van Oostendorp, H., & van der Spek, E. D. (2013). A meta-analysis of the cognitive and motivational effects of serious games. *Journal of Educational Psychology, 105*(2), 249–265. https://psycnet.apa.org/doi/10.1037/a0031311.

Yee, N. (2014). *The Proteus paradox: How online games and virtual worlds change us—and how they don't*. New Haven, CT: Yale University Press.

Yee, N. (2017, August 29). *Just how important are female protagonists?* Quantic Foundry. https://quanticfoundry.com/2017/08/29/just-important-female-protagonists/.

Young, M. F., Slota, S., Cutter, A. B., Jalette, G., Mullin, G., Lai, B., Simeoni, Z., Tran, M., & Yukhymenko, M. (2012). Our princess is in another castle: A review of trends in serious gaming for education. *Review of Education Research, 82*(1), 61–89. https://doi.org/10.3102/0034654312436980.

Zemsky, R. (2014). With a MOOC MOOC here and a MOOC MOOC there, here a MOOC, there a MOOC, everywhere a MOOC MOOC. *Journal of General Education*, *63*(4), 237–243. https://doi.org/10.5325/jgeneeduc.63.4.0237.

Zoss, J. M. (2009, December 22). *The art of game polish: Developers speak*. Gamasutra. https://www.gamasutra.com/view/feature/132611/the_art_of_game_polish_developers_.php.

Index

Note: Page numbers in italic indicate figures.

AAA games, 13, 16, 65, 207n1, 208n2
Academic capitalism and funding models, 4, 14–16, 29, 53–54, 170, 187–190, 194, 210n1, 210n2
Academic centers, game development teams in, 56–58, 62–64
Academic development, 39–40
Academic groups, values of, 39
Academic-industry partnerships, 69–73
Activision, 207n2
Activity-based budget models, 186–187
ADAGE (Assessment Data Aggregator for Game Environments), 85, 192
Addiction, gaming, 93
Administrative staff, partnership with, 193–194
Adolphus Toliver Award, 61
Aesthetic vision, shared, 23–24
Affective skills, improvement of, 11
Aging, gaming and, 7
Aleckson, J. D., 163
Alexa (Amazon), 88
Alix-Garcia, Jennifer, 111
Amateur Astronomers Association, 1
Amazon, 88, 178
American Astronomical Society, 152
American marten, 121
America's Army: Proving Grounds, 14
Amygdala-MPFC, 101

Anatomical and Physiology Exploration (APEX), 49
Anatomy Browser, 43–45, *44*
Anatomy Pro-Am, 19, 33, 182
 academic versus work-for-hire development, 39–40
 aesthetics and play, 36–37
 Anatomy Browser, 43–45, *44*
 challenges of, 50–51
 Diagnostic Detective curriculum, 45–47
 Filament Games partnership, 38–39
 integration into K–12 learning, 45–47, *48*
 iPad apps for medical/veterinary education, 47–50
 learning experiences as layers of interaction in, 52
 Oncology, 37–43
 origins of, 33–36
 patient consultation and treatment, *34–35*
 prototyping, 37–38
 role-playing scenarios, 45–47
 social innovation and transformation, 51–52
 transdisciplinary design collaborations, 51
AnatomyTable, 49–50, 70
Angry Birds, 28

APEX. *See* Anatomical and Physiology Exploration (APEX)
Apple, 108
  App Store, 16
  Siri, 88
Arizona State University, 5, 207n2
Art
  At Play in the Cosmos, 153–154
  importance of, 27, 171–172
  Progenitor X, 78
Assassin's Creed, 167, 182
Assessment Data Aggregator for Game Environments (ADAGE), 85, 192
Assessment systems, 10–11
  analytics in, 83–88
  Civilization, 133
  data design and collection, 81–88
  design of, 79–81, 175
  Econauts, 132–133
  Fair Play, 175
  future of, 88–89
  machine learning and, 11
  system design, *80*
Astronomy: At Play in the Cosmos (Frank), 140
Astronomy games. *See At Play in the Cosmos*; *Galaxy Zoo*
At Play in the Cosmos, 140–141, 170, 209n5
  art tests, 153–154
  background and origins of, 11, 139
  challenges in, 174
  context of, 139–140
  contract negotiations for, 142–143
  Cosmic Operations Research Interface (CORI), 156–158, 160
  crafting system, 158
  data integration, 158
  design jam, 142–144
  design walk-throughs and game play, 153, 164–165
  development production goals, 159
  dream features and adaptations, 161
  editorial team, 154–155
  embedded tools, 146, *147*
  flight-based game play, 152
  focus groups for, 156
  game design document (GDD), 142, 147–148, *148*
  general concept for, 142
  in-game glossary, 158
  interactive simulation design, 149–150
  missions, *148*, *149*, 160
  momentum, 163
  narrative framework, 144
  navigation and scale, 145–146, *145*
  needs of, 163
  partnership negotiation and formation, 140–143
  play-testing, 158–160
  polish, 160
  production tensions, 150–152, 173
  qualitative understandings through, 144
  review of, 1–2
  scaffolding of mathematical representations in, 155–156
  subject matter expert teams, 140
  vertical slices, 146, 152
Attentional tasks, 92, 95
Attention deficit hyperactivity disorder (ADHD), 92, 107
Audience, target, 169
Augmented reality, 3. *See also Pokémon GO!*
Autism spectrum disorders (ASDs), 92–93, 107
Avatar, 70

Bacharach, S. B., 163
Baker, David, 32, 85
Balfanz, Alex, 9
Barab, Sasha, 207n2
Bary, Jeff, 140, 149, 154, 163
Bastion, 100–101, *103*
Bauman, Eric, 47

Index

Beall, Michael, 19–20, 26, 70, 75, 76, 147, 154, 156
Berland, Matthew, 49, 70, 133
Bias, remediation of. *See Fair Play*
Bichelmeyer, B., 142
Bifurcation of economy, 114
Bill & Melinda Gates Foundation. *See* Gates Foundation
Biohazard, 36
Bird flying games, 209n3
Blackbody radiation, 149
Blizzard Entertainment, *StarCraft II*, 24
Boling, E., 142
Bots, 116
BrainPOP, 16, 135
Brain structure. *See also* Mental health games
  dorsolateral prefrontal cortex, 98
  posterior cingulate–medial prefrontal cortex, 101
Branding, 191
Breath counting game, 96–100
Brown, Ann, 119, 121
Budget models, activity-based, 186–187
Business development, investments in, 69

California (Irvine), University of, 71
Cammarata, Aaron, 208n4
Campbell, Joseph, 160
Canada, SchoolNet, 179
Cancer diagnosis. *See Anatomy Pro-Am*
Candy Crush Saga, 78, 85, 95
Canvas, 176
Capitalism, academic, 185–188, 210n2
Carnegie Mellon University, 207n2
Carnes, Molly, 53, 61
Carpenter, Stephen, 109–110
Center for Healthy Minds, 93, 96
Center for Limnology, 109
Center for the Study of Intelligence, 193
Center for Women's Health Research, 53–54

Centers for Disease Control and Prevention, 9, 86
Central Intelligence Agency (CIA)
  Center for the Study of Intelligence, 193
  Fair Play adapted for use at, 61–62
Change agents, internal, 192–195
Characters, in game design documents (GDDs), 169
Chisholm, Alex, 209n2
Chromebooks, school adoption of, 30, 130, 178, 182
Citizen Science, 110–111, 131, 174, 209n1
Civilization, 95, 109, 115, 122, 133
Civilization III, 116
Clark, Doug, 5, 7
Clash Royale, 26
Clients, Unity, 116
Climate CoLab platform, 33
Closed systems, games in, 180–183
Co.lab accelerator, 11, 122–128, 130
Colgate University, 140
Collection, data
  Anatomy Pro-Am, 45
  At Play in the Cosmos, 1519
  mobile devices, 18
  Progenitor X, 80–83
  time requirements for, 102–103
Colorado (Boulder), University of, 36
Common Core scientific reasoning standards, 119–121
Conflict management, 67
Consalvo, M., 136
Conservation Conversation Group, 111
Context
  institutional, 15–16
  Progenitor X, 83
Contract negotiations, 68, 72, 142–143
Contractors, hiring/paying, 69
Cooper, S., 32
Copyrighted materials, 29
Core services, 191–192

Corredor, Javier, 20, 28
Cosmic Operations Research Interface (CORI), 156–158, 160
Cosmos. See At Play in the Cosmos
Coursera, 178
Cousteau, Jacques, 153
Crafting system, *At Play in the Cosmos*, 158
Cramer, Katherine, 114
Credibility, 16–19
Cross-functional teams, 209n4
Cross-industry expertise, 16
Crowdsourcing knowledge games, 31–36. *See also Anatomy Pro-Am*
  EyeWire, 33
  Foldit, 10, 14–15, 31–33, 52
  Galaxy Zoo, 31
Crystals of Kaydor, 100–102, *101*, *103*, 172
Culture
  AAA versus indie, 65, 208n2
  commitment to growth in, 66
  educators, 63–64
  individualistic versus team, 65–66
  research lab, 63–64
  scientists/gamers, 63–64
  workflow rhythms, 66
Curricula, game-based, 6, 29, 130–132, 179, 181

Dalai Lama, 94
Dalson, Jennifer, 158
Dance Dance Revolution, 8
DARPA. *See* Defense Advanced Research Projects Agency (DARPA)
Databases, outreach, 191–192
Data collection
  Anatomy Pro-Am, 45
  At Play in the Cosmos, 1519
  mobile devices, 18
  Progenitor X, 80–88
  time requirement for, 102–103
Data integration, *At Play in the Cosmos*, 158

Data transformations, *Progenitor X*, 84
Davidson, Richard, 6, 11, 93–94, 95, 98
Defense Advanced Research Projects Agency (DARPA), 31–32, 188–190
Department of Natural Resources (DNR), 118–119
Design jams
  At Play in the Cosmos, 142–144
  paper-based prototypes in, 168–169
  Trails Forward, 111–112
Design leads, 169
Design models. *See also Individual games*
  assessment systems, 79–81, *80*, 175
  games for good, 5, 93–94
  importance of, 6–8
  participatory, 104–107, *105*
  preproduction, 167–170
  production, 173–175
  prototyping, 170–173
  service and maintenance, 175–176
Detroit: Become Human, 36
DeVane, Ben, 133
Development. *See also* Prototyping; *Individual games*
  academic game development production, 64–66
  challenges of, 22–23, 68–69
  constraints on, 13
  credibility in, 16–19
  generations of, 102
  grant funding for, 14–16, 29, 53–54, 170, 187–190
  green-lighting criteria for, 20–22
  indie, 65, 208n2
  institutional context, 15–16
  production, 26–27
  programs for, 15
  scaling out products, 102–104
  shared aesthetic vision in, 23–24
  starting, 14–15
  strategic alignment in, 13–14
  waterfall, 65
Development groups, values of, 39

Index

DeVry Medical International, 47, 50, 52
Dewey, John, 196
Diablo, 102
Diagnostic Detective, 45–47, 86
Dibbel, Julian, 31
Discovery Tour by Assassin's Creed, 177
Disease simulation games, 8–9
Dissemination, 190
Diversification of income, 4
Documents, game design, 169–170
Dorsolateral prefrontal cortex, 98
Downes, S., 178
Durga, Shree, 133

Eastman Kodak Company, 15
Ebert, Sheri, 45
Ecological simulation. *See Econauts*;
  Trails Forward
Econauts, 11. *See also Trails Forward*
  aesthetics and play, 123–128, *124,
    127*, 172, 181
  assessment model, 132–133
  co.lab participation, 128–130
  distributed game-based learning
    community, 135–136
  donation buttons in, 176
  game-based curricula, 130–132
  game experiences for research,
    133–134
  goals for, 123
  learning analytics in, 133, 136
  limitations of, 128–130
  market for, 182
  optimization for research and infor-
    mal use, 135
  origins of, 122–128
  polish, 175
  research versus market orientation of,
    135–136
  Trails Forward compared to, 122
Economy, bifurcation of, 114
Editorial team, *At Play in the Cosmos*,
  154–155

Educational areas, 64
Educational interventions, sustainabil-
  ity of, 29–30
Educational publishing market,
  176–183
  disruption in, 177–179
  open educational resources (OER),
    178–179
  open versus closed systems, 180–183
Educators, scientists/gamers versus,
  63–64
Eliceiri, Kevin, 36
Els for Autism Foundation, 93
Embedded tools, *At Play in the Cosmos*,
  146–148, *147*
Empathic accuracy (EA), 100–102, *103*
Empathy games, 100–102
Employee growth, commitment to, 66
Ender's Game, 177
Engelhardt, Christopher, 92
Entrepreneurial centers, challenges of,
  190–191
Entrepreneurial funding, 16
Environmental Detectives, 36
Environmental development. *See Trails
  Forward*
Eutrophication, 109. *See also Citizen
  Science*
Events, *Progenitor X*, 83
Exercise games, 5
Exploration, thoughtful, 85
EyeWire, 33

Facebook, 108
Facial recognition conversations, *Crystals
  of Kaydor*, 102
Faculty, bias education for. *See Fair Play*
Fahlgren, Erik, 155
Failure, 73, 85–86
Fair Play, 10, 53–54, 96
  academic game development produc-
    tion, 64–66
  aesthetics and play, 59–60, *60*

Fair Play (cont.)
  assessment model, 175
  Central Intelligence Agency (CIA) use of, 61–62
  challenges in, 174
  game development team building, 56–58, 62–64
  grant funding for, 53–54
  origins of, 53–54
  partnerships with Learning Games Network (LGN), 69–71
  production, 173
  prototyping, 54–56, *55*
  research lab culture, 63–64
  research results of, 54–56
  storyboarding and mockups, 56–60
  success and awards, 61
Family Educational Rights and Privacy Act (FERPA), 146
Fantastic Voyage, 37
Faster Than Light, 158
Faster than light (FTL) navigation, 145, 158
Feature engineering, *Progenitor X*, 83–86
Ferris, Michael, 111, 116, 121, 208n1
Fertig, Stanley, 1
Fidget spinners, 104
Filament Games, 18, 37–39, 64, 110, 130, 176, 181. *See also* Citizen Science
Fitness games, 5
Flappy Bird, 28
Flash, 45, 111, 175–176
Flight-based game play, 152
Focus groups, 156
Foldit, 10, 14–15, 31–33, 52
Forbus, Ken, 144
Forest management, *Trails Forward*, 117–118
"Forming, storming, norming, performing" model, 24
Fortnite, 95, 176
Frank, Adam, 140, 155
Friedrich's ataxia, 7

Fruit Ninja, 98, *99*
Fullerton, Tracy, 207n2
Full Spectrum Warrior, 209n5
Functional magnetic resonance imaging (fMRI), 91
Funding models, 14–16, 29, 53–54, 170, 187–190, 194
Funomena games, 207n2

Gagnon, David, 96
Galaxy Zoo, 31
Game-based assessment, 10–11
Game design documents (GDDs), 142, 147–148, 168–170
Game development. *See* Development
Game Dev Story, 54–56, *55*
Game feel, 175
Game Feel (Swink), 175
Game Innovation Lab, 207n2
Gamergate, 54, 208n1
Gamers, educators versus, 63–64
Games, Design, and Play (Macklin and Sharp), 170–171
Games, impact, 20–22. *See also* Assessment systems; Development; Knowledge games; Mental health games; *Individual games*
  AAA games, 13, 16, 65, 207n1, 208n2
  adoption of, 182–183
  concerns about, 4
  core services to, 191–192
  educational publishing market for, 176–183
  effectiveness of, 4–8
  emerging technologies in, 3
  future of, 195–198
  green-lighting criteria for, 20–22
  growth of, 2–4, 167
  hype surrounding, 2–4, *3*
  market for, 8–10
  motivations for, 4
  replayable, 7
  single-payer, 7

Index 237

single-session, 7
trust in, 208n4
Games+Learning+Society (GLS), 2, 10, 11. *See also Individual games*
  credibility of, 16–19
  culture of, 15–16
  funding models for, 15–16
  partnership with W. W. Norton, 140–150
Games for Health Journal, 7–8
Gamestar Mechanic, 9
Games-to-Teach Project, 31
Game studies, 64
Gaming addiction, 93
Gartner's Hype Cycle, 2–3, *3*
Gates, Bill & Melinda, 93
Gates Foundation, 93, 100, 102, 177
Gaydos, Matthew, 20
GDD (game design document), 168
Gear Games, 139. *See also At Play in the Cosmos*
GEAR Studios, 71
Gee, James Paul, 5, 8, 9, 28, 182, 207n2
Generations, game development, 102
Genres, 169
Gershenfeld, Alan, 207n2
GlassLab, 130, 207n2
Glossary, *At Play in the Cosmos*, 158
GLS. *See* Games+Learning+Society (GLS)
Good, games for, 93–94
Google, 108
  Assistant, 88
  Stadia, 177
Government organizations
  contracts with, 188–190
  game development constrained by, 13–14
  grant funding by, 186, 188–190
Grant funding, 14–16, 29, 53–54, 170, 187–190
Gravity Ghost, 59
Green-lighting criteria, 20–22
Griffiths, Ben, 208n3

Groups, focus, 156
Guardians of the Galaxy, 70

Hack, Slash & Backstab, 136
Halverson, Katja, 42
Halverson, Richard, 16, 17, 19–20, 82, 191
Hansen, Jayse, 148
Harris, Kevin, 20
Harris, Shannon, 42, 76
Harvard Graduate School of Education, 196
Heads-up display (HUD), 148
Health (mental), games for, 4, 7–8
  advantages of, 91–93
  areas for future research, 107–108
  breath counting, 96–100
  Crystals of Kaydor, 100–102, *103*
  empathy, 100–102
  games for good, 93–94
  mindfulness, 95
  negative trends associated with gaming, 92
  participatory design, 104–107, *105*
  potential of, 91–93
  scaling out products, 102–104
  Tenacity, 96–100, *97*, *106*, 174
Hearthstone, 95
Held, Kirsten, 118
Hero's journey, 160
Higher education institutions. *See also Individual universities*
  academic capitalism and funding models, 4, 14–16, 29, 53–54, 170, 185–190, 194, 210n1, 210n2
  academic-industry partnerships, 69–73
  administrative staff partnerships, 193–194
  core services to games for impact, 191–192
  enrollment, 185–186
  entrepreneurial centers within, 190–191

Higher education institutions (cont.)
  failure-averse nature of, 73
  future of games for impact in, 195–198
  game development constrained by, 13–15, 68–69
  innovation in, 11
  institutional context, 15–16
  institutional leadership, 193
  internal change agents in, 192–195
  star system in, 65–66
  traditional academic metrics, 194–195
Historical simulation games, 4–5
Hulu, 188
Hunicke, Robin, 207n2
Hype cycle, 2–3, *3*
Hyperactivity, 92
Hypothesized solutions, 168

IARPA (Intelligence Advanced Research Projects Activity), 33
Idea development, 168
IDonkey, 48–49, *49*
I MAED A GAM3 W1TH Z0MBIES 1N IT!!!1, 75
Impact games. *See* Games, impact
Implicit association tests (IATs), 60
Implicit bias, remediation of. *See Fair Play*
Imprecision, 22
Income diversification, 4
Indie game development, 65, 208n2
Individualistic cultures, 65–66
In-game purchases, 176
INK Stories, *1979 Revolution: Black Friday*, 13
Inspiration, finding, 168, 170
Institutional Review Board (IRB) specialists, 192
Intelligence Advanced Research Projects Activity (IARPA), 61

Interactive Star Chart, 145, *145*
Internal change agents, 192–195
International Statistical Classification of Diseases and Related Health Problems, 93
Interpersonal conflict, 67
IPads, 30, 45, 103, 123, 130
Iranian Revolution, *1979 Revolution: Black Friday*, 13
Iron Man, 148

Jailbreak, 9
James, William, 95
Java, 169
Jenkins, Henry, 9
John, Michael, 207n2
Johnson, Clay, 72–73
Johnson, Soren, 23, 56
JSON, 116
Junyo, 130

K–12 learning, integrating *Anatomy Pro-Am* into, 45–47, *48*. *See also Econauts*
Kairosoft, *Game Dev Story*, 54–56
Kallio, Julia, 45
Karczewski, John, 128, 136
Kelly, L., 73
Khan Academy, 176, 177, 178
Kim, Sangtae (Sang), 17
Kleenex testing, 71
Knowledge games, 31–36. *See also Anatomy Pro-Am*; Games, impact
  EyeWire, 33
  Foldit, 10, 14–15, 31–33, 52
  Galaxy Zoo, 31
  overview of, 10
  plateau of productivity, 2–3, *3*, 10
Kodu, 133
Koster, Raph, 116, 208n4
Kozma, Robert, 5, 180
Krakauer, David, 71, 76, 208n3
Kral, T. R. A., 6, 101

Laboratory for Optical and Computational Instrumentation (LOCI), 36
Land development. *See Trails Forward*
L.A. Noire, 36, 40
Lauterbach, Terra, 19–20, 77, 122
Leadership
 institutional, 193
 team, 67, 169
Learning, situated, 28
Learning analytics, 10, 80–81, 177, 192. *See also* Assessment systems
 in constructionist learning environments, 133
 in *Econauts*, 133, 136
 future of, 88–89
 in *Progenitor X*, 83–86
 in *Virulent*, 29, 86–88
Learning Games Network (LGN), 69–71, 128, 209n2
Learning sciences, 64
Learning technologies, investments in, 176–177
Leeuwen, David van, 42
"Less talk, more rock," 170
Levinson, Daniel, 96
Licensing, 29
Lightbox, 130
Linux, 179
Local partnerships, 188–190
Logging contracts, *Trails Forward*, 114, 117–118
Low, Arthur, 41
Luminosity Tool, 146
Lyons, Gary, 76, 78

Machine learning, assessment and, 11
Mackie, Thomas "Rock," 35, 43, 51, 57
Macklin, Colleen, 170–171
Mad City Mystery, 36
Madden NFL, 176
MAGIC Spell Studios, 15, 136
Maintenance, 175–176
MakeScape, 49, *50*

Malone, Tom, 33
Management, team. *See* Team building
Mario Maker, 8
Market, games for impact, 11, 176–183
 educational publishing market for, 176–177
 open educational resources (OER), 178–179
 open versus closed systems, 180–183
 questions facing, 178
Marten, American, 121
Massachusetts Institute of Technology, 31
Mass Analyzer Tool, 146
Matching games, 78
MAXQDA, 87
Mazurek, Micah, 92
McKenzie, Nathan, 96
Mechner, Jordan, 170
Mechtley, Adam, 112
Medical games, 36, 47–50. *See also Anatomy Pro-Am*; Mental health games
Medina, Carmen, 73, 193
Meditation, 94
Meeting spaces, 27
Mental health games
 advantages of, 91–93
 areas for future research, 107–108
 breath counting, 96–100
 Crystals of Kaydor, 100–102, *103*
 empathy, 100–102
 games for good, 93–94
 mindfulness, 95, 96–100
 negative trends associated with gaming, 92
 participatory design, 104–107, *105*
 potential of, 91–93
 scaling out products, 102–104
 Tenacity, 96–100, *97*, *106*, 174
Metaverse, 116
Metrics, traditional academic, 194–195
Microsoft Games, 16
Microsoft Kodu, 133
Military-training games, 91

Millar, Susan, 16
Miller, G. A., 208n5
Miller, Phil, 118
Mindfulness game, 95
Minecraft, 9, 23, 169, 177, 182
Mislevy, Robert, 207n2
Missions, *At Play in the Cosmos*, 149–150, *149*, 160
MIT OpenCourseWare, 179
Mobile game subgenres, 209n3
Model-based toys, *Trails Forward*, 111
Model map of Vilas County, 113–115
Models, game design
  preproduction, 167–170
  production, 173–175
  prototyping, 170–173
  service and maintenance, 175–176
Momentum, *At Play in the Cosmos*, 163
Monetization schemes, 175–176
Morgridge, John, 16
Morgridge, Tashia, 16
Morgridge Institute for Research (MIR), 17, 70, 76, 78
MoviePass, 178
Multiplayer games, 7
Multi-user dungeons (MUDs), 9

National Academy of Sciences, 52
National Institutes of Health (NIH), 51, 61
National Science Foundation (NSF), 29, 50, 70, 187
National STEM Video Game Challenge format, 169
Navigation, *At Play in the Cosmos*, 145–146, *145*
Ndemic Creations, *Plague Inc.*, 8–9
Netflix, 188
Neuroscience, game-based learning and. *See* Mental health games
New York Hall of Science, 49
"Next Generation Assessment" (Steinkuehler), 89

Niantic, *Pokémon GO!* 3, 8
1979 Revolution: Black Friday, 13
Nintendo
  Phoenix Wright: Ace Attorney, 40
  Wii Fit, 8
No Man's Sky, 150, 161
Northern Highland Lake District. *See Trails Forward*
Norton, Dan, 40, 64
Norton, W. W. & Company, 11, 139, 140, 176. *See also At Play in the Cosmos*
Norton Anthology series, 140
Notch, 169

Oklahoma, University of, 61
Oncology, 40–43
  academic versus work-for-hire development, 39–40
  aesthetics and play, 40–42
  Filament Games partnership, 38–39
  minimal viable product prototype, 37–38
  pilot tests, 42–43
Open educational resources (OER), 178–179
Open-source projects, 16
Open systems, games in, 180–183
Oppositional defiant behavior, 92–93
Outreach, 190–192
Owen, Liz, 76, 82, 84, 85

PAC-MAN, 80, 82
Paiz-Ramirez, Dennis, 59
Paper-based prototypes, 168–169
Paper production, 116–117
Participatory design, 104–107, *105*
Partnerships
  academic-industry, 72–73
  Anatomy Pro-Am, 38–39
  identification of partners, 168
  local, 188–190
  private-public, 69–71, 136, 139–140
  resources for, 209n1 (ch8)

Index

"three-date rule" for, 209n2 (ch8)
Trails Forward, 111
Patterson, Nathan, 19–20
PawPad suite, 47–50
Pelletier, Brian, 57, 78, 128
Perlman, Nicole, 70
Perseverence, 6
Phelps, Andy, 15, 136
Phoenix Wright, 40, 41
Pilot tests
  Oncology, 42–43
  Trails Forward, 119–120
Pilot-training games, 91
Plague Inc., 8–9, 23, 177, 182
Plateau of productivity, 2–3, *3*, 10
Playable ideas, 168
Playable toys, 170–171
PlaySquads, 191
Play-testing, *At Play in the Cosmos*, 158, 159–160
Pokémon GO! 3, 8, 92, 168
Polish phase, 160, 175
Politics of Resentment, The (Cramer), 114
Popovic, Zoran, 32
Posterior cingulate–medial prefrontal cortex (MPFC), 101
Post-test evaluations, 84
Predictive simulation, in *Trails Forward*, 116–117
Preproduction, 167–170. *See also* Game design documents (GDDs)
  At Play in the Cosmos, 140–150
  idea development, 168
  inspiration, finding, 168, 170
  "less talk, more rock," 170
  paper-based prototypes in, 168–169
  staffing, time, and results, 167–168
  stakeholder/partner identification, 168
  strategic analysis, 169
  team formation, 169
Pre-test evaluations, 84
Princeton University, *EyeWire*, 33
Private contracts, 189

Private foundation grants, 188–190
Private-public partnerships, 69–71, 136. *See also At Play in the Cosmos*
  context of, 139–140
  subject matter expert teams, 140
Pro-Am communities. *See* Crowdsourcing knowledge games
Production, 26–27, 173–175
Productivity, plateau of, 2–3, *3*, 10
Products, scaling out, 102–104
Progenitor X, 11, 177
  aesthetics and play, 77–79, *77*
  analytics in, 83–88
  assessment model, 79–83, *80*, 175
  coordination of data streams inside/outside of game play, 86–88
  correlation between learning and overall game play in, 84–85
  data collection, 83–88
  data design and collection, 81–83
  data transformations and sample features, 84
  development team, 77–78
  feature engineering, 83–86
  game data analysis, 84–86
  learning analytics, 83–86
  origins of, 75–77
  progress units, 83
  testing, 78–79
Project goals, 169
Project leads, 169
Promotions, 67
Protein-folding simulation (*Foldit*), 31–33
Prototyping, 25–26, 170–173
  Anatomy Browser, 43–45, *44*
  Anatomy Pro-Am, 37–38
  art pipeline, 171–172
  designers and researchers in, 172–173
  paper-based, 168–169
  programmers in, 172
  prototype-driven development, 54–56, 65
  rapid, 54–56, 143

Prototyping (cont.)
  team meeting patterns, 173
  Tenacity, 97, 174
  toys, 170–171
  Trails Forward, 112, *113*
  vertical slices, 170–173
Publicly traded companies, game development constrained by, 13–14
Public policy, knowledge games for. *See Trails Forward*
Public-private partnerships. *See* Private-public partnerships
Purchases, in-game, 176
Puzzle Bots, 57
Puzzle games. *See Progenitor X*

Quantic Dream, *Detroit: Become Human*, 40

Radeloff, Volker, 111
Radiation, blackbody, 149
Ralston-Berg, P., 163
Rapid prototyping, 54–56, 142, 143
Ready Player One, 177
Reagan, Ronald, 91
Rebels at Work (Kelly and Medina), 73
Recruitment tools, game development teams as, 62
Redundancies, design for, 67
Refraction, 33
Regenerative medicine, 76. *See also Progenitor X*
Reliability, game, 39
Replayable games, 7
Research assets, development teams as, 62
Research lab culture, 63–64
Research Lab Story, 54–56
  rapid prototyping, 54–56
  storyboarding and mockups, 56–58
Resilience, 6
Robinson, Erin, 57–58, 96
Roblox, 8, 9–10, 167

Robotic Advanced Medical Integrated Systems (R.A.M.I.S.),, 79
Rochester, University of, 140
Rochester Institute of Technology, 15, 136, 156
Rockstar Games, *L.A. Noire*, 40
Role-playing scenarios, *Anatomy Pro-Am*, 29, 45–47
Rosetta@home project, 32
Rothschild, Meagan, 42, 62
Ruby on Rails, 116, 122
Ruesch, Jake, 147–148, 156

Sakai Educational Partners Program, 179
Salen, Katie, 9, 207n2
Salesin, David, 32
Salkowski, Lonie, 36, 43, 45, 70, 76
San Antonio College, 140
Sawyer, Ben, 10
Scaffolding of mathematical representations, 155–156
Scaling models, 29, 102–104
Scaling teams, 10, 53–56, 169
  AAA versus indie developers, 65, 208n2
  challenges of, 63–64, 68–69
  commitment to growth in, 66
  conflict management, 67
  cross-functional teams, 209n4
  individualistic versus team cultures, 65–66
  innovative academic-industry partnerships, 72–73
  management tips for, 66–68
  prioritization of efforts in, 67–68
  private-public partnerships and, 69–71
  prototyping and, 54–56
  redundancies, 67
  research lab cultures, 63–64
  scientists/gamers versus educators, 63–64
  storyboarding process and, 56–60

Index

strategic factors behind, 56–58, 62–64
subdisciplines, 67
team leadership and promotions, 67
team meeting patterns, 173
workflow rhythms, 66
Scenario planning, 110
Schell, Jesse, 207n2
Schell, Jordu, 70
Schell Games, 207n2
SchoolNet, 179
Science knowledge games, 31–36.
  See also Anatomy Pro-Am
  Biohazard, 36
  EyeWire, 33
  Foldit, 31–33
  Galaxy Zoo, 31
Scientific domains, 64
Scientists, educators versus, 63–64
Scratch, 207n2
Self-regulation, improvement of, 11
Semantic layers, 82–83
Serious Games Initiative, 10
Service and maintenance, 175–176
Sesame Street franchise, 196
Seugn Lab, 33
Shapiro, Ben, 36, 41, 43, 112, 116, 121
Shared aesthetic vision, 23–24
Sharp, John, 170–171
Shevde, Rupa, 76, 78
SimCity, 9, 23, 130, 132
Simkins, David, 156
Single-payer games, 7
Single-session games, 7
Siri, 88
Situated learning, 28
Six to Start, *Zombies, Run!* 8
Ska Studios, *I MAED A GAM3 W1TH Z0MBIES 1N IT!!!1*, 75
Skipper-Spurgeon, Sherry, 104
Small Angle Tool, 146
Social-emotional development, 6
Social studies education games, 4
Sockowitz, Ira, 128

Soebke, Heinrich, 20
Solutions, hypothesized, 168
Spaulding, Seth, 24, 64, 207n3
Spectrum Analyzer Tool, 146
Spring play-testing, *At Play in the Cosmos*, 158
Squire, Warner, 9
Stadia, 177
Staffing, 167–168
Stakeholders
  identification of, 168
  Trails Forward, 118–119
Stanford Encyclopedia of Philosophy, 179
StarCraft II, 24
Star system, 65–66
Steam, 188
Steinkuehler, Constance, 16, 86, 88, 89, 98, 135
Stem cell game. *See Progenitor X*
Stenerson, Mark, 122, 128
Stidwell, Peter, 128
ST Math, 139, 167, 177, 178
Stone, Alex, 64
Storyboarding and story lines, 56–60, 169
Strategic alignment, 13–14
Strategic analysis, 169
Studio K project, 133
Subdisciplines, empowering, 67
Subject matter expert teams, 140
Subscriptions, 76, 176–177
Surveillance technologies, 88
Swink, Steve, 175
System events, *Progenitor X*, 83

Target audience, 169
Teacher liaisons, 191–192
Teaching tools, game development teams as, 62
Team building, 10, 53–56, 169. *See also Fair Play*
  AAA versus indie developers, 65, 208n2
  challenges of, 63–64, 68–69
  commitment to growth in, 66

Team building (cont.)
  conflict management, 67
  cross-functional teams, 209n4
  individualistic versus team cultures, 65–66
  innovative academic-industry partnerships, 72–73
  management tips for, 66–68
  prioritization of efforts in, 67–68
  private-public partnerships and, 69–71
  prototyping and, 54–56
  redundancies, 67
  research lab cultures, 63–64
  scientists/gamers versus educators, 63–64
  storyboarding process and, 56–60
  strategic factors behind, 56–58, 62–64
  subdisciplines, 67
  team leadership and promotions, 67
  team meeting patterns, 173
  workflow rhythms, 66
Team Leadership in the Games Industry (Spaulding), 207n3
Templates, game design document, 169
Tenacity, 96–100, *97*, *99*, *106*, 174
Testing
  At Play in the Cosmos, 158
  implicit association, 71
  Kleenex, 71
  pilot, 42–43, 119–120
  Progenitor X, 78–79
  Trails Forward, 119
  user, 174
Tetris, 32, 78
Thatgamecompany, 207n2
"Theme Is Not Meaning" (Johnson), 23, 56
Thomson, James, 17, 76, 77
Thoreau, Henry David, 207n2
Thoughtful exploration game play, 85
TomoTherapy, 35
Townsend, Richard, 140
Toys, development of, 170–171

Trails Forward, *118*, 119–120. *See also Econauts*
  aesthetics and play, 111–116
  Conservation Conversation Group partnership, 111
  design jams, 111–112
  as ecological simulation, 121
  Econauts compared to, 122
  environmental investigation practices, 121
  forestry and land ownership in, 117
  goals in, 115
  logging contracts and forest management, 117–118
  model-based toy, 111–112
  origins of, *112*
  pilot testing, 119–120
  predictive simulation in, 116–117
  simulated model map of Vilas County, 113–115
  single-player prototype, 112, *113*
  stakeholder group, 118–119
  technical infrastructure, 116
  vision and goals of, 134–135
Transdisciplinary design, 16–17, 51
Transgressive play, learning through, 8–9
Translational research, 190
Trust, 24, 143, 208n4
Trust Spectrum, 208n4
Tuckman, B. W., 24
Typing of the Dead, 75
Typing tutors, 75

Uber, 178
Underwood, Dean Julie, 71
Underwood, Julie, 208n3
Unity, 116, 146, 175–176, 182, 188, 209n3
Universities. *See* Higher education institutions
Unreal Tournament, 91
Unrestricted funding, 194
User experience (UX) flows, 169

Index

User testing, 174
Use Your Brainz EDU, 130

Valve, 58, 67, 173
Vaughan, Greg, 152
Vaughan, James, 9
Verbs, 181
Vertical slices, 146, 152, 170–173
Veterinary education, iPad apps for, 47–50
Video Games and Learning (Squire), 36, 168
Viewtiful Joe, 27
Vilas County (Wisconsin) model map, 113–115
Vimeo, 188
Virions, 19–20
Virtual High Schools, 178
Virulent, 10, 19–30, 177, 182
 aesthetics and play, 19–20, *20*, 27
 aesthetic vision, 23–24
 areas for future refinement, 29–30
 challenges of, 22–23
 correlation between learning and overall game play in, 86–88
 development team, 19–20
 game-based learning results, 27–30
 green-lighting criteria for, 20–22
 influences on, 24
 learning analytics, 29, 86–88
 making of, 22–23
 origins of, 19–20
 production, 26–27
 prototypes, 25–26
 release date, 19
 reviews and success, 27–28
Visual style, in game design documents (GDDs), 169

Wangen, Stephen, 121
Washington, University of, 32
Waterfall development, 65
Web services, 191

WeFold collaborative initiative, 33
Weka, 85
White, Dan, 64, 130
WIDA (World Class Instructional Design and Assessment), 210n3
Wiens, Adam, 100
Wien's displacement law, 149
Wii Fit, 8
Wikipedia, 179
Wisconsin, paper production in, 116–117
Wisconsin Alumni Research Foundation (WARF), 17
Wisconsin Center for Education Research (WCER), 210n3
Wisconsin Institute for Discovery (WID), 16–19, 54, 75, 111
Wisconsin–Madison, University of, 6, 11. *See also* Games+Learning+Society (GLS)
 Center for Limnology, 109
 Center for Women's Health Research, 53–54
 Laboratory for Optical and Computational Instrumentation (LOCI), 36
 Wisconsin Institute for Discovery, 16–19, 54, 75, 111
Wolfenstein, Moses, 20
Wood, Dave, 140
Workflow rhythms, 66
Work-for-hire development, 39–40
World of Warcraft, 56, 135
Wouters, P., 6

Yin, John, 19–20, 23
YouTube, 188

Zombie invasion game. *See Progenitor X*
Zombies, Run! 8
Zooniverse, 31